Felix Warnock spent fifteen years as a freelance bassoon player based in London, but frequently on tour around the world. He was a founder member of the Orchestra of the Age of Enlightenment, becoming its chief executive in 1988. He spent a further fifteen years as manager of The English Concert. He taught bassoon at Trinity College of Music, was briefly Head of Early Music at the Royal Academy of Music and was chairman of The Radcliffe Trust until 2019. He lives in London and now works in mental health research, a field in which he is eminently qualified after a career in the orchestral world.

Felix Warnock

PERFECTION IS NOT THE WORD FOR IT

Austin Macauley Publishers

LONDON * CAMBRIDGE * NEW YORK * SHARJAH

Copyright © Felix Warnock 2022

The right of Felix Warnock to be identified as author of this work has been asserted by the author in accordance with section 77 and 78 of the Copyright, Designs and Patents Act 1988.

All rights reserved. No part of this publication may be reproduced, stored in a retrieval system, or transmitted in any form or by any means, electronic, mechanical, photocopying, recording, or otherwise, without the prior permission of the publishers.

Any person who commits any unauthorised act in relation to this publication may be liable to criminal prosecution and civil claims for damages.

All of the events in this memoir are true to the best of author's memory. The views expressed in this memoir are solely those of the author.

A CIP catalogue record for this title is available from the British Library.

ISBN 9781398409392 (Paperback)
ISBN 9781398409408 (ePub e-book)

www.austinmacauley.com

First Published 2022
Austin Macauley Publishers Ltd®
1 Canada Square
Canary Wharf
London
E14 5AA

Table of Contents

Foreword — 7

Chapter 1 — 10
Orchestral Introduction

Chapter 2 — 37
An Oxford Overture

Chapter 3 — 65
Albion Ensemble: Five in a Bar

Chapter 4 — 94
Trials and Errors

Chapter 5 — 125
Inventing the Orchestra of the Age of Enlightenment

Chapter 6 — 161
Re-Inventing the English Concert

Chapter 7 — 189
Double Bar: When the Music Stops

Chapter 8 — 209
Coda

Foreword

It is commonplace to allow that many of our childhood memories may be inaccurate, or even completely false. One dramatic instance of a non-real memory involved the eminent Swiss child psychologist, Jean Piaget, who, by way of illustrating a point about childhood recall, gave a detailed account of his own earliest memory. This moment of melodrama occurred when he was no more than three years old: he was being walked in the park by his nanny when a malefactor leapt into their path, snatched him from his pram and made off. The nanny gave heroic chase, eventually recovering her charge and bearing him home in triumph. Although he had no other memories which dated back so long, this episode was indelibly impressed in his mind. Soon after his account was published, Piaget received a letter from the very nanny: now in old age, she wrote that her conscience was troubled and she wished to confess that the attempted abduction had never taken place. The nanny had invented the entire episode in order to cast herself in a favourable light with his parents, and with such success that her heroism had become an oft-repeated family legend.

It may perhaps seem over-cautious to open this small volume of 'punctuated anecdotes' by casting doubt, as this story surely does, on the veracity of what follows, but there is something to be said, I think, for getting such disclaimers in early. It may be noted, too, that although this foreword is presumably the first thing you, the reader, will read, it is in truth the last thing that the author has written. And now that I arrive at the foreword having, as it were, already read the book, I find that the superb confidence with which I began at Chapter 1 is now somewhat tempered by humility, or at any rate the acceptance of the possibility, however remote, of memorative frailty. So, while I cannot guarantee that everything here recounted occurred exactly as described, I can confidently say that I have written things as honestly as I can, and have not wilfully made anything up. And I might, perhaps, go further: small errors on matters of detail do not especially worry me, for even if some of what I have described is misremembered, such false memory as there might be has nevertheless become part of me, thus taking on a reality in my own narrative, just as M. Piaget's attempted abduction had for him.

In any case, childhood memories comprise only a very small part of this book, and more adult memories are likely to be more reliable. Also, this book is only partly about me: I have described it as anecdotal, and in many of these vignettes I was no more than an onlooker, or sometimes an actor with a mere walk-on part. The main protagonists are usually more colourful characters than I, but even such stars of life require their deeds to be recorded (or at least recalled) if they are to shine beyond the brilliance of the brief moment.

There are two further points to be made about the 'truth' of any story: firstly, the time of writing may be an essential ingredient I have in mind, by way of example, the somewhat anomalous eighth chapter of this book, concerning Brexit. This was written early in 2018, eighteen months or so after the referendum vote in favour of the UK's departure from the EU, and some time before the other chapters. I had voted as a Brexiteer, to the considerable astonishment and consternation of most of my friends and colleagues, and wanted to record the reasons for doing so as they appeared to me at the time. With this in mind, I have resisted the strong temptation to update my account in the light of subsequent events because, obviously, to have done so would be a kind of 'cheating'; to permit the benefit of hindsight would defeat the purpose of attempting a contemporary record. In particular, Covid-19 was unknown at the time of writing so is not referred to.

The second point about 'truth' is that people often interpret events differently, or take a different message from a story, according to what they themselves hope to hear. The title of this memoir illustrates the point: a former chief executive of the Royal Opera House, Sir Claus Moser, was obliged to visit the dressing room, post-performance, of an ageing diva who had just delivered an execrable account of a famous operatic role. Sir Claus's fawning entourage were on tenterhooks, wondering how the great man would reconcile the need to retain a modicum of personal integrity, not, in other words, utter an outright lie, with the competing need to stroke the fragile ego of the offending artiste. His solution was to embrace her warmly with the words, "Darling, perfection is <u>not</u> the word for it!" She was, of course, thrilled, as was the sniggering entourage.

And sometimes the reader himself can be guilty, finding in a story what he hopes to see, literally so in the case of the writer Michael Frayn: he confessed to a habit, which I am inclined to share, of always needing to read over the shoulder of the person sitting next to him, reading, on a train. One morning, on the London Underground, he glanced at his neighbour's newspaper, which, from its distinctive pink colour, he knew to be the Financial Times, to be rewarded by the startling headline, 'Heavy lasses keep giant company in bed'. Thrilled by the thought that the famously staid 'FT' was now covering a broader range of story, he leant keenly in for closer examination, only to be disappointed to find that the story was rather more mundane, 'Heavy losses keep giant company in red.'

Lastly, I must thank all those who helped me while writing this account, particularly my son, Daniel, who challenged me to start and my wife, Julie, who urged me to stop. Such errors as remain, are all mine, and there will doubtless be some, for I failed to follow the cautious example of the late Jeffrey Bernard who wrote to the *New Statesman* in 1975: "Sir, I have been commissioned by Mr Michael Joseph to write an autobiography and I would be grateful to any of your readers who could tell me what I was doing between 1960 and 1974."

London, December 2021

Chapter 1
Orchestral Introduction

It was mid-morning on an October day in 1972 and the phone was ringing in the little North Kensington house I shared with three other music students, all of us studying at either the Royal College (RCM) or Royal Academy of Music (RAM). Having assured the unknown caller that I was indeed the unknown bassoon player she was trying to locate, she came directly to the point, "I'm calling from the BBC Symphony Orchestra. We have a flu epidemic amongst our bassoonists—all our regulars are sick and I've tried everyone on our list of deputies. Can you come now to our Maida Vale studio to catch the last hour of this morning's rehearsal? The concert is tomorrow at the Royal Festival Hall, to be broadcast live on Radio 3." It is scarcely an accolade to be told in any context that your selection is the last desperate throw of the dice, but in this situation it was, I suppose, almost acceptable. It had, after all, the virtue of truth, and it was also true that I was amazed to be on the list at all. My teacher at the RCM was Geoffrey Gambold, long-time principal bassoon in the BBC Symphony Orchestra, so, with all options exhausted he had presumably, from his sickbed, been prevailed upon to provide a list of his pupils, and even amongst these I did not enjoy pole position as I was only midway through my college studies. None of this altered the fact that I was now accepting my very first professional engagement, utterly unaware (absurdly so, in hindsight) of what lay ahead.

I arrived by cab at the BBC's Maida Vale studios in Delaware Road at around midday, and it would be an understatement to describe the events of the next hour as challenging. Studio 1 at Maida Vale has a set of large double doors with two 'port-hole' windows near the top through which I tentatively peered. The large symphony orchestra, of 80 or so players, was arrayed facing the doors so that anyone entering would be under the eye of everyone in the room with the exception of the conductor, who was, of course, facing the musicians. I could scarcely fail to notice that there was a conspicuous gap in the ranks, this being the second bassoon chair awaiting occupation by my belated bottom. The orchestra was hard at work, so I waited for a moment until I judged that a fortissimo passage would provide reasonable cover for me to slip in unobserved, in due course applying my shoulder to the door. Silence fell instantly; so quickly, indeed, did everyone down instruments that the heavy thud of the closing swing doors made my entrance appear both clumsy and distressingly conspicuous. His orchestra having so suddenly fallen transfixed, the Maestro turned slowly to see what, or whom, had cast this spell. This was my first sight of the redoubtable M. Pierre Boulez, Principal Conductor of the BBC Symphony Orchestra. He, too, seemed struck dumb, so with what little appearance of confidence I could muster, and in a silence so intense that the proverbial pin would have dropped with the percussive effect of a cymbal-crash, I set a nervous course across the floor of the studio, around the back of the orchestra, up on to the modest platform where the back row of the woodwinds were positioned, took my seat, adjusted the music stand, opened my instrument case and, still in sepulchral silence, began the business of assembling the bassoon. Curious, isn't it, how time can appear to be 'on hold.' It has more than once been reported by survivors that at a moment of crisis, such as plunging to one's apparently certain death over a cliff, when oblivion seems imminent and inevitable, time becomes distorted. Such was the case now—my past life did not flash before me but events certainly seemed to unfold in slow motion.

At this point, as time stands still, I should say a word about Pierre Boulez because, although we had naturally enough never met, my teacher Mr Gambold had from time to time told me stories of his troubled relationship with members of his BBC orchestra. And, while I knew something of Boulez via the Geoff Gambold connection, he was also at this time the most talked-about conductor on the London musical scene not least because, prior to his appointment, he was most noted for forecasting the imminent death of the symphony orchestra…not just the BBC Symphony Orchestra, mind you, but all symphony orchestras. The age of the large-scale musical composition was, he averred, dead.

Given his well-publicised views on the pathology of the symphony orchestra, Boulez's appointment, by the then Controller of BBC Music, William Glock, had been both controversial and divisive. In the 1960s, Boulez had been the most articulate member of a post-war musical avant-garde and despite (or perhaps because of) his very left-wing politics was revered by the artistic power-brokers at the BBC and the Arts Council who were determined to 'modernise' British music-making, steering it away from its rather tweedy heritage of Elgar and Vaughan Williams, and in orchestral terms, Sir Adrian Boult. The Boulez appointment came to embody these aims. Before the days of Classic FM and the beginnings of the fightback of a more populist classical music culture, it is undeniable that the Radio 3 view of acceptable new music in the 1960s and 70s was uncompromisingly modernist, with little air-time given to 'tonal' composers such as Britten or Shostakovich. But, as with other revolutions, a determination to promote an anti-establishment position soon became the new establishment, quickly turning into a kind of cultural Stalinism in which dissent, or even the freedom to disagree, was curtailed or altogether banned. The avant-garde of the 1970s had become a closed system, swallowing up a large proportion of state funding (including BBC funds of course) yet becoming ever more exclusive (I might even use the much-abused word 'elitist' in this context), and excluding from its language everything that music-lovers actually valued. As for Boulez himself, who had earlier regarded the very idea of a symphony orchestra as a bourgeois anathema, blocking progress by constantly referring back to nineteenth-century music traditions, he had a reputation as a controversialist to live up to.

Back in Maida Vale Studio 1, I cannot pretend that such reflections were at the forefront of (or indeed anywhere else in) my mind, but the clock had begun once again inexorably to tick. My bassoon was at last assembled but I had not dared play a note to test the reed (or any other part of the bassoon's, or indeed my own, anatomy) because, although some gentle whispering had broken the absolute silence, it seemed certain that anything I did would bring an unwelcomely keen focus back on to my feebly flustered activities. So I adopted a kind of keen ready-to-play position, at which point Boulez announced that he would abandon the piece he had been working on and asked the orchestra to turn its attention to the slow movement of Brahms First Piano Concerto. Now, in my youthful ignorance and of course in the rush of being summoned so late, I had not asked what music was to be played and, even if I had, this concerto would have held few alarms. I did not know it (so much for my conservatoire training), but Brahms' works do not usually feature bassoons to a very significant extent. However, there is, as I was about to learn, an exception, viz. the opening of the slow movement of the first piano concerto.

This slow movement is indeed very slow, opening with an extended orchestral introduction in which two bassoons play, a sixth apart, a lugubrious melody against a soft string accompaniment. Thus we set sail, myself sight-reading, and my colleague, who was unknown to me at that time and also a guest because of the flu epidemic, navigating with tenacity and caution but, or so it seemed, with tolerable success. We had reached about the halfway point in the movement when the weather sharply deteriorated. Boulez brought proceedings to a stop with that singularly pained expression which the French male usually reserves for the sight of traditional English cuisine;[1] he eyed us, the two bassoons, with evident distaste. "Two bassoons," he spoke for the first time and with characteristic minimalism, "play me the opening." And with the smallest gesture for us to begin, my colleague and I found ourselves duetting, in mournful sixths and ultra-slow tempo, with an audience of some 78 musicians transfixed for a second time by this unexpected turn of events. And so we continued, *à deux*, for what seemed an age, until with a wordlessly raised eyebrow and a Gallic shrug, the maestro, or perhaps he would prefer to be *le chef*, indicated that he had heard enough.

"Now," he spoke again, quietly, and with what sounded to my sensitive ear uncommonly like menace, "second bassoon *seul*." And so began what a sports commentator (how fortunate that there wasn't one) might have characterised as an excruciating passage of play. At a desperately funereal adagio (was the tempo getting slower, or was this another instance of the clock stopping, or at least decelerating?) I played, tremblingly, an extended solo, which, in all the circumstances, amounted to a forensic examination of technical control, and I continued for so long without so much as a twitch from Boulez that the awful prospect dawned that he might require me to play the entire movement, an unaccompanied second bassoon solo lasting about 15 minutes (or do I mean 15 years, or perhaps a lifetime). Any instrumentalist will tell you that it is much easier, when under acute stress, to play handfuls of rapid notes than to maintain full control at a super-slow tempo. Eventually, after I had played for the longest

---

[1] The mirror image perhaps of the expression described by P. G. Wodehouse in one of the great opening lines to a novel: "Into the face of the young man who sat on the terrace of the Hotel Magnifique at Cannes there had crept a look of furtive shame, the shifty hangdog look which announces that an Englishman is about to talk French." *The Luck of the Bodkins*

ten minutes of my life thus far, Boulez stopped me. He glanced up briefly, then down again, evidently cast into the depths of despair.

"Second bassoon," he muttered in doleful tone, "play me an F sharp." Now, the casual reader will not know that the bassoon is an imperfect instrument in the sense that some notes work better than others, both in terms of intonation and ease of control. Briefly, the reason for this is that in the long pipe necessary to produce bass notes, the 'true' position for each note's finger hole would be too widely spaced to be reachable by anyone other than a giant; therefore these finger holes are drilled through the wood of the pipe at angles so as to bring the holes, when they surface, within reach of mortal fingers. The result is a compromise in which a few notes are less truly tuned in order to make the instrument playable at all. Needless to say, and you may have got ahead of me here, F sharp is one such and, as fate would have it, this is the note on which the second bassoon begins the slow movement of this piano concerto. Boulez, once more doleful, extended the palm of his hand in my direction, as if reluctant again to suffer the pain which the gift of my faltering F sharp would inevitably induce. I presented him with a shaky and feeble specimen. His hand held my offering, then, with a tortured expression, he turned it palm down, followed by an intemperate and rapid side-to-side cutting-off motion. Still wordless, but now with an audible sigh, his hand slowly turned upwards again, inviting a further F sharp from his hapless victim. This wordless exchange of F sharps, offered with ever-diminishing hope and rejected in silently-mimed disgust, continued for some considerable time. At first there was silence all around me but eventually I became aware of a grumbling unrest amongst my immediate neighbours. The orchestra at this time boasted two of the great figures of London's orchestral world, the eminent clarinettist Jack Brymer, who was on my right, and the brilliant but irascible French horn player Alan Civil, seated immediately behind.

Brymer was the better known to the public as he presented a weekly Radio 3 show, adopting an avuncular presentational style somewhat at odds with his real personality.[2] Alan Civil, on the other hand, was an old-fashioned trouper, blessed

---

[2] Jack's name recognition amongst the general public was attested by a story which another eminent clarinettist, my old friend Antony Pay, who was at this time the principal clarinet in the Royal Philharmonic Orchestra, told of himself. Tony was standing in a queue at his bank and the gentleman immediately ahead of him presented the teller with a cheque to be cashed. Tony, being in a rush, was leaning impatiently forward, awaiting his turn at the cashier's window, sufficiently closely to observe that the name on this

not only with a fabulous musical gift but also a fabled tolerance for alcohol (he had a specially adapted horn case incorporating a drinks' cabinet with carefully sculpted recesses for gin and tonic bottles, two glasses, serrated-edge knife for slicing lemons, and so on, though whether in those pre-technological days it boasted an ice-maker seems doubtful). These two orchestral heavyweights were becoming restive, but their rumblings only served to raise the ambient temperature, doing nothing to relieve the pressure. From behind me there came stage whispered expletives, increasingly frequent and vivid, as my F sharps continued, while from my right, I distinctly heard Jack's plummy tones (his voice did not really do stage whispers, I suppose),[3] memorably declaring this to be, "The greatest disaster since the Second World War," and other emollient thoughts along similar lines, although it was not clear whether he referred to

---

individual's cheque was Jack Brymer. The teller, on receiving the said Mr Brymer's cheque, studied it intently and his face paled, awe-struck. "Not THE Jack Brymer?" he spoke in the hushed tones appropriate for addressing royalty and other demi-gods. Our anonymous Mr Brymer appeared embarrassed and assured him, with much apology and self-deprecation that, "No", he was not THE Jack Brymer, "it is just my name." So it was with some expectation that Tony presented his own cheque, drawn on the account of Antony Pay. Not a flicker from the teller. Tony gave him plenty of time to digest the incredible possibility of serving two successive god-like clarinettists, but there was no response at all. Tony's frustration, eventually, was too much to bear, "Well…aren't you going to say it then. Aren't you going to say, not THE Antony Pay?"

[3] A flavour of Jack Brymer at this time may be gleaned from an incident witnessed (on a later occasion) in the Royal Festival Hall carpark, a notoriously overcrowded and dismal area to which entry was rarely easily achieved. Brymer drew up at the carpark attendant's booth, only to be told that there were no spaces available. "Do you know who I am?" he asked in his peculiarly resonant Radio 3 tones; "I am Jack Brymer," to which the sergeant-major manqué on duty at the barrier replied in tones strongly suggesting that a post in the Diplomatic Corps might not be his next career move, "I don't care if you're f***ing Acker Bilk, the car park's full." The extent to which Jack's blood pressure would have risen at this reply will probably only be fully appreciated by the over 50s since anyone younger will probably not know the identity of Mr Bilk, a band-leading clarinettist of the time, and the only exponent of that instrument who would have enjoyed greater name recognition even than Jack. One of the enjoyable things about this episode, on reflection, was that it revealed that our car park attendant must have known exactly who Jack Brymer was in order to choose just the right name to wind him up most effectively.

myself or to Mr Boulez. At the time I thought it was Boulez, but looking back I'm not so sure.

We had reached a point, Maestro Boulez and I, when he was indicating to me by pointing upwards or downwards that my F sharps were either too sharp or too flat but eventually he responded with a rather stagey sharp intake of breath, looking up with a pretence of pleasure and spreading his arms wide in a mock gesture welcome. "Ah," he sighed, "good", then, after a long pause he sighed again and, in a tone almost of sadness, "and now pianissimo!" and so we resumed. For the benefit of my non-bassoon-playing readers, I should perhaps explain that when this particular F sharp is played pianissimo the tendency, at least for the inexperienced or nervous player (and I was of course by now both in spades), is that the pitch will rise. So we returned, as in Snakes and Ladders, to square one with our wordless F sharp pantomime. And we could still be going at it to this day but for the fact that the leader of the orchestra[4] tapped Boulez diffidently on the shoulder and pointed to the clock above the studio door. The hands stood at 1.00 p.m. and the maestro was obliged to call time on the rehearsal. My life had been saved by the Musicians' Union rulebook.

This unhappy encounter with Pierre Boulez in one of his most misanthropic phases had a much more pleasing corollary. It must have been twenty years later, at a time when I would occasionally return to the BBC Symphony Orchestra as a guest, that one such engagement coincided with that of Boulez, of course no longer Principal Conductor, but an occasional guest conductor. There were no dramas on this occasion, indeed the former 'chef' appeared to have considerably mellowed. One of our concerts was in Paris and while sitting quietly on the orchestral bus en route from Charles de Gaulle airport to our hotel I had the good fortune to overhear the conversation of two players, whom I did not know, sitting in the seats immediately in front of me. They were too young to have been members of the orchestra in Boulez's reign as conductor-in-chief but they were discussing how challenging it must have been for the players at the time, and, to illustrate his point, one of them told the story of the young bassoon player who had appeared for the first time as a deputy and been subjected to a sadistic personal examination *pour encourager les autres*. I was a legend.

In many years of lurking, more or less unobserved, in the back rows of orchestras I never saw anything to equal this kind of conductor-led inquisition,

---

[4] At this time the BBC Symphony Orchestra had two leaders, both of whom were known as 'Belly', Bela Dekany and Eli Goren.

let alone experienced it directed at myself. Nevertheless, bad behaviour by conductors is, of course, a frequent enough occurrence, as is a degree of insubordination in the orchestral ranks. Indeed, tension between orchestras and their masters is probably as old as orchestras themselves, one of the earliest recorded instances being Haydn's 'Farewell' symphony: Haydn's employer, the Duke of Esterhazy, had built an extravagant summer palace at Esterhaza (now in Hungary) where he removed his entire court establishment for increasingly lengthy stays. The musicians wanted to return from the relatively remote Esterhaza to their homes which were at Eisenstadt in Austria, and within striking distance of the civilised world of Vienna. The 'Farewell' famously has the musicians departing two by two while the final movement is still being played, so imparting the unequivocal message to their employer that enough is enough, we are downing tools. As a small side-note on this familiar enough end-of-term story, I have always wondered if Haydn's symphonies around this period are numbered in the sequence in which they were actually composed and first performed. The Farewell Symphony is no. 45 of Haydn's one hundred-plus symphonies, and if the numbering indeed reflects the order of composition, the very seldom-performed Symphony no. 46 would have been the first of a 'new term' when normal service was resumed following the eventual return to Eisenstadt. If this is so, Haydn played a rather cruel trick on his musicians by writing their first symphony after the holidays in the virtually impossible (for instruments of that period) key of B major (with its key signature of five sharps). This would have been a rude re-awakening, especially for his horn players, for whom the writing in this work is both unusually difficult in terms of key but also lies ridiculously high in the register of the instrument. Haydn characteristically sided with his players when in dispute with 'the management', but he was making it very clear that he was in charge in their everyday working lives. It is as though he is saying, "Ok, boys, I did my best for you last summer but now you have some work to do for me. So get practicing."

Orchestral players, collectively, can find all kinds of minor cruelties to inflict on their conductors. One simple, if mischievous, example arose in the London Symphony Orchestra at the time when the young Neville Marriner was leader of the second violins. The orchestra had a concert with a visiting Japanese conductor. Just as the orchestra was taking the stage for the performance, word came from the director of the concert hall that it was customary for such concerts to begin with the National Anthem. The visiting maestro was alarmed because he had never heard the National Anthem, so Neville re-assured him, "It'll be fine. We all know it; just beat 4/4 and we will follow." A bit naughty, the Anthem being in 3/4 time. A few of the players knew what was going on but most did not, so confusion reigned.[5]

Subtle put-downs can be effective, of course, and sometimes without even being especially cruel. Into this category I would put the Mark Elder example: Mark was a guest conductor of the City of Birmingham Orchestra at the time that their principal conductor, Simon Rattle, was awarded a knighthood. The newly ennobled Sir Simon was conducting a morning session with the CBSO and Mark Elder had an afternoon rehearsal for a future concert. Two players, meeting unexpectedly at the stage door, were heard to exchange, "Hello, what are you doing here? Are you playing for S'Simon?" To which the reply, of course, was, "No, M'Mark."

And titles, or the lack of them, can be used more maliciously. I used to work occasionally in the orchestra at English National Opera at a time when two conductors, Charles MacKerras and Charles Groves would frequently alternate, each conducting an opera or two running concurrently in the season. When Mackerras was knighted (and Groves at that time was not) it was common practice for all questions from an orchestral player to conductor to begin, "Excuse me, Sir Charles", followed, according to the identity of the conductor, by a malevolent chuckle and an, "Oops, sorry…Charles." This kind of orchestral behaviour is very hard to stop because it is so collective; everyone is in this 'playground gang', except of course the victim, and the sad thing in this rather childish case was that Groves really seemed to mind.

Some maestri are made of sterner stuff and seek to take the initiative, either with a 'Mr Nice Guy' approach or its opposite, the old-fashioned martinet. The niceness of Mr Nice Guy is not, of course, invariably reciprocated: an elderly American maestro, visiting Cardiff for a first guest conducting appearance with the BBC Welsh Symphony Orchestra (as it then was), sought to win the affections of his charges with an extensive reminiscence about his enduring love of Wales stemming from his wartime visit as an American GI in 1944, nearly 35

---

[5] This is one you can try at home: hum the National Anthem with the strong downbeat falling on every 4th beat instead of every 3rd.

years previously. This saunter down memory lane was interrupted by a loud and not entirely friendly cry of, "Daddy!" from the direction of the trombone section.

And as for the martinet, the truly autocratic conductor is, these days, rather out of fashion, but it was not always so. One of the old school was George Szell, a deeply unpopular figure with the orchestra of which he was music director for twenty-five years, the Cleveland Symphony. Szell was also an occasional guest conductor at the Metropolitan Opera in New York where he was almost equally unloved. Here, though, he had a few defenders, one of whom was put firmly in his place by the following exchange with the Met's General Director, Rudolf Byng. On hearing it said of Szell by one of his defenders, "Of course, George is his own worst enemy," Byng shot back with, "Not while I'm alive, he isn't."[6]

And finally, I cannot resist including an unusually extreme example of orchestral hostility, at the other end of the scale from Marriner's understated, if effective, squib, which occurred on more than one occasion in the woodwind section of the orchestra of the English National Opera (some years before my time, this). The principal oboist had a wooden leg as a result of a wartime injury, but was occasionally known to turn this misfortune spectacularly to advantage: from time to time, when conductors irritated or simply bored him, he would seize his reed-knife, plunging it histrionically into his leg accompanied by agonised cries along the lines of, "It's all too much; I can't bear this any longer; there's only one way out." The effect on visiting conductors could be dramatic including one who is reported to have turned as white as the proverbial sheet and fainted clean away.

There are no doubt thousands of such examples, probably documented in dozens of books of reminiscences, but the truth is I was never entirely comfortable in this adversarial world of conductor-bating. My instinct was to try to build

---

[6] Szell may have been famously unpleasant but he was evidently not totally lacking a sense of humour. He was notorious for having a conducting style which involved tiny movements and a beat which appeared to be confined within an invisible box about one foot square. The story is told of a double bassist in the Cleveland Symphony who was about to retire from the orchestra. For his final concert, he attached a telescope to his music stand which he used rather theatrically during the first part of the concert to pick out the maestro's beat. As the second half began, the same theatrical business was resumed, and the bass player was taken somewhat aback when Szell 'shot his cuffs' to reveal on his right hand shirt cuff the words, "YOU'RE FIRED," picked out in miniscule capitals.

bridges, though this was often hard in the face of such deeply ingrained attitudes. I played in the Academy of St Martin-in-the-Fields for 15 years under the invariable baton (when there was a baton) of the aforementioned Sir Neville Marriner. I was generally a great fan of Neville's but my admiration was not shared by all my colleagues, and it was a source of surprise and regret to me that in all my time as a member of this great orchestra, the players never once showed their appreciation of their maestro either by applause at the end of a concert or even by the traditional tapping of bows on music stands at the moment when the conductor would take his solo bow. The effect of this on Neville himself was to make him deeply suspicious of any show of regard, let alone affection, from his players. He thought they must be up to something. The sadness of this was, it seemed to me, that Marriner's extraordinary achievement in creating such a successful group of musicians was seldom acknowledged by its own members, but had they tried to break down this barrier, this too would not have been acknowledged.

There is a wider lesson here of which all performers should be aware, and I was lucky enough to learn it early: when I was eleven or twelve, I attended a week-long holiday music course at Keele University. One of the chamber music coaches was an Oxford near-neighbour, the distinguished violinist Manoug Parikian, who had been prevailed upon to drive me home to Oxford at the end of the week. In the closing concert, shortly before this journey, I had played the Mozart clarinet quintet (this was, of course, before my bassoon-playing days) following which, Manoug graciously told me how much he had enjoyed my performance. I 'had music in my bones,' apparently. I was, of course, flattered, but responded awkwardly with much false modesty and self-deprecation. Later, on the way home, Manoug delivered a stern lecture: every performer, he said, must learn how to accept praise graciously. It will happen often that someone congratulates you for a performance when you know perfectly well that, for whatever reason, it was poor, but it does no one any favours to be honest in this situation. You must learn to smile and accept praise rather than be excessively modest or, even worse, try to explain why the congratulator is mistaken.

Parikian was, of course, right about the importance of learning how to behave properly after coming off stage. If false modesty is to be avoided, out of consideration for the bestower of praise, the converse of this problem comes when, as a manager or mere audience member, you have just heard a bad performance and have to go back-stage and find some suitable words for the offending perpetrator. As mentioned in the Foreword, the title of this memoir is a tribute to Sir Claus Moser's legendary skills in such exercises in ambiguity; the avoidance of outright lying while remaining sensitive to the vulnerability of the artiste in that immediate post-performance flush. Less inventive than Sir Claus, I used to find that, "Darling, you've done it again," served quite well in such circumstances.

On stage, of course, it is taken for granted that correct behaviour is essential. There is no hiding place there, but events do occasionally conspire...a mild enough instance was a concert in the Brangwyn Hall in Swansea, for which the Swansea Choral Society had hired the Bournemouth Sinfonietta, a chamber orchestra which I had joined the year before. The concert was conducted by the splendidly named director of the choir, Mr Haydn James. We had despatched, with sufficient aplomb, Mozart's Impresario Overture and moved on to the first of the evening's choral works, a relatively unfamiliar cantata by a young Beethoven, called Cantata for Kaiser Josef II. The opening chorus ends in a familiarly Beethovenian manner with a series of woodwind and brass chords repeated over a sustained background string chord. We reached this point uneventfully enough but in the penultimate bar it struck me that Maestro James seemed to be struggling to turn a page of his substantial and weighty score. Of course, he might be conducting partly from memory and be looking for the opening section of the following movement, but warning lights began to flash when his baton showed no sign of easing gracefully into the final cadence. If anything, it took on something of an accelerando, perhaps reflecting a growing agitation in its operator. It soon became clear to those of us who were watching (not everyone was in this class of orchestral goody-two-shoes) that standing before us was a man who was not going to stop when our music ran out. The observant ones did not include any member of the string department, who, to a man and woman, stopped playing exactly as Beethoven indicated. We in the woodwind section, perhaps being cast more in the mould of musical private soldiers and thus more accustomed to taking orders without question, made a collective decision to play on, with more repetitions of our C minor chord, for an extra bar...and then another...and another...and soon the weaker of our colleagues could play no more because, obviously, you cannot maintain an embouchure and laugh at the same time (try it!). And whether because we were the most dutiful, or perhaps just the dullest, it was the two bassoons (Ian Cuthill and I) who were the last left playing, continuing to maintain an open 5th for another bar or two before also falling victim to irresistible giggles, at first suppressed by clamping the lips together in a vain attempt to stem the inevitable, then, as the end neared, the natural warmth of our bassoons' tone mutated into a curious kind of bleating with much quivering vibrato, before a final explosive admission of defeat. You sometimes cannot be sure how much of this kind of thing is understood by the audience, but this time there was no place to hide for our hapless (and helpless) first clarinet, Frank Holdsworth, for the following movement should have been introduced by a gently beguiling clarinet melody of a dozen bars or so. However, when Mr James had sufficiently recovered his own dignity to raise an expectant baton in Frank's direction, there was no-one to be seen…Frank was literally hiding behind his music stand with his head between his knees, unable to play and indeed almost unable to breathe.

The orchestral foot soldier may be incapacitated in even more uncomfortable circumstances: as we know, a typical orchestral musician is generous and openhearted to a fault but it is nevertheless sadly true that the discomfiture of colleagues can be greeted, every now and then, with hilarity rather than sympathy. A notable instance occurred during a concert, given by the oddly named Hanover Band, at the charming London concert hall, St John's Smith Square. One of the orchestra's leading lights at this time was an opinionated, and frankly, self-important, French horn player, by name Horace Fitzpatrick. His limited technical skills as a horn player, coupled with his aforementioned character failings, meant that he was not a popular figure amongst his colleagues in the band. Horace was the soloist, on this occasion, in one of Mozart's Horn Concertos, the closing work to the first half of the concert. One of the unique selling points of Horace's account of this masterpiece, as he proudly announced to the audience before embarking on the evening's entertainment, was that he would improvise the solo cadenzas in a manner and style, as he explained, authentic to the eighteenth-century period. His performance proceeded uneventfully enough until he reached the point of the final cadenza in the last movement, whereupon he launched himself into a virtuoso cascade of ornamented scales and flourishing arpeggios which led him lower and lower into the nether regions of the French horn's register. Now, these low notes on the horn are exceptionally and obstinately hard to locate with certainty and need to be approached with caution and a kind of deference. Horace was having none of this: he plunged headlong towards the final resolution of his solo and, inevitably perhaps, as he triumphantly arrived at the very last note…nothing emerged at all.

Undaunted, he tried again, and again, and yet again, searching in vain for his elusive final note, and repeatedly digging ever deeper into his self-dug hole. In due course, as even Horace's confidence began to ebb, the sounds emerging from his horn could no longer be described in musical terms—this was a large animal in distress, from whom the life force was departing in the face of Horace's ever more desperate assault. It is, perhaps, inevitable that the musical murder being perpetrated on stage was the cause of much hilarity amongst Mr Fitzpatrick's colleagues. Eventually, though, it was over and the orchestra filed dutifully off stage for the interval. One, however, the ebullient principal oboist, Ku Ebbinge, remained motionless and yet also showed unmistakable signs of distress. At last one of his colleagues returned to ask if he was all right, whereupon he weakly nodded, then added, "But I have wet myself."

No doubt many professions have a trove of such stories, and of occasions and circumstances in which, as P. G. Wodehouse so memorably put it, 'Fate slips the lead into the boxing glove.' And those which demand some element of public performance alongside a seriousness of purpose must presumably be especially accident prone. I am thinking of the stage, of course, but the courts of law and the church must also be fairly high risk for those with a keen sense of the ridiculous and a weakness for giggles. This was brought to mind recently when that charming broadcaster, the Reverend Richard Coles, hosted a small phone-in, inviting listeners to relate occasions when they had succumbed to inappropriate giggles. He set the ball rolling with his own account of a busy Saturday when he had to perform his solemn clerical duties at three christenings, hard on each other's heels. It was only when he reached the third that it struck him that the first two families whose young persons he had just welcomed into the body of the church, were called Chambers and Potts; for some considerable time he was unable to articulate the surname of the third baptismal baby, it taking a monumental effort of self-control eventually to utter, with appropriate decorum, the word Kermode.

Returning to the orchestral context, instances of players 'corpsing' are happily rare, but of course they do happen, and in case it be thought that such human frailties are unique to the orchestral rank and file, I offer, for the sake of balance, two further examples, in the first of which it was the conductor who succumbed and in the second, even more of a connoisseur's item, the audience.

In the first example, the occasion was one of the many concerts the Bournemouth Sinfonietta gave in school halls around the West Country (there are, or were then, rather few designated concert halls in the region, so school assembly halls became familiar territory). This was a concert conducted by our engaging young assistant conductor, Kenneth Montgomery, who in the middle of a Haydn slow movement, suddenly, and to us inexplicably, dissolved into laughter. The conductor is the only one of the orchestra who faces towards the back of the stage and he later told us that his episode was triggered by the appearance behind the orchestra of a cleaning lady; not just any old cleaning lady either, but one dressed like a cartoon character, Mrs Andy Capp perhaps, with a long faded floral print skirt, hair wrapped in a kind of makeshift turban, lighted cigarette hanging precariously from the corner of her mouth, carrying a bucket and mop and, if it is to be believed, somehow also wheeling an ancient bicycle. She emerged from stage right, exiting stage left, without once raising her head or appearing by any gesture to acknowledge that there were other people present, let alone an orchestra and audience in mid-performance. The back rows of the orchestra were elevated on rostra, so by a curious trick of sightlines it was only the conductor, himself occupying a slightly elevated position on a rostrum, who had sight of this apparition. Audience and orchestra were as oblivious to Mrs Capp as she was to them.

The second, even rarer variant on this theme occurred during a small concert for wind quintet (the Albion Ensemble, see chapter 3), and this time it was the audience themselves who succumbed. The story is briefly told: my dear friend and colleague, Andrew Marriner, had recently caused one of his clarinets to suffer the indignity of a complete overhaul, involving renewal of all springs, pads and so forth. His first outing with the newly serviced instrument had been at the previous day's rehearsal for this very concert. Unfortunately, one of the new pads was not properly fixed and fell off during some especially exotic passage work (with which our Albion repertoire abounded) with the result that no further sound issued from the offending instrument. There was nothing for it but to call a halt and effect a rapid additional repair. You can perhaps anticipate the sequence of events…come the concert, we were well underway with a prestissimo rendition of a Rossini overture when an identical malfunction happened again and we were instantly silenced. A graceful Andrew, with a few words about mechanical failure, retreated to the Green Room to make the necessary repairs. Meanwhile his four colleagues were left staring awkwardly at their boots until, overwhelmed by the need to say something, indeed anything, I launched into the cautionary tale, as I extensively and laboriously recounted it (after all, we didn't know how long Andrew needed backstage) of the overhaul the clarinet had just been subjected to, of how one should never let one's instrument out of one's own hands, and, extemporising on this theme for a while, eventually reached the punch line that exactly the same accident had happened only the day before. At which point Andrew, perfectly on cue, re-appeared, calm as anything, and, before taking his seat, again apologised elegantly to the audience with the words, "Ladies and gentleman, my most humble apologies. I can assure you that this has never ever happened before." At which, of course, the audience fell about and Andrew could only glare at me, wondering what on earth I could have said to make him such a figure of ridicule. The post-mortem was painful, with Andrew maintaining, with some justice, that what he meant was that it had never before happened in a concert and furthermore holding me to account for breaching an important rule that what happens in the privacy of the rehearsal room should never be brought into the public domain. But something had to be said; we couldn't, or I anyway couldn't, just sit there in silence: a fine example of the lead-weighted boxing glove.

I had learned at an even earlier age the dangers of extempore public speaking. The occasion was another small chamber music concert, this time at a very modest music club in Southend for which the oboist Geordie Caird (another Albion Ensemble colleague) and I were accompanied at the keyboard by his then wife, Sarah. The repertoire for this combination of instruments is not extensive and, for the only time in my life, I had been talked into playing a sonata for bassoon and piano by the French composer Camille Saint-Saëns, a work for which I had no especial fondness. My moment arrived; the connecting door from backstage onto the stage was opened by an unseen hand and, just as I was stepping into the public arena, Geordie appeared alongside me, briefly halting my forward momentum, and whispered in my ear, "Felix, you do know, don't you, that they have no programme notes. You need to say something about this piece." By the time the words "no programme notes" had sunk in, I was already standing at the front of the stage, being greeted by the sparse applause of, as it seemed, a dozen or so ladies in woolly hats, and only then realising that I knew absolutely nothing about the circumstances in which Saint-Saëns came to write a sonata for bassoon, and furthermore was unable to offer any information about the composer, his life, his career, or even within a margin of error of about a century, his dates (well, can you?). So, as you can understand, a degree of creativity (or perhaps a degree in creativity) was unavoidable (I could scarcely admit such total ignorance), and I improvised with some, though I say it myself, fluency about the occasion when Saint-Saëns was commissioned to write a test piece for the annual end-of-year woodwind competition at the Paris Conservatoire, how he made such idiomatic use of the unique characteristics of the French bassoon and so on, and indeed, forth. Whatever I said, seemed to be well received by the woolly hats and it was with a renewed spring in my step that I strode confidently into the post-concert tea and sandwiches reception at the local vicarage. Before long, though, I became uncomfortably aware that the beady eye of an elderly gentleman lurking in the lee of the aspidistra in the corner was trained upon me. Worse, I soon realised that he was working his way in my direction, clearly intending to speak. What he told me is, I feel it to this today, an example of the unfairness of life. There was I, on a cold winter's evening in Southend, playing to an audience of a mere handful and before me was a gentleman who proceeded to inform me, employing some colourful language as he did so, that he had travelled from Manchester to hear this concert and that he was engaged in writing an official biography of Saint-Saëns and that if what I had said was true, he would have to re-write chapters six to ten. Not only so, but what he told me of the true circumstances of the composition of this unexceptional work, only compounded my sense of injustice. For had I known and recounted the truth to the woolly hats of Southend that Saints-Saëns created this rather workmanlike sonata while crossing the Sahara desert on a camel, they would surely have accused me of making it up. Who would guess that these post-concert receptions could be so fraught with danger?

My Southend misfortune (admittedly self-inflicted) was an acute example of another hazard (there seem to be so many) to which the orchestral foot soldier finds himself from time to time exposed: a familiar figure amongst the post-concert mêlée is the earnestly interested interrogator to whom one is bound to be polite but from whose well-intentioned clutches one yearns for release. To this inquisitor, I give the generic name 'The Gripper'.

The Gripper is, of course, a universally recognisable phenomenon but I attribute the refinement of the concept to my long-time friend and colleague, the horn player Christian Rutherford, and the unlikely location was the campus of the University of Iowa. The occasion was a tour with the late Christopher Hogwood's Academy of Ancient Music, and the University, host for that night's concert, was also generously hosting a reception afterwards, providing their staff and students an opportunity to meet the musicians. My fate that evening was to be monopolised by an earnest young lady who, it transpired, was an eager student of the baroque bassoon. All my long-rehearsed manoeuvres for the avoidance of grippers had been to no avail, and I found myself literally backing away in the face of the relentless advance of this unlikely amazon, until, trapped in a corner of the room and almost embraced (perhaps gripped) by the tentacles of a large rubber plant, all prospect of escape had been abandoned and the will to live lost. My interlocutor, it soon emerged, was not only an expert on the history and development of bassoons through the eighteenth and nineteenth Centuries, she was also, I learned, working on a PhD thesis about how they were made, with special emphasis on their internal measurements, and within this already narrow field, an analysis of the effect on overtones of the parabolic properties of the brass crooks, or bocals, which link instrument to reed. She was eager to share with me the results of the most extensive comparative survey yet undertaken, of measurements of the circumferences of finger holes of French bassoons between 1750 and 1778, and she had already generously invited my comments on her study, as yet uncompleted, of the variable quality of brass available for the manufacture of woodwind instrument keywork in mid-eighteenth-century Paris. Needless to say my excitement at these revelations was perhaps not on a par with her own, and my repertoire of interested questions and all-too-British exclamations of mild astonishment was soon exhausted. But she was now approaching her climax, an exposition of the internal dimensions, uniquely measured and recorded only the day before, of a particular French bassoon from 1772, when, as much as anything to re-assure myself that blood at least continued to course in my veins and that normal life, even after such major trauma, perhaps requiring a period of intensive care followed by gentle recuperation, had some prospect of being recovered, I contrived one further enquiry. A feeble enough question, to be sure, but the circumstances were stressful. I ventured to ask the title of her dissertation. "I'm calling it 'The Bore of the Bassoon,'" she earnestly responded, at which, I fear, I laughed, perhaps somewhat hysterically, and certainly taking a considerable time fully to recover a dignified composure. Perhaps she thought I had gone mad, for she certainly did not seem to recognise any humour in the situation, and she quickly made her excuses to bring our rather one-sided conversation to an end. For me, on the other hand, my freedom (and will to live) was restored. I had escaped both Gripper and rubber plant and made briskly for the bar in search of a well-earned sharpener.

Shaken by such a conspicuous failure to elude the attentions of the Gripper, I felt impelled at once to seek out Christian, not only to invite his sympathy at the sorry tale but also perhaps, through the catharsis of the confessional, to recover a modicum of self-esteem. I found him in conversation with another Iowa student who, it was to emerge, was both an actor and a man of action. On hearing my story, he immediately grasped the concept of the Gripper and encouraged us both to supply him with case histories and examples. Quite how this exploration developed, I now forget, but our new friend was soon volunteering to put his thespian skills to the test; he suggested that we prime him with suitable questions, then introduce him to a suitable candidate for gripping from amongst our colleagues. As Christian is a horn player and had a horn-playing colleague (I was the only bassoon in this particular concert programme) it was a natural choice to nominate his colleague as the unwitting victim of our experiment. The colleague in question was the delightful Tony Halstead, one of the kindest and politest of souls (and most eminent of musicians), and thus in every respect an ideal candidate. So it was that we drew up a list of ten questions about the early French Horn (the effect of different curvatures in the mouthpiece, for example, or the acoustics of the higher reaches of the harmonic series). Our tame gripper had, with great good humour, memorised our script and fully mastered his brief, so now it only remained to isolate our victim. We, of course, had to make the introductions, ensuring that Tony would be initially well-disposed, and then retire, but not so far that we couldn't hear the ensuing dialogue. Our *faux*-Gripper put up a virtuoso performance, not only remembering his lines but also finding intelligent-sounding follow-ups whenever the conversational flow showed signs of flagging. This might have continued even longer than it did, had not Christian been unable to contain himself (I think it was when the geometry of mouthpiece design rose to the top of the agenda) and, turning an alarming shade of pink, succumbed to such an extended fit of coughing that it was quite literally show-stopping. When the truth of the scene was eventually revealed, as I fear it had to be, I'm sorry to report that Tony, our victim, was unable to enter fully into the joke. Indeed he was so cross that I'm not sure if he has forgiven us to this day; but of course, he is too kind and polite to mention it.

No doubt the quantity of alcohol consumed would have made these kinds of events seem funnier at the time than perhaps they should have done, and looking back, it was certainly common for these tours, especially the long ones, to be fuelled by heroic quantities of liquor. Excessive drinking can, of course, be terribly destructive, and this was almost fatally the case with one colleague, who was to become a good friend later, the sublimely gifted violinist, Alan Loveday, who was, at this time, neither a glass-half-full man nor glass-half-empty. His glass was invariably emptied. My first encounter with Alan came when I was a young member of the Bournemouth Sinfonietta and he was cast as our guest soloist for the Mendelssohn Violin Concerto. The conductor was one of our regulars, George Hurst.

There were two concerts, the first in Plymouth on a Friday and the second in a small hall in Hampshire, possibly Aldershot, the following Sunday. We travelled the considerable distance to Plymouth (driving was slow going in the West Country in those days), arriving in time for a short rehearsal that afternoon. Alan had been with us in Bournemouth for rehearsals earlier in the week but had returned to London the previous day. When we reached Plymouth that Friday he had not yet arrived, but there were still several London trains which might be bearing Alan westwards, so alarm bells were not yet sounding; but as the start of the concert approached and still no soloist was to be found, management's anxiety grew. I suppose the leader of the orchestra was also alerted because strains of the Mendelssohn concerto could be heard issuing from his dressing room as he realised that Plan B would be for him to take over the soloist role. The concert duly arrived and went ahead, with no change of programme, but also with no Alan Loveday. Come Sunday, we arrived in Aldershot to find an impeccable Alan ready and waiting to rehearse, and all seemed to be in hand as we cantered once more through the concerto and Alan departed while George Hurst touched up a few details of the remainder of our programme. In those days, there were few restaurants in the smaller provincial towns and even fewer which were open for business at 6.00 p.m. on a Sunday evening, so our enterprising manager had negotiated with a local hotel to provide food for the orchestra. When we made our way to the said hotel we found Alan perched rather precariously on a bar stool, already decked out in full concert uniform of tails and white tie, and taking full advantage of the additional drinking time he had been granted before the concert. He was, unquestionably, the worse for wear. We finished our meals and returned to the concert venue, leaving Alan still located in the bar (he wasn't in the first piece, of course) but we were, by now, more than a little anxious about how he would cope with the Mendelssohn when the time came. As that moment arrived, it was re-assuring to see Alan, as beautifully turned out as ever, stepping confidently onto the stage. He turned to face the oboist, the incomparable Judy Bass, indicating his need for an A to tune to; he then spent a little time adjusting his A and E strings before launching into a thrilling account of the first movement…the only problem being that he forgot to turn back to face the audience so he delivered his virtuosity with his back to them, which I imagine, they found puzzling. In this Mendelssohn work, there is a link between first movement and the slow second movement which consists of a long held note on the bassoon, solo. As we reached this musical turning point, George Hurst, our maestro, leaving the bassoon to its own devices, gripped Alan smartly by the shoulders, rotated him through a brisk 180° turn, a musical turning point indeed. The slow movement then continued as though nothing unusual had occurred.

Years later I asked Alan, now teetotal, if he remembered anything of this. Perhaps not surprisingly he had no memory of the Aldershot concert but he did recall failing to get to Plymouth. In those drinking days, he told me, he used often to visit a bridge club, the Grand Slam Club, near Paddington Station, which was one of the few places you could get a drink after pub closing time. He seems to have spent the night playing bridge (with glass in hand) and emerged the following morning, with violin and concert clothes carefully prepared for the journey, but unable to remember where he was supposed to go. He was fairly sure, he told me, that his destination began with P. He thought it was probably Portsmouth, so it was to Portsmouth that he went that day. He out-thought himself, in a way, because he made this key decision while standing outside Paddington Station whence he could have taken a train to Plymouth. Instead, he crossed London to Waterloo Station, and the rest is history.

It was a few years before I encountered Alan again. This was after I had moved back to London from Bournemouth and was playing with the Academy of St Martin in the Fields. On my very first Academy tour to Germany Alan was playing in the violin section (not leading, fortunately). He had navigated the London rehearsals without incident, but once the tour had begun it was soon clear that his drinking was quite out of control. So much so that Neville Marriner took it upon himself to lock Alan into his hotel bedroom on the evening of each concert, thus ensuring that Alan never once made it on to the concert platform throughout the tour. Alan thus achieved a feat which many musicians would think ideal, a tour without concerts. However desirable this might seem from an individual's perspective, it was fairly obviously not sustainable, and Alan was told (he spoke of this later) that he would not be asked to play again until he had sorted out his drinking. There followed another gap, of about three years, during which he struggled with, and finally defeated his demons. He didn't speak much about these years, which must have been very tough, and I only have a few snippets.

One such reflects well on Neville Marriner. One of the first big recording successes of the Academy was with Vivaldi, The Four Seasons, with Alan Loveday playing the solo violin. This must have been recorded in the early 1960s but even today, when the piece can be heard in almost every elevator in every hotel in the world, and in the face of competition from dozens of great violinists and from the all-conquering period instrument movement, Alan's playing remains a model of melodic simplicity coupled with an apparently natural technical skill, which makes it a performance to include in any 'building a library' type of collection. Indeed, the only aspect of the disc which sounds in the least dated is the excessively florid continuo harpsichord playing (by Simon Preston, I think) in the slow movements. To help support Alan through his alcoholism years Neville signed over to Alan a share of the royalties from CD sales.

Alan later told me that he had always intended, even while in the grip of his addiction, to turn his attention to the emerging new style of period instrument performance. With hindsight, the failure to enlist Alan into the period instrument 'ranks' was quite a missed opportunity for these fledgling groups because their members were often accused of being failed modern-instrument players, and there was no doubt that the lack of solid orchestral experience in some of the early efforts at 'orchestral' baroque playing was a weakness. Alan, if sober, could have brought great critical credibility to this new world. He had an interest, too, in the technical business of recording, and an ongoing project at this time was to record himself playing the unaccompanied Bach works for violin. Sadly, this was never completed, mainly because after one session he fell over and smashed his baroque fiddle to such smithereens that it was never repaired, and he never acquired another.[7]

---

[7] This violin was not the only thing to be smashed in Alan's lost years: the Academy's recording company held a party to celebrate with a 'golden CD' the millionth sale of the Vivaldi Four Seasons disc. Shortly after taking possession of the specially made golden CD Alan slipped and fell, rising again to his feet clutching the golden disc in several

I can reveal, though, that Alan played at least one concert with The English Concert (see chapter 6) in its very early days. It must have been a concert using modern instruments, so would have been around 1972, the official foundation date of the group. The occasion was a one-off concert in Italy for which a small plane had been chartered to fly from Biggin Hill (those were the days!). All, apparently, went smoothly until the concert was done and Alan joined the post-concert celebration (he was probably in the middle of his 'non-drinking' recovery period at this time) and outstayed everyone. As he eventually retired to his hotel room in the small hours, he knew he would be struggling to meet the challenge of a 7.00 a.m. departure by bus to the airport, so, showing his considerable experience in such matters, he carefully laid out his clothes on the floor alongside his bed precisely in the order in which he would need to put them on in the morning. When the 7.00 a.m. departure hour arrived, his colleagues assembled in the hotel lobby…but no sign of Alan, and that least-welcome management phone call[8] confirmed that he was still in his room. He promised an immediate appearance, but 30 minutes later, still no Alan. Eventually, he emerged, reportedly looking dishevelled, and dressed in his concert clothes. As he later recounted, he had suffered the indignity of being sick in the night, and,

---

small pieces. What he revealed was that the CD was not an Academy recording at all; the company had simply picked the first CD that came to hand and painted it gold.

[8] In my orchestra manager role, I have often had to make that dreaded, "Where are you?" call, but my favourite of these stories did not involve me but the aforementioned clarinettist, and erstwhile Albion Ensemble colleague, Andrew Marriner, on tour with the London Symphony Orchestra: a concert in Milan was followed next day by another in Budapest, and the players were under strict orders that they must catch the one train to Budapest, departing at 10 a.m., that would get them to the concert in time. Andrew was in bed, asleep, when the phone rang…it was the orchestra manager calling from Milan central station saying that the train was leaving in 20 minutes, "We are all at the station, and where are you?" Andrew says he has never moved so fast in his life, leaping out of bed, grabbing his suitcase, running downstairs straight into a cab and sprinting across the crowded station piazza. The train was pulling away from the platform as he panted to a halt but the last wagon, the luggage van, had its rearmost door still open; he hurled his case inside and jumped, landing in a heap on a pile of other cases. He had never felt so elated in his life, but, as the euphoria subsided, he began to feel uneasy. His suitcase, he realised, had felt unusually light and, retrieving it with some trepidation, the truth was revealed; he had forgotten to pack. All his clothes, including those for that night's concert, were lost forever in the Milan hotel.

not having made it to the bathroom, had been sick over the very clothes he had so carefully laid out for the morning. So when the 7.00 a.m. phone call aroused him, he had had to wash his clothes in the shower but had been unable to dry them sufficiently to wear. His good fortune, if it can be so described, was that the morning flight was a charter, so a delayed departure time was an inconvenience merely, rather than a disaster.

Alan, now teetotal and a regular at AA groups, was gradually re-introduced into The Academy of St Martin in the Fields, starting with work based in London, almost entirely recording sessions. It was felt, no doubt rightly, that a resumption of touring life would need to be carefully handled to avoid the risks of relapse. This is where that great character, the viola player Tony Jenkins, stepped in. Alan's other great passion, apart from drink and the violin, was bridge and Tony devised an inspired and generous scheme, to be activated on Alan's first comeback tour, to keep him continuously occupied at the bridge table throughout the entire time he was not actually playing the violin. To achieve this, Tony rounded up everyone in the orchestra with even the slightest knowledge of bridge (plus a few without) and organised a rota which maintained a more or less endless bridge game over the five or six days of the tour. This was my return to the bridge table (I had learned the game while in the Bournemouth orchestra and occupied many a long bus journey with a bridge four at the back), and the time when I got to know Alan and Tony as friends. Sadly, neither is still alive, but I will always be grateful to both for re-introducing me to the game.

Alan was an imaginative bridge player: he knew the text-book rules, of course, but also had the self-confidence to disregard the 'book', as he called it, when he chose. This certainly made him an exciting partner. He attributed his disregard for conventional wisdoms to his father who had educated him at home in New Zealand. In fact, to call it education is perhaps not entirely accurate: he was brought up on the basis that he only needed to know three things, Latin, violin playing and tennis. So his education, such as it was, was an unusual one. In hindsight, it is perhaps not surprising that when he came to London as a child prodigy violinist (funded with help from the famous Budapest String Quartet whose members had been deeply impressed by his playing when they first heard him as a precocious young teenager in New Zealand) that he struggled to adjust to an unfamiliar world in which he had neither family nor established friends to keep him grounded. He achieved huge success early, playing the Tchaikovsky

Concerto at the Proms as a 17-year-old for example and making frequent appearances as a soloist in the next dozen seasons.

Typical of Alan's imaginative approach (to everything) was his preparation for a performance (again at the Proms) of the notoriously challenging Elgar Violin Concerto. The Royal Albert Hall in those days was without the air-conditioning which now makes it tolerably cool, and was famous for becoming stiflingly hot when full with 5,000 people in mid-August. Alan was concerned that his fingers would sweat, making the violin's fingerboard too slippery, so he devised an ingenious practising method which involved pouring linseed oil in various concentrations onto the fingerboard, thus replicating 'battle conditions'.

Needless to say, Alan had a finely honed sense of the ridiculous, but as with any gifted raconteur the manner of the telling contributed so much to the effect of the story that a more pedestrian, written account can only hope to capture part of this. There was the time on tour in the States when he found himself in a New York diner for breakfast—he was served by a typically hard-faced waitress with a voice like a pencil-sharpener and was intimidated by the multitudinous menu choices of breads and eggs which can be challenging even at the best of times, let alone first thing in the morning. He opted, eventually, for two poached eggs on brown toast, an order which he carefully relayed to his server, who proceeded to holler through a hole in the wall to the kitchen, "Boy and girl on a raft, on brown!" After a while, Alan, although amused at this image, found that he had nonetheless changed his mind and, with some trepidation summoned his server again, apologising in typically British style for being a nuisance and so on, to enquire whether he could possibly, if it was not too much trouble, change his order to scrambled eggs. Without breaking stride the hard-boiled harridan hollered down to the kitchen again, "That boy and girl on a raft…wreck 'em!"

Then there was the recital tour in Australia and New Zealand in which he had to play sixty-four concerts in sixty-five days (and the 'free' day was spent travelling by boat from Australia to New Zealand). This was both physically but particularly mentally exhausting, so much so that he remembered standing in the wings of a school concert hall somewhere in Australia pondering what to play as an encore. And he realised that he couldn't remember if he had played his recital. He had to ask!

More dangerous, even life-threatening, was a similar recital tour, this time to South Africa. In those days, travel to South Africa was by ship which, for the drinking man, presented plentiful opportunities and risks. After a series of escapades during which Alan had to be restrained by crew members from harming himself, annoying other passengers and damaging sundry items of the ship's furniture, he was summoned before the ship's captain, to be informed that the last person 'of his sort' to be aboard this ship had been thrown overboard by the crew, never to be seen again and his name expunged from the passenger list. For his own safety, Alan was to be confined in the ship's slammer for the remainder of the voyage. He would be checked twice daily by the ship's doctor. That Alan accepted these strictures with as good a grace as he did, was helped, as he reported, by the knowledge, which he held but which was unknown to the captain, that the said medic was a fellow alcoholic. Not only so, but he was already in the habit of visiting the slammer approximately twice daily in order to consume a bottle of scotch undisturbed. He was glad to share this indulgence with such a convivial companion as Alan (and was even persuaded to bring Alan his violin so that he could practice Paganini Caprices in the intervals between drinking sessions).

And a final word on the great Alan Loveday; I once asked him, long after he had altogether given up drinking, whether he ever missed it and he surprised me by saying that he did, "The thing is, Felix, that when you woke in the morning with a filthy hangover you had one comfort, the certainty that the day could only improve. I do not now like waking up each day knowing that things will never be better than this." He was one of those great musicians who, despite all eccentricities and absurdities, was absolutely serious about the need for music in his own life (he could be nothing other than the musician he was) and the absolute conviction of the vital importance of music to all of us. And he shared this wonderful combination of eccentricity and seriousness of purpose with another of my one-time colleagues and musical giant, Francis Baines.

Francis, in the 20 years or so that I knew him, was the double bass player in many of the burgeoning period instrument orchestras in the 1970s and 80s. By this time he must already have been in his 60s, and had already enjoyed an extraordinary and varied musical career of which many of his younger colleagues were doubtless scarcely aware. He was a man unlike others. Earlier in his life he had been, amongst other things, the principal double bassist in the London Philharmonic Orchestra and a composer of some distinction. He played on an Amati bass, one of the vary rarest of instruments, which for years he parked overnight in the left luggage office of Waterloo station before boarding his train home. Home at the time was a canal boat with, as he so reasonably explained, no space to store a double bass.

Anyone who has seen Francis on stage, let alone worked with him to any extent, will recognise how challenging it is to describe his character in words. Any 'Francis' performance was a little piece of theatre, entirely self-contained, but also a vital part of the whole. For a man who could have been a grandfather to many of his young period instrument colleagues it is a tribute to his passion for all kinds of music that his enthusiasm never dimmed. Embarking on a long series of recording sessions, a complete cycle of the nine Beethoven symphonies, might have been daunting, but not for Francis. As they prepared for the first 'take' his young desk partner asked how he felt about embarking on such an arduous recording journey, no doubt expecting the jaded response of a typical battle-weary orchestral hack. Not a bit of it; Francis was delighted that he and his wife June, a violinist, were both engaged for the recording sessions and that, "Beethoven's going to buy us a new car." Perhaps this was the same series in which Francis, very unusually for him, arrived rather late for a rehearsal. He made his way to his double bass stand at the back and, with a determined air, but without apology, unpacked his bass and took his place. His desk partner pointed to the spot the orchestra had reached but Francis shook his head, in his characteristically exaggerated manner, rather as a dog might shake itself after a swim, and began, pianissimo but prestissimo, at the beginning of the movement, so that every note was played, *sotto voce,* until he had caught up with his colleagues, whereupon he resumed the usual tempo. It would have been disrespectful to Beethoven, he later explained, not to have attended to every note the master had written.

Chapter 2
An Oxford Overture

Oxford in the immediate post-war years was a place of tremendous intellectual intensity. My parents, in common with many of their generation, had been obliged by national service to postpone their undergraduate studies, so when they did eventually go up to Oxford they were considerably older, and vastly more experienced, than a typical undergraduate just out of school. They were hungry, literally and intellectually, and determined to get started as quickly as possible on their peace-time lives. Also, the academic climate of the university was very different in 1945 from the complacent traditionalism of a generation earlier. Throughout the 1930s Oxford had been welcoming substantial numbers of refugees, academics from Continental Europe who brought with them intellectual traditions and methods quite new to English academic life. These accidents of history, a uniquely experienced and motivated student body entering a newly invigorated academic environment, meant that the university at the start of the 1950s, still a time of widespread rationing and chill austerity, was an intellectual hothouse; this was my parents' world.

My father, an Irish Guardsman, had fought in Italy, buried the dead in The Netherlands and defended his fellow soldiers in Courts Martial on all sorts of charges, trivial and serious, and all of this before his undergraduate studies began. My mother had begun her undergraduate studies in 1942 but interrupted them to take a 'protected' teaching job at Sherborne School (in order, she said, to avoid National Service which might have seen her recruited by Bletchley Park[9]). She returned to Oxford in 1946 and, amongst other things, became

---

[9] Bletchley Park was to be avoided because in 1943 it was assumed that the war with Japan, and the need for intelligence services at Bletchley, would continue for many years, even after the defeat of Germany. That the atom bomb would bring hostilities to an end

secretary of the philosophical Jowett Club. Here she met my father. Their relationship initially got off on the wrong foot, as a result of my father being unable to resist a joke: my mother was rather in awe of the young Geoffrey Warnock and had written him a formal letter inviting him to speak at a Jowett Club event; she had given much thought to how to open this dialogue, eventually opting for, "Dear Mr Warnock, may I call you Geoffrey?" to which in due course he replied, "Dear Mary, may I call you Miss Wilson?" Despite this awkward start, Miss Wilson was apparently soon to be found writing Geoffrey's Greek history essays while he wrote some (she says "most") of her thesis for the MPhil degree she took in a single year (rather than the usual two).

My parents married in 1949 and so began an unusually equal partnership. This was helped by the fact that, shortly before the wedding, my mother was offered a lectureship at St Hugh's. My father, at about the same time, was awarded a prize lectureship at Magdalen, so they knew they would be staying in Oxford and no issue would arise, or at least not immediately, about whose career would take precedence. Equality of esteem there certainly was,[10] but equality of pay was another matter altogether: my mother was the first ever married lecturer at St Hugh's and she recalled, with some bitterness even long afterwards, how dreadfully little she earned in her first job. One reason, of course, was that her pay assumed that she would be living and dining 'free' in college alongside all the other spinster fellows.

In terms of my parents' professional philosophical work, the post-war intellectual atmosphere was hugely stimulating. Optimism was in the air, and there was a new style of philosophy which it then seemed possible to believe might 'solve' many of the old problems; this was to be achieved by paying close attention to, and analysis of, language. For the pre-war logical positivists this had involved 'translating' problematic statements of everyday language into logically rigorous empirically verifiable statements. For the new Oxford

---

as quickly as it did was unknown, of course, so it was assumed that the Japanese would have to be defeated Pacific Island by Pacific Island, a kind of hand-to-hand combat which would have been painfully slow and brutally costly in terms of lives lost.

[10] Equality also featured, in due course, in my parents' approach to childcare: they developed a concept which they called 'the equality of suffering' based on the recognition that each parent hated certain essential tasks but that the hated tasks were different. The key to a harmonious relationship was therefore to ensure a fair distribution of the 'hated' tasks.

philosophers however, no such translations seemed necessary. A rigorous attention to the facts of language was going to be a sufficient, indeed the only, suitable philosophical tool. These two philosophical approaches, of course, shared a conviction that the analysis of language was an essential part of philosophical enquiry, but the important distinction lay in the purpose of such analysis. For the logical positivist this was held to be the key to metaphysical truth. For the new Oxford school, linguistic analysis was simply to be a tool to enable clearer thinking.

Oxford was the centre of this new style, and at the heart of it in Oxford, the undisputed leader of the new, was J. L. Austin, White's Professor of Moral Philosophy, who followed in, but also significantly diverged from, the path of Gilbert Ryle, who was nevertheless a continuing *eminence* during the 40s and 50s, and author of the influential book, published in 1949, 'The Concept of Mind'. My father was a friend and admirer of both Ryle and Austin, but was perhaps closest to the latter, and when Austin died suddenly in 1960, he became the executor of his literary papers.

Some years later, my father wrote the introduction to an assessment of Austin, in which he described something of the work, and in particular the philosophical approach, which the group around Austin were encouraged to adopt, "Austin believed that what had descended to our time under the name of philosophy was the tangled residue of a formerly even vaster tangle; there had been, as it were, an original gaseous mass of undifferentiated problems from which, as certain kinds of questions and methods gradually became clear, planets broke away in the form of independent disciplines—mathematics, the physical sciences, formal logic, psychology and so on. If so, what remained in the domain and under the title philosophy was at least highly unlikely to consist of any one kind of problem, and no single method was likely to be, quite generally, the key to progress. Problems, then, ought simply to be approached with no preconceptions, set out in the clearest light and discussed in any way that might seem to be relevant and effective; the needed virtues were truthfulness, and above all, industry and patience; the typically fatal philosophical failings were inaccuracy and oversimplification, and above all the impetuous proliferation of bogus 'solutions'."

Indeed, the need to proceed slowly and carefully in any given enquiry was a recurring theme, and one which the Oxford philosophers have been much teased about since.[11] In the same article, my father returned to this theme, "[Austin] had not at this time, indeed he never had, any doctrine of his own as to the nature of philosophical problems in general. Nor had he, as perhaps he had later, any general views about philosophical method. His general belief, then as always—and this scarcely amounts to a doctrine—was that both the statements and alleged solutions of philosophical problems were characteristically unclear, and that this was owing partly to human frailty but chiefly to the ambition to settle far too much, far too quickly. He believed that if progress was to be made, many questions would have to be raised, many facts surveyed, and many arguments deployed step by step and narrowly criticised: questions ought to be distinguished and considered strictly one at a time, and no effort spared to make it wholly clear what question was being asked and exactly what answer was proposed to it."

As for my mother, she shared the Oxford philosophers' passion for clear thought and ordinary language. The 'mission', she later said, was, "the deflation of pretentiousness and philosophical jargon." It is a surprise, therefore, that her first published works were on Existentialism. She claimed to have started on the demystification of Existentialism simply because she was asked to do it and she needed the money, but it is probably also true that the different style of this philosophy was the very quality which presented such an interesting challenge to render it, so far as could be done, into ordinary everyday language.

It was in the 1960s that I first heard her distinguish my father's professional philosophical work from her own: he did 'real philosophy', requiring original thoughts, while she was more of a journalist, reproducing the ideas of others in a form digestible to a general audience. The truth is, I think, that she did not want fully to commit to the small group of Austin acolytes; even in these early days her interests were broader, leaning more towards the history of ideas and the application of philosophical methods to moral questions, especially those with impact on public policy which required policy-makers and legislators to make decisions. A kind of applied philosophy.

One of my mother's main preoccupations in the 1950s must in any case have been babies. There were four born between 1951 and 1956, then a fifth, Boz, in

---

[11] Many years later, my father told me that he felt he had "arrived": there had recently been a Monty Python sketch in one of the Flying Circus TV shows which featured a pair of policemen pedantically debating some more or less futile procedural point while standing at the station desk. Their names were Sergeant Strawson and Sergeant Warnock.

1961. I was the second of the five, following about 18 months after my older sister, Kitty. I remember the arrival in our household of my youngest two sisters (although I was only four when my late sister Fanny was born), but of my brother James's arrival all I know (and naturally this was learned some time later) is that he was delivered into the world by two aptly named midwives, Nurse Paine and Nurse Screech.

Domestic life must have verged on the chaotic, but somehow my mother always managed to find nannies at the right moment to keep crises more or less at bay. Also, my sister Kitty and I were, I think, fairly biddable children in our early years, inclined simply to accept what was given. Although it was unusual, in the early 50s, to have a working mother, it may be that our upbringing differed little from that of earlier generations of middle-class children who were brought up by nannies and domestic staff. In earlier generations, the mothers would certainly not have worked, as ours did, but this did not necessarily mean that they chose to spend much time with their offspring. My mother, for example, grew up in the same house as her widowed mother (my grandfather had died a few months before my mother was born) but Mither, as she was for some reason known, certainly did not want to see a great deal of her children. The real upbringing happened in the nursery, under the strict eye of a nanny, the remarkable Emily Coleman. This was 'Nan' who remained a part of our lives in Oxford because she continued to live with one of my mother's sisters, and was present to offer domestic support at the time of the birth of each of the five Warnock children.

The Warnock tribe was not untypical of North Oxford families. The author, Peter Snow, wrote in his book about post-war Oxford,[12] "North Oxford folk have large families and to accommodate them have to drive around in cars as big as their living rooms…the archetypal car is the Volvo estate…however, big old Daimlers will do at a pinch as will old Saabs which rather resemble the dons who own them, being heavy, round-shouldered, slow but powerful, and going on forever." My father was a good deal fitter and leaner than a Saab, but our family cars did conform to this stereotype; they were indeed memorable, starting with a Sunbeam Talbot (complete with running-boards), then a characterful Citroen (of the type called *Traction Avant* made famous in the original 'Maigret' TV series), followed by the living-room-sized Standard Vanguard Estate and finally, graduation to the Volvo Estate. My mother had at different times, cars of her

---

[12] 'Oxford Observed' (John Murray)

own of varying degrees of eccentricity. There was an extraordinarily rare kind of Citroen, the Bijou,[13] with a fibreglass body to a design by the creator of the Lotus Elite, and a bubble car, I think a Heinkel,[14] which was essentially a three-wheeled motorbike covered by a flimsy shell. Excitingly, it had a front-opening door. Eventually this collectors' item was abandoned out of sheer frustration at its unreliability in Oxford's High Street, and my mother recalled that she did not dare return to the High Street for months afterwards for fear of being shamed into reclaiming her recalcitrant car.

These great cars came into their own as the family became more numerous and holidays consequently more complicated: my parents had bought a quite primitive but wonderfully located house on the North Yorkshire coast, near Whitby, to which we de-camped usually twice a year. The journey from Oxford to Whitby, in those pre-motorway days, was an adventure in itself, although, as time went by, the landmarks became increasingly familiar and are, to this day, etched into my consciousness: the first leg was the 22 miles to Banbury, followed by a tedious slog up to Rugby, always leading to tears, or close to tears, of frustration at the impossibility of navigating through the heart of Leicester without getting utterly lost. With the challenge of Leicester behind us we were in properly unfamiliar territory and it was usually time to stop for lunch, which was invariably an extensive picnic to be eaten on a moth-eaten rug laid out in a roadside thistle-infested field. Post-lunch we began to hit some of the places I have not visited since but which, if I hear or read their names now, immediately take me back to these journeys: Bawtry, for instance, or Thorne (near Doncaster) which boasted a very narrow and ill-maintained toll bridge. We were in Yorkshire by this time and could begin to tick off the remaining legs of the drive: Selby, then York, about 20 miles to Malton, then Pickering and the final 20 miles up onto the purple-heathered North Yorkshire Moor, the first glimpse of the sea, then down the steep Blue Bank into Sleights and, within a few minutes, Whitby and our ultimate destination Sandsend.

These were wonderful times with beach life in the summer and in winter the ever-present hope, never I think realised, of being snowed in and unable to get back across the moors for the beginning of a new school term. One of the many

---

[13] Only 210 Bijou cars were ever built!

[14] Strange, how two great German aircraft builders, Heinkel and Messerschmidt, were reduced to producing these pathetic little three-wheelers. Was this some kind of post-war humiliation contrived by US business interests?

joys was the independence we children had to roam the village and play in the stream at the bottom of the valley along the banks of which it stood. We would be sent down to E. Stanforth and Son, the village store, to collect the newspaper for my parents, where young Mr Stanforth would tend the seaside shop dressed almost invariably in a traditional brown apron. When the weather was fine the beach was a fabulous expanse of sand, covered twice a day by the incoming tide, so perfect for beach cricket and sandcastles and my favourite complicated civil engineering projects involving diverting the stream as it flowed down to the sea, or creating doomed fortifications against the incoming tide.

Of course, the weather was not always kind, but this allowed for other pleasures such as dodging the waves as they broke over the car park on the rocks above the beach. Our exploits would nowadays probably be banned as too dangerous, but it was a large part of the fun of it that we were more or less unsupervised for such long periods of time. The daily routine was not invariable, but typically would involve a drive into Whitby for food shopping, including the makings for an afternoon picnic, the most essential ingredient of all being a plentiful supply of lemon buns from Elizabeth Botham in Skinner Street. The taste of the lemon icing (sampled, in the interest of research, several times in recent years) remains to this day unrivalled. The picnics would usually be consumed in some discomfort, for instance sheltering from howling gales in a shooting butt on the top of Danby High Moor, or suffering plagues of flies somewhere near the ancient stepping stones in the low-lying Egton Bridge, or, more sedately, sitting amongst the ruins of Mulgrave Castle a mile or so inland up the Sandsend Valley. As years went by there were new pleasures, for me at any rate, including my first rounds of golf at the Whitby course (exposed on the cliff-top to the cruellest winds), occasional visits to watch the cricket at the end-of-season Scarborough Festival which in those days attracted some of the very best international players, or walking the two or three miles from Sandsend to Whitby along the beach, or in the opposite direction along the disused railway line with its plentiful supply of blackberries.

Those long summer holidays in Sandsend were a time of great happiness, but the truth is (and I feel somehow guilty in admitting it) that I was a curiously unreflective child, not giving any thought, for example, to whether I <u>should</u> be happy or sad. On the other hand, I do not think I was self-satisfied; this was just life, and I seemed to be content simply to exist within it.

Returning to Oxford at the end of the summer holidays my parents would resume their typical North Oxford life, of which the most characteristic social event would not be, say, the drinks party as in London or neighbourly life as one might imagine it in typical provincial cities but the dinner party..."Small enough," to quote Peter Snow again, "to be socially controllable and to permit conversation (or that attenuated blend of disputation and allusion which passes for it in North Oxford) to flourish." I remain rather fond of this, 'attenuated blend of disputation' which was, I suppose a professional hazard of the kind of philosophy in which my parents were then engaged.

As mentioned earlier, the prevailing style and practice of linguistic philosophy has been subjected to unkind criticism in subsequent years. For example, Ernest Gellner[15] has written of its 'utility as a weapon of defence', providing a 'rationale for anyone wishing to have nothing or as little as possible to do with one or more of the following things: (1) science and technicality (2) power and responsibility (3) ideas'. The last of these certainly goes too far but the first two undoubtedly resonate. North Oxford types did not warm to technology, nor to industry and commerce, and as for power, there was something vulgar about the exercise of authority or getting elected,[16] for example. But it is certainly true that the defining characteristic of the intellectual culture was of argument and dispute, deriving no doubt from the university's adversarial tutorial system. This disputational attitude also seemed to develop its own rather exaggerated verbal style, manifested in a fastidious exactitude of speech and a habit of italicising certain words in certain contexts. For example, "I *completely* disagree...", "In my view you are *quite* wrong...", "His arguments are *utterly* ridiculous," and so on.

I must say that I am inclined to defend my parents and their colleagues against such strictures. What is missing in Gellner's critique is any sense that the subject of philosophy could, and perhaps even should, be fun to do. 'Fastidious exactitude' was certainly a characteristic of my father's literary, as well as conversational, style, which can now seem a bit dated, but an essential adjunct

---

[15] 'Words and Things', a critique of linguistic philosophy.

[16] This sense of the vulgarity of elections was not shared by the Warnock siblings. I well remember my own bitter disappointment when my father failed, by a single vote, to be elected President of Magdalen.

was the obvious enjoyment of absurdities, which can give pleasure to this day. In my father's case there is, I must admit, an additional pleasure I get from his distinctive tone of voice; in much of what he writes his conversational and literary styles are scarcely distinguishable.

As an example, here is a short passage from his book 'The Object of Morality.' The context is a discussion about Rules, and in particular why one should, or in this case might not, comply with a rule. He gives three examples of non-compliance: firstly, the rule may be particular to a group of which one is not a member (for example, a rule that 'undergraduates must wear gowns'); secondly, a rule may not be complied with by mutual agreement (for example, in an ordinary friendly round of golf not every rule of golf, of which there are very many, needs to be adhered to); and I will quote the third example in full because it conjures up such an image, both enjoyable and absurd, of the philosophical parent creeping out at dead of night to tiptoe across a manicured college lawn dressed only in plimsolls (trainers, I suppose, for younger readers) in pursuit of empirical and phenomenological data for the advancement of philosophical enquiry:

"Then, thirdly, perhaps we should take note of a different sort of reason I might have for supposing that compliance by me, here and now, does not really matter. The object, so to speak, of a rule against smoking in the ammunition store is, no doubt, strictly that *no one* should smoke there; and if there is good reason for that, then there is good reason why I should not. But one might argue that the real object of a rule against, say, walking on the grass is not really that no one, but rather that not *too many* people, should do so: for the occasional transient would do the grass no harm, and the general prohibition is really a mere surrender to the difficulty of otherwise limiting transients to a harmless number. If so, why should I not, harmlessly, break that rule? Well, in such a case non-compliance can be argued against, and often effectively. Perhaps my example would undermine the desirable general practice of complying with the rule; perhaps it is not for me, or for any other individual, to be judge in his own cause as to whether or not to comply; perhaps, if I break this rule, my own character will thereby be nudged along the downward path; perhaps it is simply unfair for me not to do what other people, as I concede rightly, are required by the rule to do, or perhaps I cannot get away with it. But that such arguments must always be effective seems excessively strong doctrine. If occasionally, alone and in pitch darkness and wearing plimsolls, I nip across the forbidden grass, I will surely have a very tender conscience indeed if I do so in the conviction of doing wrong."

I suppose I have inherited, from my father, a taste for this combination of rather self-conscious exactitude, even in everyday matters. I'm sure he would have enjoyed Steven Pinker's sentence, allegedly uttered by his own child and cited in support of his argument that our grasp of grammar is, at least to an extent, genetic rather than entirely learned, a sentence which <u>ends</u> with five prepositions. The picture you have to conjure is of a careworn father trudging upstairs to read his hard-to-please child a bedtime story, to be greeted with, "What did you bring the book that I don't want to be read to out of up for?" This is (just) a grammatically tolerable construction but one which no adult would ever use, so could not have been 'picked up' from adult usage, even by so precocious a child as Professor Pinker's would doubtless have been. On the other hand, there are sentences which can comprehensibly be uttered by an adult, but share some of the absurdity of the five-preposition sentence; for example, there is the curious sentence containing five successive 'ands'. The narrative here being that the landlord of the 'Lamb and Flag' public house, emerging from his pub, finds a sign-writer at work on a replacement sign. The landlord asks, "Could you please leave more space between Lamb and and and and and Flag?"

Jokes, or more particularly word-based jokes rather than the practical sort, must have been an ingredient of Oxford academic life, long before the post-war dinner parties, and probably also pre-dating the Edwardian-era building boom which made North Oxford the spiritual home of the Oxford academic, following hard on the heels of a change of statutes which permitted dons to marry and no longer reside, monk-like, within college walls. One only has to think of Charles Dodgson, author of 'Alice in Wonderland' and fellow of Christ Church, or the Rev William Spooner, Warden of New College, to see that a love of absurdity must have been deeply ingrained in the Oxford psyche from at least the nineteenth-century.

Spooner was, of course, Oxford's most celebrated mangler of language. Sadly, almost all of the better-known Spoonerisms are apocryphal, or were at least vigorously denied by Spooner himself. He admitted to having once announced the hymn in Christ Church Cathedral as, "The Kinquering Kongs," but claimed that the majority of his most famous so-called utterances were made up. What a shame, for they should be true. Surely, he should have reprimanded an undergraduate for, "Fighting a liar in the quad", announced the title of his forthcoming sermon as, "Our Lord is a shoving leopard," or offered a loyal toast to, "Our Queer Dean." May sod rest his goal.

Spooner may have been no more than somewhat absent-minded but he seems to have carried this off in a rather endearing way. He was reported to have stopped a young colleague in the street and invited him to tea to meet the new archaeology lecturer. When this invitation was greeted with a surprised "But, Dr Spooner, I am the new archaeology lecturer," Spooner reportedly replied "Oh, never mind, why not come anyway." And his greeting of an ex-undergraduate with the words, "I'm trying to remember if it was you or your brother who was killed in the war," is very believable and strikingly similar to my own introduction to a long-retired teacher when I first went to Winchester. The venerable 'Jacker', whom I gathered had once been my father's form-master, looked me up and down before carefully venturing, "Ah, yes, Warnock, the son of your father, I believe." I can see what he meant, and in any case it was not an unreasonable belief.

~~~

At about this time, the mid-1960s, my mother had made an unusual career move, abandoning university teaching to become Headmistress of the Oxford High School, and once again, as at St Hugh's, she was the first incumbent to be married (I believe they had to alter the school's statutes to permit the appointment). The new headmistress had few fears, but one was that if her daughters were in her school they might laugh at her during assembly. So Kitty, who was already in the school, was swiftly dispatched to boarding school while Fanny, five years younger, briefly joined that exclusive band of Dragon School girls before moving to Downe House, near Newbury. Thus Boz, the youngest by five years was to suffer a rather solitary childhood without siblings in term-time and very reliant on an odd assortment of nannies and other minders. The most vivid of these were two Irish sisters, Anne and Peggy, who came to us in succession, for three or four years each before marrying their boyfriends and moving on. Peggy was followed by a highly competent and reliable nanny called Biz, but by this time I was not only away at school during term-time but often also in the holidays on National Youth Orchestra courses, so the regime of Biz and Boz was only observed by me as might a visitor from another planet, that other planet being Winchester.

But I have digressed from my parents' dinner parties which, as young children, we used to listen to and observe (so far as we could) from a concealed position seated at the top of the stairs. I always assumed that we <u>were</u> unseen, but perhaps we were simply tolerated so long as we did not create a disturbance. Certainly, as we grew a little older we were gradually permitted to be introduced to the more child-friendly guests. One of these, whom we were always especially pleased to see, was Frank Packenham, Lord Longford, who at that time lived with his considerable family in the Iffley Road. Lord Longford was an infrequent visitor but his immense popularity with us may be attributed in no small part to his welcome habit, extraordinarily old-fashioned even then, of tipping the children half a crown (quite a lot of money in our childish eyes) which, given the number of substantial families in post-war Oxford, must have been a significant drain on the Packenham purse.

A little later, when I was perhaps eleven or twelve, I would sometimes be invited to join the pre-dinner drinks (sadly, in my case, minus the drink). My parents' guests were almost always colleagues, and usually philosophers. Conversation, though, was more often than not dominated by academic gossip (certainly not by philosophical discourse). Even without knowing anything about the personalities involved, this kind of routine chat amongst professional colleagues was at a sufficiently un-elevated level as to be unintimidating; and it also gave a pleasurable sense of being included, trusted even, with a certain privileged kind of information. A comparable sense of inclusion was enjoyable when one could share in their quasi-academic jokes. For example the (probably quite well-known) Descartes joke, even if this was initially puzzling and required some research on my 11-year-old part to work out why it was thought amusing: René Descartes walks into a bar, orders a beer and drinks it at a gulp. "Would you like another?" the barman asks. Descartes considers the question carefully…"I think not," he says and disappears.

It was on one of these occasions that I was introduced to the legendary Isaiah Berlin, who was deeply engaged in conversation with the more familiar figures (because more regular visitors to the house) of Peter Strawson (whose children were more or less the same age as we were) and, I think, a near neighbour, parent of similar-aged children and fellow of Christ Church, Oscar Wood. There must have been others too because the room seemed quite full. The conversation was led by Berlin and with remarkable kindness he contrived matters to allow me to contribute. Having somehow learned that I was at that time captain of the Dragon

School cricket team he began asking questions about cricket, which must have been one of the very few subjects in the world about which he knew nothing whatsoever. He questioned me (and I suppose there was some kind of philosophical curiosity here) about the difference between the rules of cricket and some of its conventions (for example, there is no rule which says that the fielding side must open the bowling with fast bowlers rather than slow, but it is almost invariably so), but quite soon we had moved on to the duties and responsibilities of a captain, including what skills and what character traits would tend to make a successful team. By now, everyone was engaged in this debate, and I found myself expounding to a roomful of Oxford's most eminent philosophers on how opening batsmen should have a sound technique and a certain obstinacy of character capable of fearless resistance in the face of the most severe and intimidating examination by the fastest and meanest opposition bowlers. And our modern-day philosophers now had sufficient with which to begin selecting a philosophical cricket team, with all their historical predecessors, from Plato onwards, available for selection. Having chosen two openers we moved down the order; next our team required a no. 3 batsman with a bit more elegance than our openers, probably our most stylish player, whereas in nos. 4 and 5 we should seek more reliability and consistency. These would be the men whom you would trust to pass 50 for you if your life depended on it, or, in our philosophical XI, who could be relied upon to make a completely solid argument even if lacking the greatest flashes of insight. Then of course you come to the brilliant all-rounders, capable occasionally of winning a match "off their own bat," but not necessarily the most reliable in a crisis. Finally, to the bowlers who need to be terrifyingly speedy or to enjoy some special quality of mystery or capacity for bamboozlement. Far be it from me to pick a full philosophical team but I can perhaps give a flavour of our North Oxford selection committee with a few tentative suggestions: for our top-order players, as I have said, we require sound stylists who can demonstrate a 'class' which sets them above your average journeyman, so I think worthy of consideration would have to be those 'big names' of philosophy who also write well, for example, David Hume, Descartes, Plato. Nietzsche certainly writes well but I am inclined to place him as one of our aggressive fast bowlers aiming to strike fear into the opposition. Berkeley also writes with great clarity but would, I imagine, fall into the more metaphysical class of spinner with a touch of mystery.[17] Having said this, if it is bamboozlement that we seek we might have to overlook Berkeley in favour of, say, Sartre or Hegel, both of whom share in their different ways a remarkable ability to sow confusion. As an outside 'pick' we might perhaps consider Machiavelli, a potential match-winner certainly, but also highly unreliable; and our philosophical umpires might raise a question about whether he is even properly eligible to join our philosophical team. Of one thing I am fairly sure, though, namely that under Berlin's rather individual and discursive chairmanship our committee would never have reached a unanimous conclusion. It was a great game, generously played, and kindly in its purpose to find a central place in it for an eleven-year-old boy otherwise in danger of exclusion. Not only so, but Berlin remembered the occasion and returned to the improbable cricket theme during a future visit. This time he broadened the scope by seeking my views on the value of sport; in particular, I remember his interest in whether it was primarily about building character or whether a certain strength of character was a necessary pre-condition for sporting success. What a wonderful teacher Berlin must have been—there may have been no definitive answers, but after more than fifty years his questions and his method of questioning remain with me.

Not all such games were based on sport. There was one word game, inspired, I think, by Vladimir Nabokov, which required the invention of manically mangled aphorisms or well-known phrases, such as, "People who live in glass-houses shouldn't try to kill two birds with one stone," or the rather sinister, "Cats which are not let out of the bag often become skeletons in the cupboard." I was reminded of this years later when the then Archbishop of Canterbury, Robert Runcie, was cruelly congratulated for nailing his colours firmly to the fence on the matter of gay clergy (or was it women priests?).

In a different vein again, was the challenge, issued on another dinner party occasion, to imagine the most frightening thing that could ever happen to you,

---

[17] I had been aware of this quality in the philosopher Berkeley from a very young age because I used to read a strangely memorable little book of verse entitle 'Verse and Worse', which included the following unforgettable lines:

'A philosopher named Bishop Berkeley

Declared, metaphysically, darkly,

All that we see

Cannot possibly be,

And the rest's altogether unlarkly.'

the only rule being that it must be something which either had actually happened or which credibly might happen (in other words no supernatural events permitted). I forget, now, how the competition was judged but I do remember my own choice of winner which was a story about the famous tightrope walker, Blondin.[18] He made a living in America by charging admission to view his death-defying exploits which, in order to keep attracting audiences, had to become ever more outrageous. For a time, Blondin's speciality was to walk the tightrope across the Niagara Falls: his manager, one Harry Colcord, assembled a huge crowd every day for a fortnight, so Blondin had to vary his act, becoming more outrageous each day. He would ride a unicycle one day, cross it in a sack the next, cook an omelette on a primer stove when halfway across and so on. For the final *tour de force* the manager had excelled himself and, through extensive newspaper advertisement, attracted the largest crowd. The *pièce de résistance* was to be for Blondin to carry a volunteer piggyback across the Falls. A volunteer was sought from amongst the onlookers and, perhaps unsurprisingly, no-one stepped forward; whereupon Blondin turned to his manager, who had himself never stepped onto a tightrope, and said, "It has to be you," and, positioning his nervous manager on his back, the two of them soon set off down the rope. Now, when stretched across so wide a distance the rope has a certain 'give' in it and with the unusual weight they had to negotiate a steep-ish downslope to reach the middle. Of course, the upside was also steeper than expected and it soon became clear that Blondin was in some difficulty. The weight was greater than he had anticipated and the gradient more severe, and about halfway up the upslope he came to a halt, turned his head to address the man on his back and said, "I can't do it. You will have to walk." So, never before having walked a tightrope, you find yourself having to climb off another man's back, on to a rope with a steep gradient, high above the Niagara Falls, and being told to walk. Don't look down. This is, in fact, a true story, as I later learned, and there is even a photograph of the two men arriving at the opposite side of the Falls, with Blondin walking backwards with both hands extended to hold those of the other man walking forwards. It may be the poor quality of the photograph, but the manager's eyes have sunk so deeply into his head that they appear only as two black holes. It's almost enough to put you off your dinner party food.

---

[18] Charles Blondin (1824 – 97) retired to England, eventually dying of diabetes at home in 'Niagara House', Ealing, West London. He is buried in Kensal Green Cemetery.

Although in this particular game no supernatural events were allowed, Oxford did have its fair share, perhaps more, of ghosts. The Strawson house in the Banbury Road was a typical tall, narrow town house and was believed, at least by the Strawson children to be haunted. I don't recall whether a ghost was ever seen, but there were several occasions when, with all the family downstairs, mysterious footsteps were to be heard pacing the corridor upstairs. Of course, there may have been any number of banal explanations, but it was enough to set a childish imagination racing. The truth is, though, that I was never sure what lessons we were supposed to draw from such brushes with other worlds, although there was no mistaking the moral of the famous ghost of Brasenose Lane: a fellow of that college saw an undergraduate, a well-known member of an atheist society, being hauled out of his ground-floor window by a tall man in a black coat; the don had a not-entirely-accountable feeling of horror, and rushing into the college he found that only a few moments before the undergraduate had burst a blood vessel in the middle of a blasphemous speech, and fallen dead on the floor.

Even now, when my visits to Oxford have become rare, certain locations continue to have a particular resonance. For instance, the walk from Beaumont Street along the Broad towards the Radcliffe Camera recalls Osbert Lancaster's memoir of his undergraduate days. He describes the odd assortment of undergraduates plus a few dons who assembled at the Saturday lunchtime receptions hosted in his Beaumont Street lodgings by one Colonel Holkhorst, a Reader to the University in Spanish and Portuguese. Very few dons shared the undergraduates' enthusiasm for the colonel, but a notable exception was, 'that great and good man,' R. M. Dawkins, the Professor of Byzantine Archaeology and Modern Greek,[19] 'No eccentric professor of fiction could possibly hold a candle to the reality of Professor Dawkins whose behaviour and appearance placed him, even in an Oxford far richer [in eccentrics] than now, in a class by himself. Ginger-moustached, myopic, stooping, clad in one of a succession of very thick black suits which he ordered by postcard from the general store of a small village in Northern Ireland, he always betrayed his whereabouts by a cackling laugh of great carrying power. (Once when passing alongside the high wall of Exeter, startled by this extraordinary sound, I looked up and saw the Professor happily perched in the higher branches of a large chestnut tree hooting

---

[19] Richard MacGillivray Dawkins (1871 – 1955), Director of the British School at Athens, 1906 – 13.

like a demented macaw). His claims to scholarship were indisputable...[but]...of his powers as a lecturer it was difficult to judge as he had managed over the years successfully to discourage anyone from reading modern Greek. When, very occasionally, some misguided female student, despite every obstacle he could devise, inscribed herself for the course, his first, and last, lecture of the academic year was always of such shattering indecency that the unfortunate young woman immediately decided to take up Icelandic. The Professor...was much in demand as a luncheon and dinner guest not only for the sake of his engaging personality but also for his reminiscences...Unfortunately it was seldom easy, and always demanded much patience, to appreciate these at their full worth owing to his tendency to be overcome by helpless mirth provoked by the absurdity of the situations and characters he was recalling which rendered the end of his stories virtually incomprehensible. Occasionally, much to the astonishment of those present who were meeting him for the first time, he would slide, completely overwhelmed, under the table, hooting madly; there to remain for a couple of courses to re-emerge with the savoury, articulate but with tears of laughter still trickling down his cheeks. In the last years of his life, his mobility, formerly excessive, was much impaired by a broken hip imperfectly mended, which he found infuriating. But his end was blissful; one fine June day, having lent down to smell a rose in Wadham College garden, he suddenly drew himself upright, cast aside his crutches and with his face irradiated by a seraphic smile fell back dead at the feet of Maurice Bowra.'[20]

Not all Oxford characters were members of the university. It was the Oxford buses which gave me my earliest encounter with transvestism: we always hoped our journey would coincide with the rota of a particularly flamboyant bus conductor, with blond curly hair, startling eye make-up, often a pink chiffon scarf and always a broad Welsh accent, who would greet the passengers, especially if male, with a cheery, "Hello darling!" and keep everyone entertained on the journey. I later learned that this was one Thomas Joyce, and something of a local legend, who, according to the Oxford Mail, was sacked by the city transport

---

[20] Sir Cecil Maurice Bowra (1898 – 1971), Warden of Wadham from 1938 to 1970, was a well-known homosexual who is credited with the remark, "Buggers can't be choosers", explaining his engagement, later abandoned, to a plain girl, Miss Audrey Beecham, niece of the famous conductor. He also said, of Sir Isaiah Berlin, "though like our Lord and Socrates he does not publish much, he thinks a great deal and has had an enormous influence on our times."

authority for attempting a version of the Dance of the Seven Veils which involved a striptease while standing on a table in the staff canteen of the Gloucester Green bus station. The same Oxford Mail piece describes him preparing for an appearance in court, doing his make-up in the reflection of the glass of the court notice board, dressed in fishnet tights, pink top and that already familiar pink chiffon scarf. This was in the 1960s and thirty years later I spotted, by chance, his obituary in the local paper in 1994. Sadly, he had fought a losing battle with alcohol in his later years and was living in the Cyrenian Hostel in the Jericho district of the city at the time of his death.

~~~

Thomas Joyce was perhaps an extreme example of the newly liberated spirit of the 1960s. My own conscious sense of freedom coincided with my six year spell, between the ages of seven and 13, of fulfilment as a pupil at the extraordinary Dragon School, a wonderful institution which somehow created a culture of kindness, politeness and humanity as well as academic achievement despite, or more probably because of, the bizarre collection of characters on the teaching staff. These colourful figures undoubtedly encouraged and supported me, but I feel now that a sense of limitless possibilities is actually a defining characteristic of childhood in general, not solely attributable to school. As a child, the very fact that you do not quite know who you are enables you to imagine that everything is possible, but once you grow up, marry, have children, go to work, all defining activities of adult life, the options are narrower, the choices more restricted. Life itself becomes more limited.

The Dragon was very conveniently located at the end of our road, with the result that I would often spend entire days there, from dawn until dusk. This was largely, I suppose, because my interests and talents, such as they were, were focused on sports and music, both activities to be pursued outside formal school hours. I loved the Dragon with one single exception which I confess with a degree of shame, felt even to this day. This was swimming, a compulsory activity which involved learning to swim in the hateful murk of the River Cherwell which ran, or rather dawdled, fetid and sluggish, at the bottom of the school playing fields. The water was always cold, but also filthy, and I took against it for ever (indeed I have never overcome my dislike of swimming) when a dead sheep floated by, becoming stuck in the riverbank reeds, while I was attempting my 'test', a challenge which every boy had to achieve. This involved swimming a width of the river and back fully clothed in an old Dragon School uniform. The test was indeed considerable for the weaker swimmers, and in any case not for the faint-hearted, because the uniform in question consisted of heavy blue corduroy shorts and jacket which when soaked in river water felt like lead weights dragging you to the muddy bottom. The horror of it was compounded by the schoolmaster in charge of instruction in swimming, the universally disliked and feared Mr Dyson, Slimey Dyson as he was known to us, a man over-keen on corporal punishment, especially of the boarders.[21] My shame arose during a week in mid-term when I had a cold and, with great delight, was permitted a note exempting me from swimming on medical grounds. I contrived to re-use this note every week until the end of term. Having got away with this modest deception I was mortified to find that my end-of-term report lamented my extended absence from swimming and, in true Dragon style, wished me a speedy recovery from my, clearly rather serious, affliction. This tender concern, of course, had to be explained to puzzled parents who, I think, only partly forgave me when I laid on rather thickly the mildly traumatic incident of the transient dead sheep.

It may or may not be common in large families that the siblings are cast at an early age in a role, for instance, "She's the clever one," or, "He's the dreamer," but this was certainly the case in our Warnock clan. The Darwinian view of growing up in a large family is that it should force each individual to be sufficiently assertive to secure its needs and fight for attention. In my case, and I think it may also have been true of my brother and sisters, almost the reverse was true: the consequence of such a substantial childish population was that we were allowed to exist relatively undisturbed in our own interior worlds, having been pre-assigned, as it were, certain character traits and a perceived role in the family which was not re-examined, even in the face of contradictory evidence. My elder sister, Kitty, was always described as an independent spirit and so, whether she liked it or not, she was more or less obliged to be so. By contrast,

---

[21] Dyson all-too-closely resembled the ghastly Captain Grimes in Evelyn Waugh's 'Decline and Fall', dismissed from his prep school post for the offence of "aiming low at the leapfrog."

my brother James was cast as the clever one (which indeed he is), and as for my sisters Fanny and Boz, the former was musical and Boz, quite a bit younger than the others, was of course the clown. In my case, I was the stupid one though not without some redeeming non-academic skills, notably on the sports field and, later, as a musician. So the Dragon School (swimming excepted) suited me perfectly because it wore its intellectual pretensions so lightly.

The Dragon's approach was exemplified in a story told by Lady Antonia Fraser (whose father, Frank Packenham had tipped his way so handsomely into our childish affections as a visitor to our Chadlington Road home) in her reminiscence of the school: competitiveness in academic matters extended to the parents, some of whom were rumoured to be extremely helpful with homework, and on one notable occasion a popular master named Jacques awarded his form prize to a Mrs Arrowsmith instead of to her apparently precocious son. This was applauded as an excellent joke but the applause was also, I suspect, in part for the excellence of Mrs Arrowsmith.

If excellence in intellectual matters was treated lightly, perhaps because taken somewhat for granted, sport was taken with the greatest seriousness, and the highest importance was attached to winning. My own intellectual pretensions were negligible so I was fortunate that sport could become, for better or worse, my *raison d'être* at the school. In my last two years as a Dragon, in 1964 and 1965, I played in all the 1st XI (1st XV) teams of all the sports which were permitted, namely cricket and rugby in the Summer and Autumn, and in the Spring term soccer and hockey sharing centre stage.[22] I was particularly fortunate, as captain of cricket, that the coaching of the team was in the intense, almost professional, hands of Clarkie, whose brother was the manager of the England teams on tour in Australia, South Africa and the West Indies. Clarkie was of the Mike Brearley school of captaincy, which for non-cricketers can be characterised as a rather cerebral management style aimed at getting the best performances out of one's colleagues rather than necessarily leading by example. Of course, if one could also lead from the front in performance terms, so much the better. To this day, I often feel that the grounding I was given in the mysterious arts of cricket captaincy would enable me to captain the England cricket team better than quite a few of the modern-day captains. As for the

---

[22] Tennis was tolerated as an occasional pastime, but never treated with the same seriousness as team games, always being dismissively referred to simply as "the woolly ball," clearly a game for girls!

coaching of the practical cricketing skills, these were delegated, for most of my time, to Dougie Henderson, a useful[23] university blue and Minor Counties batsman, and Guv (Mike Gover, later to become Headmaster), an out-and-out enthusiast, if more or less devoid of cricketing skill.

Returning to the important matter of winning, I learned a harsh lesson on this in my final cricket season at the Dragon, a lesson never forgotten, although, as will be revealed, my interpretation of the central incident has become more nuanced over the years. As already mentioned, I was captain of cricket and the point in the season had arrived for the annual match against arch-rival Horris Hill. Ours was almost a spectacular triumph of record-breaking proportions: my role in the side was as opening batsman and, as captain, to marshal the team's bowling resources, determine the field settings and so on. This we handled to such good effect that our highly rated opposition were dismissed for a relatively paltry score of 85 (if memory serves). On going in to bat with my opening partner, Charles Alexander, we were invincible, rapidly bringing our score up to 79 for no loss, within six runs of achieving a maximum ten-wicket victory. The opportunity to clinch such a big win by striking a maximum six does not come around very often and I couldn't resist, but sadly (and predictably) was bowled in the attempt and we won by nine wickets instead of ten. The following day, I was summoned to a kind of tribunal of the masters responsible for the team and received a dressing-down, the likes of which I have never since suffered. My death-or-glory effort was deemed, amongst other offences, an irresponsible dereliction of leadership duty, arrogant, setting a bad example to the younger players, vainglorious, frivolous, risky, a futile gesture and so on and on. It was a humiliating carpeting and I was duly mortified (even though, in private I continued rather to despise my successor at the crease who dutifully prodded around, scoring the few remaining winning runs in singles).

The instructive corollary to this sorry tale took place in the 1980s. By now, in my 30s, I made a very rare appearance as a member of an Old Dragon cricket team and amongst the spectators was none other than Mike Gover, one of the members of the tribunal which had delivered that bracing post-match dressing-down, who had by this time risen to become the school's headmaster. We had not met for twenty-five years, and he greeted me with, "Felix, dear boy, I shall

---

[23] I use the word 'useful' here because I was always amused by its use in a cricket context: the brilliant spin-bowler turned cricket commentator, Jim Laker, would often refer to "a useful crowd" at, say, the Oval Test, but its use was never explained.

never forget the day you won the Horris Hill match with that magnificent six." A perfect example of unreliable memory improving on reality and the clearest possible lesson that apparently futile gestures may turn out to be less futile than supposed.

～～

By this time, the 1980s, my father had risen to the vice-chancellorship of the university. He was, in truth, a somewhat reluctant administrator, claiming that he was only doing it for the pension, but he never lost his enjoyment of the ridiculous. One of his duties as Vice Chancellor was to host distinguished, or at any rate wealthy, visitors to the University. One such was a prospective donor, a potentate of uncountable riches from one of the oil states of the Gulf. The potentate had been given a tour of Oxford in the afternoon of his visit and it fell to my father to dine with him that evening at high table in Magdalen College. Conversation was a struggle, on account of the potentate's limited English, but my father grappled manfully with the challenge, in due course enquiring politely about the afternoon's tour. The visitor seemed tolerably pleased but had clearly been struck by the traffic congestion, unknown in his part of the world. "You have so many drivers. You are all drivers." Feeling on safe conversational ground my father responded, and choosing words which had the best chance of being understood, remarked that, "There are indeed many drivers, but we are not all drivers."

Thereupon the potentate surveyed the company around high table and asked, "Which of you here is not a driver?" Following his gaze, my father, an impeccably honest man, was becoming uneasy at the dearth of non-driving fellows, but at last his gaze lighted with relief upon the distinguished white head of the elderly Professor of Divinity and Fellow of Magdalen who was regularly to be seen cycling the streets of Oxford. He appeared to be the only one amongst the present company whom my father could say, with confidence, was a non-driver, but nevertheless it was with a sense of impending trouble that he ventured, "That white-haired gentleman over there is not a driver." Our potentate leant forward, now showing a keen interest, "Ah, so he is not a driver." Pause for thought. "And what is this man's name?"

My father, as he reported these events, was now aware how sticky the wicket had become: the Fellow in question was Oxford's leading biblical scholar and eminent editor of The New English Bible, none other than Professor G. R. Driver. This was perhaps the moment at which my father might have saved himself, but with an honesty which does him great credit but which, in these particular circumstances, might be thought ill-placed, he offered, "His name is Professor Driver."

A long silence ensued while this information was digested. "You mean he is professor of driving?"

"No, not that."

"So everyone is a driver?"

"Well, in a sense, but the professor does not drive, he is just called Driver." And so the conversation stumbled on, drying from trickle to drought, with our potentate retreating into silent non-understanding of this bizarre place of learning, or, in the light of what he had just been told, he may have felt it a place of bizarre learning. I don't recall whether a donation was eventually forthcoming.

When, ten years earlier, my father had become principal of Hertford College, the one drawback of living in the generously proportioned 'tied cottage' which was the Principal's Lodging was that its entire frontage, including all the bedrooms, was on Catte Street where the noise, especially from undergraduate revelry on Saturday nights, eventually became intolerable. There was also the difficulty which 'living above the shop' presented of never being able fully to escape from college life. My parents therefore decided to buy a weekend cottage as an escape from continuous college life and lighted on an old school house in the village of Great Coxwell near Faringdon. Faringdon is an attractive, if somewhat faded, market town but one of its claims, at least from a musical point of view, is that the great Lord Berners had lived there, at Faringdon House. Berners can certainly stake a claim to be one of the great eccentrics, but he was also not without substance in his time as a noted composer, novelist and painter. His music is now seldom heard but in his day he was taken seriously enough to be described by Stravinsky, no less, as the leading English composer of his generation. His output was not large (about 50 works in all) but included five ballets, two of which were commissioned by Diaghilev and choreographed by Ballanchine, and the other three were choreographed by Frederick Ashton. Not a bad record for someone now regarded as a mere dilettante, with a reputation for doing his composing while on country drives, seated at a clavichord specially installed in the back of his chauffeur-driven Rolls Royce.

Whatever doubts there may be over Lord Berners standing as a composer there can be no such equivocation about his place in the very top rank of eccentrics. Examples abound. He liked to build things, and one of Faringdon's notable architectural features is a curious folly tower which stands in the grounds of Faringdon House. Berners had commissioned the architect Lord Gerald Wellesley[24] to create this tower to a particular Gothic design but, on returning home from an overseas trip, was enraged to find that Wellesley was building to a Classical design and was already half finished. Berners insisted that the top half of the tower be re-modelled to conform to his original Gothic intentions. Thus, Berners' folly became a kind of double folly, and, to complete the picture, when finished, Lord Berners placed a notice at its entrance, "Members of the public committing suicide from this tower do so at their own risk."

His reputation (and perhaps also his interest in things falling from heights) was established early, for as a child he once threw his mother's dog out of an upstairs window. He had been told, he said, that if you throw a dog into water it will learn to swim, so, applying this logic, he wanted to test whether if you threw a dog out of a window it would learn to fly. Famously, too, he kept doves on his estate and dyed them turquoise, pink and gold, an idea he might have stolen from another bizarre member of the land-owning classes, Sir George Sitwell (father to Osbert, Edith and Sacheverell), who elected to improve the view from his study by acquiring a herd of white cows and painting them in Chinese willow pattern.[25]

And finally, in this diversion into eccentricities, no discussion of musicians and folly building can be complete without an honourable mention of William Beckford, a century earlier than Berners. Before he reached the age of ten, Beckford had inherited £1 million from his father and an annual income of £100,000. At the age of five, he had piano lessons from the nine-year-old Mozart, then on his one and only visit to London in 1764 – 65. Beckford's promising development as a musician was interrupted in 1784 when in his mid-20s he had

---

[24] Gerald Wellesley was, according to an acerbic John Betjeman, "the only modern architect to have a style named after him—the Gerry-built style."

[25] I was reminded of the Sitwell cows on a recent visit to the charming Milton Keynes Museum where they maintain in their grounds a 'herd' of five concrete cows painted as Aberdeen Angus. It occurred to me that the surreality of this installation might be further heightened by the addition of five real Anguses painted to look like concrete.

to flee the country having been scandalously caught *in flagrante* with a 15-year-old boy, and he spent the next dozen or so years touring Europe with a large retinue of hangers-on. He clearly missed his home comforts, though, because he invariably travelled with his own bed and he was in the habit of having the walls of the hotel rooms in which he stayed, re-papered with his choice of prints. On one visit, to Portugal, he took with him a flock of sheep—not to keep himself supplied with English lamb, but so that they might graze outside his bedroom window, *à la Sitwell*, to remind him of home. History does not record the colour of the sheep, whether white, black or indeed willow pattern.

On his eventual return to England, Beckford embarked on his famous folly, Fontwell Abbey, a huge Gothic structure with a 300-feet central tower making it one of the tallest buildings in the country at that time. Unfortunately, Beckford was so impatient to complete it that he caused too many corners to be cut in the construction (as well as constantly plying the workmen with liquor in the improbable hope of increasing their stamina and output) and the tower collapsed even as he dined for the first time within the 'abbey'. The tower was re-built no fewer than four times before being abandoned as a picturesque ruin in the 1820s.

And so we return from such country diversions to the Oxford of the late 1960s. This was, of course, the decade now associated with student protest (for those of a political bent) and flower power for the hedonistic, but no one told me at the time. I had progressed from the Dragon School to Winchester, and my life was henceforth dominated by a hatred of school for which I sought compensation in music, principally, and to a lesser degree, cricket (I made my highest score when playing as a last-minute substitute for the Old Wykehamists against my own team when the former arrived at the game a man short) and beer (there were more than 70 pubs within walking distance of school). I prefer, though, to draw a veil over the three grim years that I spent at Winchester. I give enormous credit to my mother, at this point, who somehow persuaded herself to allow me to leave school at 16, to complete my A Levels at the Oxford College of Technology (my subjects were the not-overly-technological Music, German and French). My mother must have called in a few favours, both to sort out my peculiar education and to rescue that of my brother James who was expelled from Winchester at the same time as I resigned. The school behaved especially badly in my brother's case, chucking him out not for anything he had done but because they thought he might bring them into disrepute in the future (which indeed he might have, but to be convicted, as it were, of a crime before you have committed it seems disgracefully unfair). Not only did they dispose of him without due cause, they also allowed him to leave without ensuring that he went home (he disappeared up to London) and then tried to intervene with the school which had agreed (as a favour to my mother, I think) to take him by advising them against doing so. Fortunately, their advice was ignored.

My mother was able to pull such educational strings because, as already referred to, she had moved out of University teaching to become headmistress of the local High School, the Oxford High School. Exactly why she did this is disputed…her children believe that she applied for the job primarily because we had bet her that, if she did, she would not get it. Her own version is scarcely more high-minded: she once wrote that, "It was a way of letting me off all the awful graduate students who perpetually beleaguered me. With the undergraduates, you talk to them for an hour, give them an essay, and they go away. But these graduates wouldn't leave me alone."

It is extraordinary how often I still meet women who claim my mother as their one-time headmistress. Considering that she was in this job for a mere five years it seems almost impossible that so many of my more-or-less contemporaries could have passed through the school in that time.

It was to be no more than a five-year stint because, in 1970, my father became Principal of Hertford College and my mother left the High School in order to fulfil a role as wife and co-worker at Hertford, which was almost a requirement of his job. At the time I was doubtful of the wisdom of this very conventional step: it seemed improbable that my restless mother would be satisfied with such a traditional 'wifely' role, but with hindsight it turned out to be a brilliant move. She began writing again, starting work on one of her best books, 'Imagination', and within a short time she was 'discovered', by whatever mysterious processes civil service appointments committees function, to be one of the 'Great and Good': as an academic with administrative experience in education, with an interest in public policy matters and, above all, with time to spare, she was an ideal candidate for membership of government advisory committees of all kinds. She was appointed a member of the Independent Broadcasting Authority, she chaired a committee of enquiry into the treatment of laboratory animals (including the brief *cause célèbre* of the smoking beagles), sat on a Royal

Commission on pollution, delivered a Dimbleby lecture, awarded Harkness Fellowships, but she first came to public attention as chair of a report into the education of handicapped children (as we then referred to them). Most controversial, though, and certainly the most high profile and 'political', was her chairmanship of the Royal Commission on Human Fertilisation and Embryology. This was a challenge, but I suppose one for which she was as well qualified as could be: it required great clarity on the issues themselves, and a skill at reducing these to their essentials; an ability to look at emotive subjects without excessive emotion, it required administrative skill, political wisdom, and educational gifts which brought as many of her committee members as possible to a consensus position. At the heart of the inquiry was the question of whether 'spare embryos' from IVF treatment could be used for research purposes, and it is a tribute to the report that its main recommendation, that research should be permitted under license up to 14 days from the time of fertilisation, has stood the test of time. The 14-day limit, though still controversial, remains with us, as is the licensing authority, established on the recommendation of the Warnock Report, which has proved a reasonably successful mechanism whereby government can keep abreast of scientific developments.

I should have paid closer attention to my parents' lives at this time. My father was Vice-Chancellor of Oxford University and my mother was becoming a well-known public figure, as well as Mistress of Girton College in Cambridge, both at the top of their games. But others certainly took notice. One of these was the distinguished American columnist, George Will, who had been a pupil of my father's a dozen years previously and was one of the most widely read and widely syndicated columnists in America, with a twice-weekly column in The Washington Post. This is what he told his national readership in December 1984, and there is little to add:

"Oxford, England—Geoffrey Warnock, vice chancellor of Oxford University, explains why politicians so frequently ask his wife, Mary, to reason about moral dilemmas: 'They seem to think she knows the difference between right and wrong.'

"The vice chancellor is not like the vice president of the United States. The vice chancellor is grander. He runs the place—to the limited extent that an ancient institution requires running. The office of chancellor is, with lovely illogic, honorific. The current occupant is Harold Macmillan, who recently wondered aloud whether, now that he is 90, he should step down. He promptly answered himself with a firm 'no'.

"But splendid though the vice chancellor undoubtedly is, in his black suit and white clerical necktie, he is no more splendid than Dame Mary, DBE, Britain's savant for all seasons. Thatcher, Warnock…is there no room for men at the top of British life? There should be a national enquiry into this question, but it would be conducted by yet another Warnock committee of enquiry.

"Mary is about to become principal of a college in Cambridge, but presumably will continue as a cottage industry producing solicited advice for the perplexed. When a British government knits its brow about education for the handicapped, or in vitro fertilisation, or some other thorny issue, the government eventually exclaims, 'It is too deep—send for Warnock!'

"Regarding, for example, in vitro fertilisation, the most recent Warnock committee sought criteria by which to limit research on human embryos conceived outside the mother. The committee report emphasised an early stage in the development of the embryo—a stage at which there appears an arrangement of cells called 'the primitive streak.' It occurs about 15 days after conception and is a stage in the multiplication of cells that marks the last point at which identical twins can occur. Hence, it marks the beginning of individual development of the embryo and is, the committee concluded, an appropriate outer limit for research on embryos produced by in vitro fertilisation…

"…the Warnocks, both of whom are philosophers by training and inclination, seem to be constantly bumping into public questions that call for philosophic subtlety. Geoffrey was a philosopher before he was elevated to the vice chancellorship, and presumably still is: one can hardly stop being a philosopher once one has got the habit…only one thing is clear. There are too many questions, and not enough Warnocks to go round."

Chapter 3
Albion Ensemble: Five in a Bar

With the Albion Ensemble, we enter a very different world from that of the orchestra. Here was not the war of attrition between conductor and orchestra, nor the struggle between players and management. Our adventures were those of the gang, although, of course, a gang more from the pages of Enid Blyton than of the more modern kind. We did not roam the streets armed with heavy drugs and light artillery, but we were mutual friends willing to support each other through thick and thin. We were a wind quintet, the core of the group comprising the colourful threesome of Philippa Davies, Geordie Caird and Andrew Marriner, all National Youth Orchestra contemporaries; I was not their original bassoonist (Jeremy Ward, another NYO alumnus, and subsequent colleague in the period instrument world, held this distinction, if such it was) and the horn players came and went periodically, Robin Martin when I first joined, Peter Francomb when I finished, with the intervening period enlivened by a brilliantly high-octane cameo from the extraordinary Jonathan Williams. But it was Philippa, Geordie and Andrew, playing flute, oboe and clarinet respectively, who rather literally set the tone.

We were rehearsing at Geordie's Halliford Street studio one summer's afternoon in 1995 when a message arrived from our agent that a US TV station was on the phone enquiring of our availability the following morning. Intriguing, and, needless to say, irresistible. It turned out to be the iconic breakfast TV show 'Good Morning America' which was broadcasting live each day that week from the garden of Cliveden Manor to celebrate the 50th anniversary of Victory in Europe (VE) Day. Cliveden, now an upmarket hotel, had housed the US military headquarters in 1944/45 and famously, in the intervening years, its swimming pool had been the setting for the key events involving the young 'dancer' Christine Keeler, Minister for the Army John Profumo and Eugene Ivanov, a

Russian military attaché (a spy, in other words) leading to the notorious 1960s Profumo scandal. In an earlier age, Cliveden was also supposed to have been where the eighteenth-century composer Thomas Arne had written 'Rule Britannia' (part of the finale of his cantata 'King Arthur'), and the Good Morning America production team, having unearthed this historical nugget, had decided to feature this quintessentially British music on their breakfast menu. It was to be literally an outside broadcast, the entire show being delivered in the garden, so it was decided that music for wind instruments would have the best chance of success. I don't know how they lighted on the Albion Ensemble, but here they now were on the phone, and it was not long before we had agreed to present ourselves as a wind octet (2 oboes, 2 clarinets, 2 bassoons, 2 horns) the following morning at 9.00 a.m. in the Cliveden Hotel gardens in Berkshire. 'Good Morning America' was to be broadcast live, starting, if memory serves, at 6.00 a.m. East Coast time, 11.00 a.m. for us.

There was a fair amount to do in the hours leading up to our 11.00 a.m. deadline. Our ensemble was usually a quintet of course, so we had to engage some additional players at extremely short notice. There was also the awkward fact that there was no version of Rule Britannia for wind octet, so we had to write it. For this task we threw ourselves upon the mercies of our friend and colleague, Gordon Davies, an ace arranger of a number of our more popular tunes, to rise to the challenge of this shortest of deadlines. It actually had a kind of eighteenth-century authenticity that the ink should scarcely be dry on the page as the first performance began.[26] So it was that our hastily assembled team, with our even more hastily assembled repertoire (filled out by some real eighteenth-century music in the shape of a Mozart serenade for the same instrumental combination) rocked up in carefree mood ready to deliver a world première to an unsuspecting audience of bleary-eyed Americans. There was time enough to canter through our short programme and I remember how relieved we were to have had the foresight to bring a bag of clothes-pegs…we were positioned in an exposed spot at the very bottom of the garden across an expanse of manicured lawn, some distance from the big house, in a windy corner. Our main worry was that our music would blow away, or stands blow over; of other pitfalls, into which we were imminently to tumble, we were blissfully unaware. As has often been observed, foresight has its limitations, and in any case it is the completely

---

[26] Mozart was famously still writing the overture to Don Giovanni on the day of the opera's première.

unforeseen, the unknown unknowns, that you need to look out for. Having honed our clothes-peg techniques, Geordie, Andrew and I were called over to meet the show's director and presenter, and for a short conference with Randy, the 'floor manager'. They had been so delighted with our run-through that a hurried conference had decided we should have an additional, and more prestigious, slot: we were to play the programme out as the credits rolled. We agreed readily enough (after all, coast-to-coast exposure in the US did not come around every day) and it was only after we had settled on the extra music (and a tiny haggle over additional fees) that the first alarm bells faintly sounded. The director explained that the advertisements which immediately followed the close of the show, were sourced in the US and cut in at a fixed time over which the UK production team had no control. Since he did not have the technical wherewithal to fade our performance out it would therefore be essential for us to finish our performance no more than four seconds before the commercials automatically took over. The cardinal sin, we were firmly told, would be to finish too soon, for this would mean that the show's credits would roll in silence, but almost worse was the indignity of being cut off while still in full spate.

"OK," we said, confidence still brimming, "just tell us how long you want us to play for and we will arrange something accordingly."

"Ah," came the reply, "this being a live show we can't be sure. It could be anything from 30 seconds to 90 seconds." After a moment's consternation, the ever-resourceful young Marriner had the solution: Randy would be responsible for telling us when to play (the talking parts of the programme were taking place on the terrace of the big house, too far away for us to hear anything) and, when the time arrived, would also tell us whether we needed to fill 90 seconds, 60 seconds or 30 seconds. We would play a little Mozart Minuet and Trio which divided itself neatly into six eight-bar sections, each lasting about five seconds. Thus, if we played it straight through at a brisk tempo we could cover the ground in 30 seconds; the same music at the same tempo, but with each section repeated, would give us, our arithmetic suggested, 60 seconds or, by taking a more leisurely speed and repeating each section, including the reprise of the final Minuet, we could spin matters out for almost a minute and a half. Perfect. What could possibly go wrong?

Our director clearly had no understanding of why finishing a performance involving eight players at a fixed time without a fixed starting time was a tricky challenge, but nevertheless the sun was shining, the wind seemed to have dropped and we were in confident mood, beaming even, as 'Good Morning America' was itself beamed across a somnolent Atlantic to its audience of American early birds. All went well, as Randy, ambling across the luscious Cliveden turf, gave us the thumbs up for 'Rule Britannia' (he couldn't speak, of course, because we were going out live) which we delivered with a self-consciously British *sangfroid* in the teeth of a re-gathering gale. Our clothes pegs, though, ensured that our music was as dutifully unflappable as we ourselves.

We could relax now, awaiting our carefully choreographed play-out music; some forty-five minutes later I was immersed in a leisurely book, propped on my music stand, when my peripheral vision picked up trouble: hurtling in our direction across the manicured grass from the direction of the Cliveden house a panicked, arms-flapping figure hove into view. Randy was on the move, at the topmost speed achievable given that he was also bent double to avoid being caught on camera, clearly no longer the debonair ambler; as he came into breathless earshot his message was unmistakable; ignoring the liveness of the situation his cries were an urgent stage whisper, "You're ON. Play, NOW. GO. Now, please. PLAY!" So saying, he fell to his knees, though whether in supplication or because he could no longer sustain his curiously crab-like posture, there was no opportunity to establish.

In a flurry of unpreparedness books fell to ground, reeds and mouthpieces were retrieved, instruments applied to lips and we were away…but, as the attentive reader may have spotted, Randy had omitted to tell us which version we were playing. Our collective sense seemed to be that this was a long version: remembering the instruction that our worst outcome would be to fall silent before the credits finished rolling, our tempo was sedate. To my relief, I saw that Randy, aware of our dilemma, was once again on his knees on the grass, not praying so much as scratching us a message with a black marker pen on a piece of cardboard. Moments later, he held his message aloft…'4 MINUTES'. This was scarcely believable; no contingency had been discussed for anything outside our agreed parameters of thirty seconds to a minute and a half, and it scarcely needs saying that, live on coast-to-coast TV, we were in no position to stop to hammer out a new plan. It was clear to us all, I suppose, that we would, at the very least, have to play the whole movement twice, and slowly, but this still wouldn't fill the dreadful eternity of four minutes with what was essentially thirty seconds of material. We were about to test to destruction Parkinson's Law that work expands to fill the time available to do it. Well, I can tell you it doesn't. And worse, our long version involved making the repeats of both sections of the Minuet both times we played it. Thus, if we were to play the Minuet and Trio twice through we would, in this thinking-on-your-feet version play the Minuet four times in sections (with both sections repeated twice). Or would my colleagues revert to normal and abandon repeats on the reprise. Each double bar (and they came around every five seconds, remember) was an agony of uncertainty, waiting to guess what one's colleagues might play next while simultaneously trying to calculate how many variants of our three schemes were divisible (perhaps I mean multiplicable) into four minutes. The tempo of our performance had slowed to a crawl, and the gaps at each double bar became ever more extended and thoughtful as each player grappled with this ghastly game of bluff and guesswork. But we battled on, communicating via eyebrow movement (a kind of locked-in syndrome) and any other available body language, managing, with only minor mishaps, to stay in touch with each other. We had reached the Minuet again, for the fourth and final time now and the finishing line was surely in sight. Randy, meanwhile, was at work on another sign, eventually holding aloft, '2 MINUTES'. Impossible; we had already played for three minutes and fifty-something seconds and were now stuck in an endlessly repeating loop of the final five-second section of the Minuet. By now, our melody instruments (mainly the clarinets, but manfully supported by the oboes) were engaging in ever more bizarre, baroque, ornamentation in a fruitless attempt to disguise the fact that we were playing the same eight bars over and over again in the desperate hope that Randy would relent and bring the curtain down on an episode that would surely end in disaster or, at the very best, humiliation. Meanwhile, our guest players, no doubt already planning to dine out on the horror of our plight, were, depending on their basic character traits, either scarcely concealing their laughter or displaying the pasty, palely sweaty complexion of the condemned man facing imminent execution (but without hearty breakfast). To this scene of mounting, if suppressed, hysteria Randy at last brought relief with a new sign saying, 'TEN SECONDS', at which point Andrew, with an enormous effort of eyebrow language and the nerves of steel which had kept our leaking ship afloat, embarked on a fortissimo and adagio final rendition of the Minuet. I confess that the final moments are now lost in the red mists of fearful memory but it was with no little sense of achievement that we brought matters to a none-too-unanimous close. In the uncannily absolute silence which followed our final chord, I felt as the shocked survivor of a car crash must feel as he sits blankly at the roadside surveying a heap of crumpled metalwork which had been, only moments earlier, his prized automobile.

Astonishingly, the TV moguls expressed themselves delighted with our show. Not only had we, somehow, given satisfaction on the day, there was, sometime later, some even more startling feedback. One of our oboists at the Cliveden Massacre was the eminent principal oboist of the Philharmonia Orchestra, Gordon Hunt. Being something of a perfectionist, he had been less amused than horrified at the experience (i.e. one of the 'facing imminent execution' characters) and some days later, at the end of a Philharmonia rehearsal he was called over by Ricardo Muti, their principal conductor, who told him that he had recently seen him on American TV. Muti had been in Los Angeles a few days previously and, suffering from jetlag, had switched on the East Coast breakfast show at 4.00 in the LA morning. Gordon was, of course, convinced that his execution was imminently at hand but, incredibly, Maestro Muti, had loved it (his jetlag must indeed have been severe) and wanted only to know how the event had come about in the first place. Gordon had the good sense, at least as he later reported, to do what all sound orchestral players learn at their mothers' knee, namely, when the conductor says something ridiculous, just smile and nod.

~~~

It was soon after this lamentable episode (perhaps even because of it) that the Albion Ensemble's capacity for resilience and self-preservation came to the attention of the British Council. The Council's role (in those halcyon days when it could be said to have had one) was to fly the flag for British cultural life. We, it seemed (it was never quite overtly stated), were thought to be a group with a strong enough survival instinct to be dispatched to some of the more difficult postings (difficult either because of perceived resistance to matters British and/or cultural, or difficult simply in terms of geography, climate or logistics). These would be countries in which self-reliance and an ability to deal with the unexpected would be at least as important as giving concerts.

The first of our British Council assignments was a five-week tour in Asia, beginning with a fortnight in China followed by a week in South Korea and shorter visits to Malaysia, Hong Kong and The Philippines. These tours were of course intended as a form of soft diplomacy, a window onto British arts and

British values.[27] In truth, it was just the kind of hard-to-measure investment for which Mrs Thatcher's government had little time, and even as we embarked on our overseas mission, we were uneasily aware that such cultural diplomacy was unlikely to survive for much longer. I had not been to China before, my experience of communist regimes, such as it was, being limited to the East European communist bloc countries, particularly East Germany and the Soviet Union (as it then was); the abiding memory of this Chinese adventure was the much greater openness of the Chinese themselves compared with their East European communist counterparts. Naturally, we were very carefully monitored, indeed were assigned our own minder, a delightful man named Junbang. It was an odd experience for us (obviously professional diplomats grow accustomed to it) to know that one's every move was being noted and, presumably, reported up the management line but, even despite this constraint, our conversations were much less inhibited than they would have been in communist Europe. For example I recall several discussions with Junbang about population control and the single child policy. Even with the benefit of hindsight his frankness was startling: he said that the one child per family policy was probably a mistake (this was the 1990s, remember, and the policy only began to be relaxed some twenty-five years later), and would certainly create difficult problems for the next few generations. There were many reasons, not all of which I remember, but the principal risk was the creation of a top-heavy social structure which would put impossible burdens on an ever-reducing number of wage-earners: China was a country with no social welfare whatsoever, so care for the elderly and the sick, as well as for children, was entirely the responsibility of families. Limiting families to a single child, while helpful in the short run in allowing more mothers to work, would inevitably place a heavy responsibility on the child, when reaching working age, to support a potentially huge family 'superstructure' out of a single wage or salary. At the same time, Chinese society was becoming industrialised, leading to a migration of younger workers from the rural regions to the ever-expanding cities. The social consequences, which, of course, included the weakening of traditional family bonds and responsibilities, had not,

---

[27] Exactly what impact the wind quintet has had on British cultural life is perhaps debatable, and we learned rather too late in our tour that our performances of Malcolm Arnold's 'Three Sea Shanties', one of the works we had selected as our national cultural showcase, was rendered more than usually baffling to our Chinese hosts by virtue of being translated into Mandarin as 'Three Little Houses by the Sea.'

according to Junbang, been properly evaluated or planned for. A different kind of issue arising from the single child policy was the question of enforcement: the people most easily persuaded/coerced into abiding by the policy were the urban educated classes. As you moved into China's more remote regions, the party's control became less effective, so the 'peasant' population, as Junbang rather dismissively described it, was still rapidly growing with many large families. The Party's ability even to communicate with these 'peasants', let alone alter their behaviours, was surprisingly limited; many couldn't read (there was no nation-wide education system in the rural areas) and China has more than seventy spoken languages and no common language. Consequently, the principal method of enforcement was economic, rather than through persuasion and education (only later becoming more draconian, with enforced abortions, sterilisations and so forth). The state would pay for all the health and education needs of a first child but nothing towards the same needs of subsequent children. However, in the rural regions there were often no schools to go to and little formal health care, so most families had to be self-sufficient, living off the land. Consequently, there were few costs for the state to meet. It followed that the financial penalties for having larger families were less burdensome and the economic levers commensurately less effective in the rural areas than in the cities. I also asked Junbang about the stories we sometimes heard in the West of parents allowing their girls to die, or even killing them, so as to ensure the single surviving child would be male. He replied rather carefully that he didn't himself know of anyone who had done this, but later the same day, pointed out to me a sign standing at a river's edge just outside Beijing which he translated for me, "No drowning babies in this part of the river." He made no further comment.

Junbang also explained something of his personal circumstances when questioned about how he came to be looking after this oddball group of itinerant musicians. He had been in the Chinese diplomatic service, posted to Toronto, and became engaged to be married to a colleague who was also posted in Canada. They were then faced with some tough choices: if they wished to continue their careers in the diplomatic service they would have to accept that they would never again be posted to the same Embassy at the same time because of the perceived likelihood of defection (he denied that this would be a temptation because both he and his wife would not abandon their parents back home, but we are dealing here with bureaucratic perceptions). The alternative, which they had accepted, was to leave the diplomatic service and transfer to the domestic agencies, which allowed them to live together in China. Furthermore, they had signed a contract to have no children, in exchange for a promise of more rapid career advancement and better housing. The stark reality of these kinds of decision made a deep impression, but most surprising was the fact that we were discussing them in the first place. One further question which I perhaps should have asked Junbang was when his move to domestic agencies had been made: it seemed open to some doubt whether he truly felt that acting as nursemaid and spy to a visiting wind quintet could properly be categorised as 'rapid career advancement.'

Despite the niche nature of our 'mission', we were treated with extraordinary generosity by our Chinese hosts. For our first 'welcome' dinner in Beijing, we were taken to a celebrated specialist duck restaurant (there were seven floors for dining and we were proudly informed that three thousand ducks were slaughtered every day for consumption on the premises).[28] At these formal receptions, we were never permitted to choose what to eat, so we simply accepted what we were given, sometimes having to deal with some strangely unfamiliar foods as a consequence. One of the many dishes that evening was a kind of soup, rather along the lines of *minestrone*, which contained some ingredients which puzzled me. By way of making conversation with my neighbour, I asked her to identify a little pink-coloured vegetable (as I supposed it to be) with a slightly rough surface and shaped a bit like the inner sole of very small shoe. This great delicacy, at least according to my informant, proved to be a cat's tongue. Washing it down with strong liquor seemed a good solution at the time, possibly because copious quantities of such liquor were constantly available. This was another surprise: perhaps we had not been properly briefed, but I was quite unprepared (though in truth rather easily persuaded to adopt local custom in this regard) for the truly impressive quantity and strength of the alcohol which was consumed. Every few minutes, it seemed, there was a pause in the meal for someone to propose a toast ('to eternal friendship', 'worldwide harmony', 'the universality of music', and similar earnest philosophies) each of which was celebrated with a downing in a single shot of a tumbler of the local, and lethal, firewater, a type of grain-based spirit called Baijiu, and it was only somewhat deep into the evening that I noticed that after each such toast our empty tumblers were removed from the table, to be replaced with something a little larger; so by the evening's end we were dispatching seriously damaging measures of the said

---

[28] I believe this must have been the celebrated Quanjude Roast Duck Restaurant, near Tian'anmen Square.

firewater just as the speeches, toasts and celebrations gathered pace. Needless to say, our hosts' glasses had not been substituted, so they had contrived, no doubt by virtue of long experience, an unassailable competitive advantage. And it was only as we reeled out, that the British Council's Beijing representative revealed that this was a traditional testing-of-the-mettle of recently arrived visitors. Not only so, he continued, but Philippa, our wonderful flautist, had just equalled the British all-comers record. This fine example of the British competitive spirit (I use that word advisedly) did not go unappreciated, because when we progressed from Beijing to Shanghai we were given an especially magnificent banquet by the mayor of that city, whose welcoming speech referred, lyrically, to Philippa as, "She of the capacity of oceans."

Before we left London we had been given some guidance about local customs (although, as I have said, alcohol consumption was not mentioned), including the instruction that under no circumstances should one eat with one's hands when in China. This would, we were told, be regarded as the last word in ill-mannered philistinism. This injunction was put to the sternest test in Shanghai where we were promised a special local delicacy, crab, only available at a particular market and then only if one arrived before 6.00 a.m. to buy it. This meal received a substantial build-up from our hosts, so when the moment arrived for the great treat there was an air of expectation. There were, I think, ten of us altogether around the table and we were each presented with a substantial crab (fortunately for us no longer alive) on a dinner plate, and nothing else but chopsticks. This was to be special. Once everyone had their crab before them, there was an awkward, and increasingly embarrassing, silence. No-one moved...perhaps our hosts, out of politeness, were waiting for us to start, but wait...the troubling question was how to start. You may never have given much thought to how you would tackle a whole crab armed only with chopsticks, but I can assure you it is an intellectual as well as practical challenge which we did not solve. All we knew was...no hands permitted. Eventually of course, our host, chuckling contentedly at our discomfiture, leant forward and grabbed his crab in both hands and began to break into its shell. This was, it seemed, the single exception to the no hands rule and once again we were being rather mischievously tested.

In truth, much of the China leg of our tour revolved more around food and drink than around concerts, and as we neared the end of our Chinese fortnight we had promised Junbang, of whom we had grown fond, that we would buy him a final meal at a restaurant of his choice. We had travelled south to Canton (aboard a plane which, in my seat at any rate, was without seatbelts despite having all the correct, 'Fasten your seatbelts,' signs) from where we were to take a train the next day across the border to Hong Kong. Junbang was not a native of Canton and he told us that one of his dreams was to eat a seasonal local delicacy, not available in most other parts of the country, and here only available for a few months of the year: snake. So we had agreed, in a spirit of adventure, to take him to a snake restaurant; we had, of course, dug this hole for ourselves by incautiously offering him the choice of cuisine, and perhaps the only redeeming fact, which we learned later, was that the specialist snake restaurant was, when out of snake season, a dog restaurant, which might have presented an even sterner culinary challenge. And so it was with excitement mixed with no little anxiety that we found ourselves sitting around a Cantonese table being invited to select our snakes, very much still alive, from an assortment of bags and cages. There was no way to make an informed choice; how, after all, to decide what makes a tasty snake, but eventually we each had pointed a trembling finger at the slithering ball of snakes and our fatal (for the snake, certainly, but, for all we knew, perhaps also for ourselves) choice was then seized by the neck and deftly skinned alive. There was then a little recovery time (for us this time, not the snakes) before our first dish, a three-snake soup, arrived at the table, closely followed by snake steaks, not unlike a tuna steak in appearance but tasting more like chicken. Not bad so far as taste went, although the texture was predictably rubbery. All in all matters were proceeding pretty well when the restaurant manager, who had naturally enough taken a close interest in our unusual little group, returned to our table and fell into an earnest exchange (of written messages[29]) with Junbang, our guide and, on this occasion, also our guest. While the wordless exchange was continuing, with messages passing back and forth on the back of a menu, I became a little uneasy at the frequency with which both protagonists would pause and allow their gazes to fix, with some intensity, upon myself. Eventually, I asked Junbang what was up. "The entire snake is used in the cooking with the exception of the gall bladder. But the contents of the gall bladder are highly regarded in traditional Chinese medicine as a cure for poor eyesight. As you are the only wearer of glasses amongst his honoured guests the

---

[29] It continues to surprise that our highly cultivated minder was unable to communicate in speech with the manager of a substantial restaurant in the heart of a major city. But they had no common language, so written messages it had to be.

proprietor is planning to offer you the very special privilege of drinking the contents of the gall bladder..." And there was more along these lines but I'm afraid I don't remember it; my mind was already elsewhere, wrestling with the diplomatic niceties of how to decline this generous offer while minimising the offence given. Before I could contrive a solution, our man was back, now, or so it seemed to me, with a more narrowed eye and ruminatively brutal look than hitherto, bearing a tray on which, in solitary glory, was a wine glass about half full (or it may have been half empty, but definitely fuller than I would have chosen) with an extraordinarily dark green liquid. Its appearance was not unlike a metallic paint (very much full gloss) in British racing green, but even more glitteringly intense. It was borne inexorably in my direction and I felt myself turning green, although in my case it was not a racing green but something much more bilious, the waxen pallor of the poisoned, as my diplomatically compulsory pick-me-up approached. But wait...just as I had reconciled myself to the inevitable, mentally summoning the priest to forgive my sins and administer, as it were, the final rites, my immediate prospects took a more favourable turn. A second waiter now hove (I think this is what waiters do) into view, bearing a second tray with a second solitary *objet*. Encouragingly this was a bottle (a bottle, mind you, not merely a glass) of the very same viciously and anaesthetically effective firewater, Baijiu, which had wrought such destruction in Beijing: if not salvation, this at least might offer oblivion. To my growing relief our host transferred a very small quantity of his vivid liquid to a second glass, then topped it up with a satisfactorily large slug of the contents of the baijiu bottle. If this were an ordinary cocktail I judged the proportions to have been about 20:1, and I was sufficiently encouraged to accept with what good grace I could command what was in any case clearly inevitable. If I was to die, I reasoned, it would be preferable to be poisoned by a lethal dose of alcohol than be subject to the unknown agonies of snake poisoning. While these events were unfolding I found myself reflecting on my parents' recently deceased cat, Simpkin, who, in the Wiltshire countryside, would occasionally murder a rabbit. On these occasions little would remain of the deceased other than a few bones and some skin, with the alarming, in my present predicament, exception of the animal's gall bladder which was always very carefully set aside by our murderous pet. Simpkin clearly knew something of the medical effects of gall bladder ingestion which was unknown to Chinese medical practice. To prevent my thoughts running too imaginatively on my <u>own</u> mortality, I turned for distraction to thinking of the recent sad demise of Simpkin himself, after whom the Hertford College student magazine had been named. My father, then Principal of the college, had provided the next edition of the eponymous journal with a most touching obituary:

'The Principal's cat Simpkin, whose name this magazine bears, died on 16th November.

'Believed to have been born in the rural West Country, he was admitted to the College as a very small kitten early in 1972, donated by a family friend who had failed to persuade her London landlady to tolerate a cat. In his younger days, he was alarmingly wide-ranging—observed once as far south as Merton Street, and keen on exploring the Bodleian and Camera at a time when, with through traffic in Catte Street, there were risks in that enterprise. In early days, too, he was liable sometimes to climb, as kittens will, to perilous heights from which, with much fuss and bother, he needed to be rescued. But he soon settled down happily in College, taking meals in the Lodgings and perhaps other places too, and establishing almost a second home with the Bursar of New College, an easy trip for him over the wall behind the College.

'He was a notably affectionate cat, who could do with any amount of manhandling by college members and tourists. He never quite learned to miaow, but the touch of a hand always called forth a good 'basso' purr—except to one tactless tourist who, last summer, enquired when 'her' kittens were due. However, in spite of his urban and gregarious life-style, he remained, on his country holidays, a formidable carnivorous predator, and will be unmourned by the rabbits and voles of Wiltshire (of which there are far more than conservation requires).

'His amiable presence in the quad and elsewhere, in his invariably impeccable academic dress of black and white, will be greatly missed.

'G. J. Warnock.'

With such sombre reflections I returned to the reality of my present predicament and the need to cheat, if I could, immediate death by poisoning. With a great effort of will I drained the proffered (substantial) glass, closed my eyes, and was at peace. As the fiery liquid coursed around my frame I allowed myself the pleasure of opening first one eye, then another, to be greeted by enthusiastic applause not only from my colleagues but also from the proprietor, the waiters and even some of the other customers in the restaurant who had all gathered round to observe the drama unfold. I contrived to beam, Cheshire cat-like, at least until the realisation dawned that my medicine was to be repeated, not once but several times. I am unable to say for certain whether snake's gall is or is not beneficial for the eyes. It may, after all, have been more a consequence of the alcoholic medium through which it was administered that I stumbled from that snake pit quite cross-eyed.

My encounter with snakes might belie the assertion but my role in the Albion Ensemble at this time was to provide the occasional reality check; although my four colleagues had a pretty good instinct for the location of that invisible but vital line dividing acceptable from unacceptable behaviour, we did not always agree on where the line should be drawn.[30] Somewhere in Shanghai the line was for a while lost, with over-indulgence beginning to impact on the quality of concert performance. It was possible, too, that we were becoming over-confident in our hosts who had provided such a beautifully detailed and exhaustive written schedule that we felt that nothing could occur to disturb it. So it was that we arrived at the concert hall in Shanghai having dispensed with the usual pre-concert rehearsal except for the shortest of acoustic check shortly before the audience was to be admitted. As we set up our music-stands it was in unusually subdued tones that Philippa revealed that she had left all her music in her hotel room. I may have volunteered to go back to fetch it, or maybe I was simply delegated to do so, but in any case I soon found myself hurrying back to find the driver and car which had brought us on the 20 minutes-or-so drive from hotel to hall. The timing was tight but not impossible: the concert was an hour away and the drive 20 minutes each way; I would have to run into the hotel, take the lift to

---

[30] There was one morning in Shanghai when an excursion by boat on the Yang Tse River was scheduled. This took place hard on the heels of a more than usually self-indulgent evening, again involving copious quantities of drink, and we had been afloat no more than ten minutes on the very gently undulating Yang Tse when both Philippa and Andrew announced that they were sea-sick and needed to disappear below deck, "to throw up." This was overheard by Junbang, who questioned Andrew about the meaning of this, to him, unfamiliar expression, "to throw up." To fill the awkwardly ensuing silence, and perhaps because he was dangerously close to illustrating the concept there and then, Andrew prattled, mentioning, with suitable gestures, the ancient art of juggling which, "as I'm sure you know, Junbang," requires intensive practice in private. Thus, did 'juggling' acquire a coded meaning in the language of Albion to the mystification, no doubt, of many.

the 25th floor, then return and change for the concert. All do-able so long as nothing unexpected happened, but I certainly didn't want to waste any time and I was uneasy. Junbang instructed that day's driver but the latter spoke no English (and I, no Mandarin) so I had to hope that he understood that the situation was urgent and that I did not want to see the sights of Shanghai at this moment. Shortly after we set off back to the hotel I realised, too, that in my haste to get started I had left in our dressing room at the hall the schedule on which I had come to rely. This was the age before mobile phones, of course, so the schedule was the essential reference source for the addresses for all the hotels, halls and contact people for various emergencies, so I knew that, without it, should anything not go perfectly right I could be in real difficulty. As we pulled up at the Peace Hotel I indicated as best I could by signs, that I would be as quick as possible and that the driver was on no account to move from where he had stopped outside the hotel entrance. The Peace Hotel occupied a full block and was constructed to a symmetrical pattern with four entrances, each one at the midway point of each side of the block. I sprinted in, hoping that I would find the music where Philippa had said it would be (and not strewn about the room). I realised that I wasn't sure exactly which programme we were to play that evening, so I would have to bring everything. These things were passing through my head as I waited for the lift which seemed to be taking for ever to descend from the top of the building (and there was only one), and it took me a while to realise that it was not going to arrive at all. It was out of order. So now it was a climb of 25 floors via the stairs which were located in one of the corners of the lobby. Launching myself vigorously at this new challenge I was soon panting and sweating, but at last I reached Philippa's room and was relieved to find her music in a neat pile on a table, so, grabbing it all, I ran downstairs again to the strangely symmetrical lobby. I was a little disorientated by having had to climb the stairs rather than use the familiar lift, so I was no longer quite certain which entrance I had used. This one, it must be…so I hurried out, only to find myself in a street teeming with people, but no car to be seen. By now, I was concerned, thinking that perhaps my driver had thought he was simply dropping me off at the hotel, and he may have driven off. Also, I realised, with a sense of impending doom, that even the name of the concert hall, carefully written on the aforementioned schedule, was now unknown to me, so even if a taxi could be found it wouldn't help me. I tried the second of the four identical exits, then the third, with identical results…plentiful people but no white cars. The last exit at least produced a different result…emerging from the hotel I found myself in a street with, very strangely, no people (quite a rarity in Shanghai) but, to my astonishment a line of thirty identical white cars drawn up one behind the other along the entire length of the street. Could one of these be mine, and if so, which? So, I found myself walking to the street corner then slowly working my way back, stopping at each car to stare with what I hoped was a friendly and intelligent eye into the inscrutable gaze of each of the thirty drivers. This was the moment when I realised that westerners all look the same to Chinese (I believe it is our sunken eyes which make identification difficult) just as oriental features can be hard for Westerners to distinguish. Time seemed to be standing awfully still, but eventually (at about car number twenty) I detected, or so I thought, a small nod of recognition from one of the drivers. Interpreting this as an invitation to climb into the car I hesitated only momentarily. Should I just check the other ten cars? The driver, if indeed he was my driver, would probably think me quite deranged if I walked past him, and the last thing I could risk was that he would give me up as mad and drive off. So I climbed in, we set off and I spent an uncomfortable few minutes wondering if I recognised any of the buildings on our journey (I didn't, of course). I was late, by now, but I had achieved a kind of calmness which only arrives when further worry is pointless: I didn't know if I was in the right car, nor could I communicate with its wordless driver, nor did I know where I was supposed to be going, nor, wherever it was, whether this car would take me there, and I didn't have any way of contacting anyone, so what choice was there but to let the fates decide. Just as I had reached this high level of karma, we drew up outside a building and the driver, bless him, indicated with silent gesture that I might care to alight. So, feeling somewhat drained, I re-joined my highly unsympathetic colleagues ("Where HAVE you been?" "You do realise we've had to delay the concert because of you," and so on). Sometime later that evening Junbang offered the driver's apology: apparently, and most unusually, the police had corralled all the cars waiting for passengers outside the hotel's four entrances and insisted they park all together in a neat line outside a single entrance. My driver had had no choice but to comply or face unspecified, but no doubt dire, consequences.

    Following our wonderful (with the solitary exception just noted) fortnight in China and a restful day or two back in the 'free world' of Hong Kong, our next touring destination was South Korea. Our first duty on arrival in Seoul was to dine with the British Council representative, a Mr Newton, his wife and a few colleagues. It turned out that the 'few colleagues' were, in truth, all of their friends and colleagues: the Newtons were moving to a new posting the following week, and it became increasingly clear that they were hugely delighted to be going; so much so that this very evening they were throwing a party to celebrate their imminent liberation. Copious quantities of alcohol fuelled ever more articulate disenchantment with diplomatic life in Korea, with special focus on impossible language barriers and dreadful food, but not neglecting the appalling political tensions, the unlikelihood that Seoul would manage the upcoming Olympics (they did so very well) and the disparagement of Korean cultural prejudices not only against Western (and especially European) influence but also against Japanese and Chinese cultures which Koreans, we were told, regarded as youthful upstarts. There was something disturbingly colonial about this general low regard for 'the natives' but also something quintessentially British about the Foreign Office's lack of effective response…there was only one Korean speaker at the Foreign Office, apparently, and he had been posted to Nigeria for the last three years.

And so, nursing our all-too-familiar hangovers, we set off next morning from Seoul, the capital city, into the 'interior', to the provincial town of Jeonju, with the unhelpful cries of the previous evening's hosts (along the lines of "Good luck, you'll need it,") still ringing in our ears. The Korean leg of the tour differed from the others because the logistics were organised by a local music entrepreneur, a Mr Kim. This meant, amongst other things, that we were without the neatly typed diplomatic schedule of each day's activities on which we had so heavily depended in China. We knew we were to be at Seoul's main station for an 8.20 train but there our certainty ended. We found ourselves gazing in bleary bewilderment at a departure board which appeared to show two 8.20 trains departing to unreadable destinations which in any case changed every 30 seconds or so. Fortunately, or so it seemed, Mr Kim appeared and, without any great show of confidence, suggested that the train to Kuangzu would probably be the best. I asked him when we were due to arrive (I was worried, given our difficulties at reading the destination boards at the main station, that the provincial stations might not have their names transliterated, making it challenging to know where we were). Again he didn't inspire huge confidence by replying that it really depended at what time the train departed Seoul. Further enquiry elicited an estimate of "sometime after 11.00." And with this, we climbed aboard and were on our own.

The carriages were in an old-fashioned style, with the train divided into dingy self-contained compartments with no inter-connecting corridor. One of the features of our compartment was a faded map of the railway route pinned behind brown-ish plastic to the carriage wall. Re-assured, we settled in for our journey and only later did I study the wall-map. On closer examination it was far from re-assuring. Not only did the city of Jeonju not appear, nor did our train's alleged ultimate destination, Kuangzu. The five cities listed, at which it had to be assumed the train would stop, were transliterated as Chŏngju, Chŏnju, Sonjju, Kwangju and Changju. As 11.00 a.m. approached the tension mounted in our compartment. The train slowed and came to a Halt (to describe it as a station would be misleading), so it was not hard to decide not to disembark, hoping that the next, or at least one of the next stops would offer something more substantial. We spent the next thirty minutes or so wondering if we had made a mistake but in due course found ourselves trundling through what looked like the outskirts of something which could conceivably have been described as a conurbation. We decided to alight, which we had to do very fast because one thing we had already observed was that this train might meander sedately through the Korean countryside but when it came to a city station it suddenly adopted a Japanese-style efficiency, stopping for a few seconds only, before resuming its rural idyll. By this stage of the trip, we were burdened with a substantial amount of baggage…six weeks' worth of clothes, including concert gear, musical instruments, music, music stands, video recorder and far too large a caseful of Chinese souvenirs including, if I remember correctly, a complete dinner service which Peter Francomb, our horn player, had acquired in Hong Kong. We found ourselves, breathing heavily as the train puffed lightly into the distance, the only passengers on a long platform. And then, as in an exercise in perspective, a tiny dot could be discerned on the distant horizon at the very opposite end of the platform and, labouring under our loads, we struggled in the direction of the dot. This must be Mr Koh (or so we hoped) who was to be responsible for us for the coming two days. Mr Koh regarded us, impassive and immobile, as we floundered in his direction, groaning under the weight of our burdens (especially the dinner service), and greeted us with the incredibly welcome line, "Good morning…I am your interpreter." We had been so starved of any information about what we were to be doing in this place whose name we didn't know that Mr Koh's welcoming words prompted an instant volley of questions about our immediate future, especially the location of our hotel, the prospects for lunch, the schedule for the rest of the day and so on. Sadly, it quickly emerged that Mr Koh's command of the English language extended to no more than six words and with 'good morning' and 'I am your interpreter' he had run through his full repertoire and had nothing further to add.[31] We had no idea what we were supposed to do...had this been China we might have anticipated a day, or even two, of guided tours before a little light teaching and perhaps a concert and, undoubtedly, some excellent dining, but, somehow, we now felt a long way from China.

The impassive Mr Koh led us to a small bus which took us to a truly dreadful hotel. The ceiling of my room sagged alarmingly and the walls bulged claustrophobically inwards with damp, and as for the carpet it actually squelched as you walked on it. I didn't dare explore the quality of the bed, partly because I had put all of my possessions on it to protect them, so far as I could, from the flooding, so I hurried out again, having observed, on arrival, that the hotel boasted some kind of restaurant which, it was to be hoped, might be persuaded to provide some food. Here we met Mr Koh again, flanked this time by two young female interpreters, neither of whom, it soon emerged, spoke English. Nor did the hotel staff of course, although they proudly presented us with a menu in English. It emerged, in due course, that this menu must have been written a few years previously because whatever we ordered, by pointing at a number, the answer was, firstly, an eagerly nodded, "Yes", and then, after lengthy silence (and no further enquiry amongst chefs or other staff), a crestfallen, "We have not."

While some of us worked our way through the entire menu, concluding eventually that 'they had not,' a single item on it, Geordie had valiantly taken up the struggle to divine what we were supposed to be doing in this godforsaken spot. "Today pran," was Mr Koh's opening. Geordie has a smile of the utmost charm which he now shone upon one of Mr Koh's soubrettes. "Would it be possible for us to have a rest for an hour before we do a workshop?" Silence, then, "Yes, 2 o'clock rest." This was welcome news indeed but was quickly followed by, "2 o'clock pianist time," then, "r'sal." Dialogue (if such it can be called) continued along these lines until Geordie had the bright idea to ask our

---

[31] Mr Koh's six-word vocabulary was memorably extended at the very end of our excursion into provincial Korea: as he stood at the departure gate to send us on our way back to Seoul he suddenly broke the silence of the preceding days with the words "Goodbye Albion, I am on a high cloud."

trio of interpreters to write it on the back of a menu. By now Andrew was unable to contain his growing desperation; a combination of tiredness, frustration and hilarity, with hilarity about to win explosively. He decided to escape and he and I left the room purportedly to get our own schedules (which, of course, didn't exist) from our rooms. Once out of the door we were overwhelmed. We leant against opposite walls of the corridor, weeping with laughter, and gradually subsiding to the floor, at which precise moment a diminutive Korean waitress, bearing an immense tray laden with crockery, came around the corner into our corridor and, at the sight of two large Englishmen in paroxysms on the floor, apparently in the throes of noisy and simultaneous heart attacks, uttered a terrified shriek, dropped her load of crockery which shattered spectacularly along the length of the corridor, and fled in confusion.

Meanwhile, back at the dinner table, Mr Koh's team had written out a hymn-sheet for the day which read:

14.00	rest
14.00	leson
15.30	pianist time
17.00	rersal
19.30	concet
21.30	hotel

The other three were still puzzling over this when Andrew and I, partially recovered, rejoined them for our, "Yes, we have no bananas," lunch. Some food had arrived, served in bowls, and so hot and highly spiced that it was impossible to identify ingredients. We concluded that the '14.00 rest' should probably be discounted, having been added to the list as an attempt to respond to our pleas, but that '14.00 leson' was probably in the implacable Mr. Koh's plans. 'Pianist time' was indeed baffling, since pianists had not featured in any of our plans to date. In a moment of rare optimism, I speculated that what was intended might be 'quiet time' with the word quiet having somehow been translated, perhaps with some musical reference muddled up in it, as 'piano'. I was clutching, by this time, at any straw, and was in any case quite desperate for a bit of space before the 'rersal' for another 'concet'.

14.00 duly arrived, to find a tired and hungry, and above all reluctant, Albion Ensemble assembling in the hotel lobby laden once more with instruments, concert clothes, music case, music stands and all the paraphernalia, only to be greeted with astonishment by Koh and Co. who shooed us back to our rooms. Moments later as I lay on my bed, literally surrounded by my possessions (anything to avoid the soaking-wet floor) there was a knock on the door and, stepping gingerly across a kind of lily-pad arrangement of hotel towels to open the door I was confronted by two Korean teenagers bearing bassoons, in the company of one of the non-English-speaking interpreters. To describe the next 90 minutes as a nightmare would not do justice to the awfulness of the experience. My two Korean students were eager; they stood with their instrument cases gazing expectantly at this curiously rumpled foreigner, who appeared to have been asleep in his suitcase, then simply advanced through the reluctant space, dumped my ever-so-carefully protected suitcase in the pond that was the bedroom floor, set their instrument cases in the limited space just vacated and began to assemble their bassoons. Meanwhile my efforts with their chaperone-cum-interpreter were not going well. English was clearly impossible but I thought I detected a small glimmer of understanding when I desperately offered a little French, and a sound emerged which could originally have been intended as 'un petit peu'. So we proceeded...My students were beginners (or at least players of minimal skill), the room, already oppressively small and dangerously inwardly bulging, seemed to have shrunk further, with its four occupants, to the size of a telephone box, and one about to be submerged in a flood. There was one chair, and a desk so small that if you sat on the chair there was no room for your knees under it. I had never attempted to teach in French, nor attempted to teach a pupil, let alone two, in a flooded telephone box. These girls had brought no music with them and I had nothing suitable with me, so the going was heavy, but I struggled on, all the time wishing that I had played dead when the knock had come at the door; but it was already clear that a mere locked door, and possibly even an actual corpse, would have been insufficient deterrence for a determined Korean on a mission. Of the final half hour, I remember little, other than looking at my watch three times within a single minute and finishing with an attempt to retrieve the Weber bassoon concerto from a fallible memory and delivering it furiously to my startled visitors.

It had been wisely decided to abandon any attempt at 'rersal' so we left for the concert intending only to play a few notes in the hall as an acoustics check. We left ourselves about 30 minutes between this check and the concert, to allow the audience to come in and ourselves to explore possible options for drinks, snacks etc. (we hadn't yet cracked the food issue and I was by this time exceedingly hungry). Just then there was another knock at the door, "I am bassoonist from Seoul; I have driven five hours for lesson"; "I'm sorry, it's a little difficult; concert in half an hour, you know"; "Lesson after concert?" and so relentlessly on, until I found myself giving my five-hours-from-Seoul bassoonist the benefit (if so it was) of 29 minutes of bassoon wisdom before our first Korean concert. The idea of a post-concert lesson was out of the question because we had scarcely eaten anything for 24 hours and I had become obsessed with worry about where the next meal might be coming from, a common enough touring anxiety even at the best of times, and this was certainly not one of those times.

All in all, Korea was terribly hard work; it was surprisingly exhausting to wake up each morning without the slightest idea what that day held in store; one had to be prepared for anything, but our days were mostly filled with endlessly hopeless teaching when we were not playing concerts; and of course the insuperable language barrier made everything so much more challenging. It didn't especially help us, either, that the difficulties we encountered were shared by the diplomatic and ex-patriot community, not much in evidence in any case outside Seoul, all of whom had come to regard Korea as a hardship post. Their default response was invariably to ease the pain by despatching copious quantities of strong liquor.

However, whatever one's own problems, it is usually possible to find someone even worse off, and so it proved in Ulsan. At the end of another long day[32] we descended on the deserted hotel bar in search of a nightcap. After an

---

[32] Our journey had been enlivened by a long coach journey aboard an alarmingly elderly Greyhound bus, no doubt dumped on the unsuspecting Koreans having seen many thousands of miles of service quartering the American continent, on which there were no other passengers than our five selves. Our proud hosts had attempted to give the rattlesome superannuated Greyhound a touch of class by providing aboard a kind of air hostess, in figure-hugging uniform, who, every fifteen minutes or so, would elegantly sashay the length of the aisle from her front seat to ours at the back to enquire whether we had any needs, bearing a tray full of Kia-Ora orange juice and crisps. Riveting though this performance was, my attention was constantly drawn instead to our driver…above his head, and set slightly behind him, a television was suspended from the ceiling for the benefit of the absent Korean passengers. This television was showing a succession of Westerns, dubbed in Korean (including one, strangely enough starring Michael Cain, that well-known cowboy) and our pilot was watching these, a considerable gymnastic feat,

extended negotiation with the barman, who seemed unable to imagine that someone sitting in a bar might perhaps be hoping for a drink, we realised that we were not quite alone. From a dark recess emerged a forlorn figure who approached us at first hesitantly, and then with a kind of desperate hope. "My God", he gasped, "You're English." At which point he drew up a neighbourly stool and his story began to unfold. In brief, he was an employee of the Thames Water Board who had been seconded for a six-month term to assist the authorities in Ulsan in building a new sewage system in the city. He complained, and it was easy to sympathise, that he had been in Ulsan for six weeks and had so far been unable to communicate with any of his Korean colleagues. Worse, on the day of his arrival he had been unable to buy a meal (sympathetic nods at this too) and had finally just pointed at something on a menu which, when it eventually arrived, had poisoned him for the next three days. After this experience he had next time pointed at the first item on the hotel restaurant menu, which turned out to be something akin to a minestrone soup, so he had eaten this and nothing else for the last five weeks. As his tale drew to a close, our disconsolate water worker capped the sorry saga, observing that he had never in his life been abroad before, and if this was abroad, he hoped he never would again.

After Korea, our week in the Philippines was, by contrast, a relaxed affair apart from the small matter of a brush with death in the middle of a concert at the British Embassy in Manila. That day had begun with a long planned trip by minibus to the Pagsanjan rapids, a drive of several hours made to seem much longer by the attentions of a guide who gave us, uninvited, a relentless flow of touristic information, an unstoppable stream made mesmerising, for me at any rate, by the incredible whiteness of her teeth. The rapids were, it must be admitted, somewhat disappointingly unrapid but we did manage some good swimming at the foot of a spectacular waterfall, then discovered, to our pleasure, that the trip we had booked included a modestly palatable lunch including clam soup and various bits of meat on sticks.

Returning to Manila by early afternoon there was even time for a short rest before leaving for the Embassy, and it was only as we re-grouped for our departure that there were the first signs of trouble. Peter enquired if we all felt

---

requiring him to lean backwards at a 45 degree angle and stare straight up at the ceiling for what seemed like many minutes at a time while his ancient bus, apparently unguided, careered through the Korean countryside.

ok because he was struggling. Until that moment, I had felt fine but as soon as Peter mentioned (actually he launched into a detailed and intimate account of) the state of his bowels and that he was simultaneously feeling sick I suffered what I hoped would turn out merely to be a psychosomatic sympathetic reaction. On arrival at the Embassy we were presented to a few of the guests and Peter, by this time looking quite ill, retired upstairs to save what energy he could for the approaching concert. By the time the concert began I was undeniably ill, and the most important activity before the concert was to discover the nearest toilet to the stage in case of emergency. Peter was now worse, and although bravely carrying on as normal Andrew was sinking fast. We began our programme with Rossini's 'Silken Ladder' overture arranged (by my bassoonist colleague Graham Sheen) for wind quintet. Peter by this time was able to contribute no more than a few heroic bars of horn solo but thereafter he played not a single note until having a brave, if not especially accurate shot at the very last chord. As soon as this ended he left the stage, not to be seen again. This was the moment that our planning back in London came into its own. Anticipating some such event as this we had packed at the bottom of our music bag a few works for combinations of instruments other than the standard wind quintet. Next to exit the stage was Andrew, so Philippa, Geordie and I hacked through a Beethoven trio which none of us had played for several years. On Andrew's re-appearance we played a quartet by Jean Francaix and after that I lost track. I departed the stage to attend to my urgent functions and at one point Philippa was, literally, the only Albion left standing, so she delivered a splendid performance from memory, and playing as slowly as she dared, of Debussy's 'Syrinx' for solo flute. After quitting the stage (the only time I can remember doing this mid-concert) I retreated to the green room to find Peter lying on the floor. I have always believed that to describe someone as 'as white as a sheet' is to employ a figure of speech, but I have never seen anyone so unnaturally white as Peter at this moment. He was also unnaturally immobile and it was with real anxiety that I found myself checking that he was still breathing. That he might die seemed a real possibility, and struck rather urgently home with me since my own symptoms had, hitherto, mirrored his with an approximate 30-minute time lag! Luckily, I was able to find someone from the Embassy staff and asked them to call a doctor immediately, and after that I don't remember much at all, although we did apparently bring the concert to a close with four of us on stage. Soon afterwards a doctor duly arrived and gave Peter an injection and the rest of us some pills, before questioning us about what we had eaten that day. He seemed to find the whole thing hugely funny and eventually pointed an accusatory finger at our lunchtime clams, implicated partly by the obvious unwisdom inherent in eating shellfish in this part of the world but also by the fact that Philippa, alone amongst us, had not eaten them and had survived unscathed, while the unfortunate Peter had had seconds.

Recovery from food poisoning was mercifully swift and the even tenor (what a strange expression) of our touring lives was soon resumed. We were by this time four weeks into our assignment and I confess that my appetite for the wind quintet repertoire, limited at the best of times, was sated. I had become tired, for the time being, of sharing what few bassoon skills I still retained with eager young players (although one of my students in Kuala Lumpur was one of the most beautiful girls I have ever seen as well as being the daughter of the Malaysian Minister of Culture) and I was certainly tired of the constant round of receptions and quasi-diplomatic dinners. In other words, I was looking forward to stepping aboard the plane home. I had found our stay in Manila rather oppressive; it was, of course, the end of a long tour, but my spirits were certainly not lifted by the fact that we were housed in a diplomatic compound with an armed guard of heavily be-weaponed Filipino soldiers lolling in extraordinarily humid heat at each end of our street. If I had been in their shoes I would have been at the highest risk of running murderously amok. And the humidity really was extraordinary…under grey leaden skies each afternoon the temperature rose inexorably until, precisely on cue, the heavens opened at 5.00 p.m., delivering the most devastatingly powerful downpour. But when it was over, nothing was different except that steam now rose threateningly from the ground as the downpour was turned into a form of smog. This was climate as pressure cooker.[33]

From Manila we moved on to Kuala Lumpur with a brief stop to give a concert in the exotically named Kota Konabolu. This place used to be called Sarawak, a name familiar only to those of my generation who used as boys to collect stamps. Sarawak, as I continued to think of it, was built by British

---

[33] One redeeming feature was the pleasure to be had on our daily drive into Manila as we passed a small hospital, evidently run by the nuns from the attached convent, which boasted a little outbuilding alongside the central cluster of buildings. Above the entrance of this unassuming structure hung a painted sign identifying it as 'The Antenatal Clinic of the Immaculate Conception.' It always seemed a rather bustling place, certainly busier than its singular name suggested that it should be.

imperialists and if you held your nose (the sewers seemed to run down the middle of the main streets) and covered your ears, you might have imagined yourself to be in Eastbourne, so typically urban-Edwardian was the terraced banality of the architecture. A sense of colonial throw-back seemed also to apply to people's names: the British Council employs as many locals as it can, especially in its regional offices, and, true to form, we were met at Kota Konabolu airport by two very elegantly besuited Malaysians, who proudly introduced themselves as Basil and Ronald. We took to them immediately and it was a great regret that we could share their company and hospitality for so short a time. Had we had an extra day, Basil would have taken us into the jungle to meet his grandfather who had been a head-shrinker until this pursuit fell out of fashion; but apparently he still liked to show off his trophies. The oddness of this place was somehow captured by the airport signs that politely asked passengers, "Please, do not litter indiscriminately." You have to wonder how a discriminating litterer should proceed; perhaps by fastidiously placing an item in a carefully chosen spot, then retiring to await developments.[34] And so to Manila, and, via my beautiful bassoonist pupil, home.

Of our next British Council trip I have little to say. The truth is that I found India depressingly squalid and grim and I was pining for home from the very first day, but our eventual departure nearly came a day early and in coffins: at some point in the tour we had collectively decided that we could not leave India without having set eyes on the Taj Mahal, so on the very day of our evening flight back to London from Delhi we made a rather reckless plan: our final concert was in the old-fashioned splendour of the Doon School at Dhera Doon in the foothills of the Himalayas, and we had persuaded our British Council driver to take us back to Delhi airport via the Taj Mahal. The problem with this was that the Taj was a considerable distance the other side of Delhi, so we had to set off in the small hours of the morning on a four hundred mile drive. Our descent from the mountains in the dark was scary enough but in the end uneventful and, as we reached the flat northern plains, still in darkness, my colleagues in the back seats of our Land Rover were dozing contentedly and our long-suffering driver could at last pick up some speed. I was in the front passenger seat and suddenly, out of the darkness, I was staring death in the face,

---

[34] A comparable public message, which never fails to give pleasure, can sometimes be heard on London's Underground, "When boarding the train please use all available doors,"…well, I've tried, but I'm just not quick enough.

in the form of the huge radiator grille of a large unlit truck bearing down on us at speed on our side of the road. Our heroic driver reacted in the only way he could by heaving the steering wheel to the left and we plunged off the road into…as it miraculously turned out, a grassy field. I turned to look back to see the truck disappearing into the distance and, much closer, but moving laboriously in the same direction, was an ox-cart, laden high with hay bales and utterly without lights. The truck had clearly been trying to avoid this unseeable, until the last minute, obstacle and in doing so had almost killed us. Had we been forced off the road only a few minutes earlier we would have plunged to our deaths down a Himalayan ravine. We may only have been in the foothills, but foothill is a relative term. A Himalayan foothill is a serious mountain in any other context. In truth we all owed our driver, whose reaction to this near-death experience had been impressively phlegmatic, a huge debt of gratitude, but my slumbering colleagues, only now stirring themselves and looking about them in surprise, seemed only to half-believe my account of the event. They clearly suspected that our driver had fallen asleep and that I had failed in my duty as watchman to prevent exactly this eventuality.

As for our Indian concerts, they were lent a slightly bizarre character by the curious regulation that the British Council, the promoter of our tour, was not permitted to sell tickets; the concerts had to be free. This meant that our audiences were unpredictable, both in number and in level of sophistication, ranging from the extraordinarily Anglophile Parsee, Mrs Jeejeeboy, whose elegant Mumbai drawing-room was dominated by large photographs of the Queen and Duke of Edinburgh, to the kind-looking gentleman in Madras (now Chennai) who approached the stage at the conclusion of our recital to request that we play an encore. As we politely prepared to accede to this flattering appeal, he continued, "Please play, 'I wandered lonely as a cloud.'" Then, seeing that we were momentarily non-plussed by this unusual request, our gentleman admirer clambered up to the stage and at once began to declaim Wordsworth in a strong, if heavily accented, baritone. We could do little other than let events take their course, which they duly if unexpectedly did: four men in white coats hurried on to the stage and dragged our orator, still declaiming, into the wings. This alarmingly militant development was later justified on the grounds that this poetic soul was an escaped lunatic for whom the white-coats from the asylum had been scouring the city since dawn.

Our UK and European concerts never reached such heights of unpredictability. In the UK, these often involved driving great distances, all crammed into Geordie's latest magnificent motorcar, and back home after the concert. And this was also the pattern for some of the nearer French, Belgian and The Netherlands engagements. The epic encounters with French cuisine, which had entered a kind of Albion legend, pre-dated my time with the group, but there was a notable festival in the Belgian Wallonia region which we visited more than once. We stayed each time in a plain hotel called Hotel Orange which had an unexpectedly terrific restaurant from which we always emerged with heavier gait and lighter wallet. The last time we were there we had been paid in cash a handsome enough fee, but when we came to divvy up on our return home we found there was left just £1 each from the two-day trip having played two concerts (and eaten three dinners).

Despite our experience of near-starvation in Korea, over-eating while on tour is something of an occupational hazard. When your schedule is in the hands of others it is probably natural to suffer some mild anxiety about where the next meal is coming from, hence the tendency to over-compensate when the opportunity arises. There was no such worry at the Hotel Orange, of course, and there was another notable Belgian day when the culinary tables (as it were) were turned. Our concert was in Oudenard (I think it was Oudenard, but certainly one of the Duke of Marlborough's triumphs). Andrew had a friend who lived nearby. Because she was unable to come to the concert it was decided we should drop in for tea between our afternoon rehearsal and concert. As it turned out we were a bit pushed for time; not only did 'living nearby' require a longer-than-expected drive out of town but also the Mayor of Oudenard had sent a message, only that day, that he had arranged a short reception for us immediately before the concert. This meant that we had to be back at the Town Hall earlier than anticipated. We bowled up at English teatime to discover that our friendly hostess had interpreted 'dropping in for tea' as only a Belgian could. She had laid on the most magnificent spread of meats, cheeses, baguettes, puddings, wine, beer, cakes and fruit. Of course, it would have been rude not to fall upon this unexpected feast with enthusiasm, so we set to, explaining through full mouths that we had to hurry because we had a date with the Mayor at 7.00 p.m. Departing in due course with fond thanks and incipient indigestion we retraced our steps to the Town Hall in time for the mayoral event. To our dismay we were greeted with another simply magnificent spread; no mere buffet this, but a sit-down affair, a virtuoso display of the culinary brilliance and, well, sheer capacity of Belgian hospitality. Of course, it was a daunting challenge, manfully tackled, to put up a decent show of appetite, but by the time the cream cakes and chocolate puddings arrived we (unlike the Duke of Marlborough before us) simply had to admit defeat, and were reduced to claiming that we couldn't eat more before a concert. The Mayor seized on this tiny opening to invite everyone to return <u>in the interval</u> for the pudding course, explaining that it couldn't be after the concert because he had arranged another reception post-concert in which the focus would be on sampling the local beers in all their agreeable variety.

So, after one of our more breathless concerts, we re-grouped with the burghers of Oudenard to address the serious question of beer. And as our rather strenuous evening was finally drawing to a close I fell into conversation with two distinguished-looking gentlemen who enquired where we were staying. When it emerged that we were driving back to Brussels one of the silver-haired pair issued an earnest warning about the chances, likelihood even, of being breathalysed, a relatively new area of law enforcement in Belgium which it seemed they both regarded as a bitterly unfair assault on civil liberties. Divining that they were speaking from some personal experience I enquired further and learned that my eminent interlocutor and his distinguished colleague were the local magistrates. My initial reaction was alarm, of course, but my two new best friends were by now offering some useful tips. To be precise, they said that at this time of night the chances of the traffic policemen (and they knew them all personally) themselves being sober were very small indeed, so the advisable course, if challenged to submit to a breathalyser test, would be to insist that the investigating officer should also take the test. Apparently one of these excellent upholders of the quality and essence of Belgian life had, that very morning, dismissed a case in which the prosecution's witness, a police officer, had failed his own breathalyser, and he gave me to understand that, should I be arraigned before him the following morning, he would gladly repeat the medicine.

Chapter 4
Trials and Errors

It was 1980; Margaret Thatcher had recently been elected Prime Minister and we had entered a turbulent period, politically speaking, in which right wing certainties were to produce a much more confrontational government style than the previous (Labour) administrations had dared adopt. Yet, despite these certainties, or perhaps because of them, we seemed to live in an age of ever-increasing anxiety.

My own life at this time, while neither particularly confrontational nor especially turbulent, was nevertheless unsettled in a way which will be familiar to all freelancers, in whatever field. Despite being constantly busy, I remained uncomfortably troubled by the small but persistently nagging fear that my working life was more fragile than it appeared, that each engagement, to put it starkly, might be the last. Part of the problem was that I had several competing strands of work which were always hard to reconcile with each other and required some deft juggling of the diary. It might be argued that such diversity should be a source of strength, but it felt more like a house of cards which could collapse at the slightest unfavourable gust. My main orchestral diet was now primarily as a member of the Academy of St Martin in the Fields, with frequent excursions into the English Chamber Orchestra too. The Albion Ensemble provided my main, but not my only, chamber music interest and I had recently begun teaching at Trinity College of Music. Cutting across all of these threads, and often conflicting with them, was a growing interest and curiosity in 'period instrument' performance.

A number of distinct paths were leading in this direction. The study of eighteenth-century performance practices had until recently been a quaint backwater frequented by amateur musicians with more curiosity than technical skill, but it had suddenly been given an injection of professionalism and intellectual rigour by the writings, concerts and recordings of the extraordinary Viennese cellist Nikolaus Harnoncourt. The novelty of his insights and the revolutionary new sounds of his Concentus Musicus group were at once thrilling and impossible to ignore. Here was a scholar who was not satisfied with mere academic research amongst the musicological cobwebs, he was intent on discovering what an eighteenth-century orchestra might actually have sounded like. And his explorations were not simply confined to the orchestral instruments themselves, some of his most penetrating insights were into intellectual and cultural attitudes in the eighteenth-century. In other words, how musicians of the time thought about their music. In the context of my own professional life, mainly concerned with the music of exactly this period, the bright light which Harnoncourt shone was both revolutionary and fascinating.

As a bassoonist, I was leading a sheltered life in the comparatively gentle world of chamber orchestras whose repertoires were built on the baroque and classical foundations of, for example, Bach and Handel, Mozart and Haydn. And this music gave rise to a particular technical issue so far as the bassoon player is concerned. In Bach, say, or early Haydn, the bassoon often finds itself doubling the bass line, in effect playing as an extra cello. It was known from contemporary accounts that having a bassoon (sometimes more than one) amongst the string section was a normal eighteenth-century practice, but to make a success of this, in other words to find a sound quality which blends into the cello sound rather than steps into the foreground as in a bassoon concerto, requires a particularly delicate touch and soft-speaking reeds, which do not come naturally to the modern German-system bassoon. Similarly, when playing chamber music of this period I would valiantly attempt to stay discreetly in the background when providing a bass line for, say, an oboe sonata, but it was hard to believe that the practical difficulty of such unnatural exertions was really what composers of the time had in mind when writing what was in other respects quite simple music.

The seeds of my thinking about these kinds of issues had been sown early. I had had the good fortune, while still at school, to be taught by a very eminent bassoon player, Cecil James, formerly principal bassoon of the Philharmonia Orchestra amongst others. Cecil was the very last professional player in the UK to play on a French system bassoon, everyone else having by now transferred their loyalties, if not all of their affections, to the German bassoon (a new design and new fingering system invented by Willhelm Heckel in the 1830s), and it was his playing which gave me an early taste for the distinctive French bassoon timbre which was by then almost extinct in the 'modern' world. The soft-edged quality of this sound seemed to have more in common with a cello sound, blending effortlessly into a string section and removing altogether the troubles which were causing me such difficulty on my German bassoon. This was significant because the French bassoon is unquestionably a direct descendant of the instruments in use in Handel's time, while the German bassoon was more or less a new creation of the nineteenth-century designed to cope with the increased range and dynamic demands of the orchestral music of the time.

So, I began looking for further evidence that something valuable was in danger of being lost if this type of instrument were to disappear forever, not just in England (where the battle was already lost) but world-wide, and even in France itself.[35] One thing I did know for certain was that no one, at least no one in the UK, had yet mastered the technical demands of the recalcitrant eighteenth-century bassoon, and yet surely it could be done. I wanted to do it, if only to prove to my own satisfaction that my instincts about it were correct.

One rich source of circumstantial evidence was to look at the music itself from the baroque and classical eras, for surely composers would only write music which satisfied them in performance. So what did they write? The answer seemed to be bassoon concertos: the output from these times (roughly from 1720 to 1800) was simply enormous. In the first half of the eighteenth-century the most prolific composer of such works was Antonio Vivaldi who wrote at least forty of them for his talented pupils at the Ospedale della Pièta in Venice. But later composers continued to contribute numerous concertos to the growing bassoon repertoire, including many good pieces from minor masters such as Danzi, Fasch, Graupner, Devienne, Stamitz, Vanhal and, in London, Bach's

---

[35] That the French instrument was indeed an endangered species, even on its home turf, was confirmed by a painful episode at the Aix en Provence Festival in 1979: the Academy of St Martin in the Fields had been engaged as the pit orchestra for the Festival's production of Mozart's opera The Marriage of Figaro. My colleague, Graham Sheen, and I were approached by a solemn group of five gentlemen who introduced themselves as the bassoon players of the prestigious Orchestre de Paris. They had been instructed by their newly appointed conductor, Daniel Barenboim, to forsake their native French-model bassoons and spend their summer holiday learning to play German instruments. They had come to our concerts, they said, to hear "how it ought to sound." I was sorely tempted to urge them to put a bit of steel in their spines and mount a proud defence of their national heritage but it was clear that they had already given up any thought of such resistance.

youngest son Johann Christian. And to prove the point, if further proof is needed, an analysis of the programmes in the 1790/91 season at the famous Vauxhall Gardens concerts[36] on the south bank of the Thames shows that they included eighty violin concertos, eighty-two oboe concertos and <u>sixty-nine</u> bassoon concertos, and the next most featured solo instrument was the basset horn (and this only because of a special visiting overseas player) with sixteen. There was a total of seven trumpet concertos, a few for clarinet (the same visiting artist) but for the flute, cello, French horn, viola etc. not one. 1791, the same year as these Vauxhall Gardens concerts, was the year Mozart died. He wrote only one concerto for bassoon[37] but his orchestral writing for the instrument, especially in the piano concertos and his operas, is simply wonderful. Such beautifully idiomatic writing and melodic inspiration would surely not have been written if

---

[36] Vividly described in Tobias Smollett's *The Expedition of Humphrey Clinker* through the eyes of the gushing Lydia who declared herself "dazzled and confounded with the variety of beauties that rushed all at once upon my eye. Imagine to yourself spacious gardens, part laid out in delightful walks, bounded with high hedges and trees, and paved with gravel; part exhibiting a wonderful assemblage of the most picturesque and striking objects, pavilions, lodges, groves, grottos, lawns, temples, and cascades; porticoes, colonades, and rotundas; adorned with pillars, statues, and paintings; the whole illuminated with an infinite number of lamps, disposed in different figures of suns, stars, and constellations: the place crowded with the gayest company, ranging through those blissful shades, and supping in different lodges on cold collations, enlivened with mirth, freedom and good-humour, and animated by an excellent band of music…" This lively scene appealed less to Lydia's grumpy uncle, Matthew Bramble, "Vauxhall is a composition of baubles, overcharged with paltry ornaments, ill conceived, and poorly executed, without any unity of design or propriety of disposition. It is an unnatural assemblage of objects, fantastically illuminated in broken masses; seemingly contrived to dazzle the eyes and divert the imagination of the vulgar—here a wooden lion, there a stone statue: in one place a range of things like coffee-house boxes covered a-top; in another, a parcel of ale-house benches; in a third, a puppet-show representation of a tin cascade; in a fourth, a gloomy cave of a circular form, like a sepulchral vault half lighted; in a fifth, a scanty slip of grass-plat, that would not afford pasture sufficient for an ass's colt. The walks, which nature might have intended for solitude, shade, and silence, are filled with crowds of noisy people, sucking up the nocturnal rheums of an aguish climate; and through these gay scenes a few lamps glimmer like so many farthing candles."

[37] There are some reasons to believe (judging by Mozart's letters) that he wrote four bassoon concerti (as he did for the French horn). Wouldn't those scores be a great discovery for a musicologist of the future?

it was not capable of satisfactory performance. Then, as we move into the nineteenth-century, the bassoon almost disappears as a solo instrument, a retreat into obscurity which coincides strangely with the rise of the new version of the instrument.

~~~

While still at school, and still under Cecil's benevolent eye, I had played in the pit orchestra for a groundbreaking annual series of Handel opera productions at the tiny Abbey Theatre in Abingdon. This minimalist band was an eclectic mixture of locals, such as myself, who were either still at school or at music college, and a smattering of slightly older players who had finished university or conservatoire and were just embarking on their professional careers as players. This was my first encounter, for example, with Nicholas Kraemer who was directing from the harpsichord, and Colin Kitching who fixed the band and whose father had made new translations of the libretti. I was quite star-struck of course, and it was amongst this group that I first heard about the move which some were making into period instrument performance of repertoire such as this Handel opera. It was also where I first heard about some of the big characters who were starting to make names for themselves, and who were to play important roles in my future professional life, such as Christopher Hogwood, the singer Roger Norrington and the oddly named John Eliot Gardiner[38] to name but three. Jiggy, as Gardiner was known, was at this time attracting some ridicule: he had recently married and had evidently insisted on conducting the choir at his own wedding, causing liturgical confusion as well as confirming the early onset of the hubris with which all conductors seem, to a greater or lesser degree, to be afflicted.

Over the next few years, as I moved on through the Royal College of Music and into my first (indeed only) contracted orchestral job in Bournemouth, I tried to follow as best I could this parallel musical universe. The real pioneering work was happening not in the UK but in Austria and The Netherlands, led, as already

---

[38] Gardiner was initially hostile to period instruments. I had the dubious privilege of playing in what I think was his very first period instrument performance (Henry Purcell's Ode for St Cecilia's Day at the Innsbruck Festival). It was widely believed amongst the choir and orchestra that Gardiner had accepted this engagement without realising that Innsbruck was a 'period instrument' festival. In other words, it was a mistake.

mentioned, by the remarkable Nikolaus Harnoncourt in Vienna and Gustav Leonhardt and Frans Brüggen in Amsterdam. Tied as I was to the daily routine of regional orchestral life, I was envious of the apparent ease with which some contemporaries who had not rushed headlong, as I had, into full-time employment, seized the opportunity to visit these precocious musical centres to sit at the feet of the leading lights in this exciting new world. So my resignation from the Bournemouth orchestra after a mere two-year stint may have seemed at the time somewhat impulsive, but in truth the need to escape from the orchestral treadmill had become insistent. I needed to find some time and space to explore and experiment.

And a final push, had one been needed, came from that ebullient genius, David Munrow. Along with many of my contemporaries I had been inspired by the brilliance with which Munrow had enlivened the music of the medieval period with his unique combination of exotic noises, clever programming, intellectual curiosity, irresistible enthusiasm and presentational skills. And as if this were not enough, Munrow had made a second career as the 'voice' of early music in his extraordinarily eclectic radio programme, 'The Young Idea'. Shortly after I had moved back to London, he called me, quite out of the blue, to enquire about my progress and my plans. He had heard that I was starting my exploratory journey and he wanted to encourage me, he said, by telling me about his next project (he had just finished a monumental TV series, a related book and a world tour covering the history of medieval music), to advance into the eighteenth-century with the launch of a baroque-instrument orchestra. Munrow was so full of enthusiasm for his plans that it was extraordinarily shocking to hear, only two weeks later, that he had committed suicide. Munrow's baroque orchestra is one of the tantalising might-have-beens of this experimental period and, although it never happened, it certainly did encourage me to redouble my efforts with my own poor fumblings. History will record, of course, that it was Christopher Hogwood who took forward the orchestra that Munrow had planned (Munrow had asked Hogwood to be his keyboard player in the venture) which became the Academy of Ancient Music.[39] And, even before Hogwood's Academy saw the light of day, Trevor Pinnock had, in 1973, launched, with a

---

[39] AAM, whose mission was to perform eighteenth-century music on period instruments, was named after a group established by the energetic organist and author, Dr Charles Burney. By a nice symmetry his orchestra was founded to revive interest in earlier music by giving it up-to-date performances on modern instruments.

minimum of fanfare, The English Concert, the orchestra (as it eventually became) of which I was to become manager more than twenty years later.

There was a sense of adventure in the air but, even so, knowing how to set sail in these largely uncharted waters was surprisingly hard. So far as I could learn there was one man in the country at that time who could make a copy of an eighteenth-century bassoon, so I placed my order with the notoriously slow and, in terms of time, unreliable Hans-Jörg Lange. But I was warned that this instrument, if it arrived at all, would take years, so I bought, in the interim, an old English-made bassoon from an antique shop in Hampstead. These English instruments, as I was soon to discover, were much more limited in range and in every respect less sophisticated than their French counterparts but, with much trial and extensive error, I was able to make a start on a primitive instrument probably made for a church, or perhaps military, band by one William Milhouse.

The Lange bassoon never did get made, but before long I had acquired two French instruments, of which my favourite was an original 1820 French bassoon by Jean Savary[40] which I bought because I had most rashly (the absurd confidence of youth appals me now) promised the clarinettist Alan Hacker that I would play the Schubert octet with his period instrument group, The Music Party, while knowing that it would be impossible on any instrument I then owned. This Savary became, over the next 15 years, my more or less constant friend, and I loved it partly because I could speculate about its history and, in particular, its previous owners. The maker, Jean Savary, whose father was also an instrument-maker (and also called Jean), was himself the principal bassoonist at the Opéra Comique in Paris until c. 1828, whereupon he took over his father's oboe and bassoon-making business and continued making bassoons into the second half of the nineteenth-century. I like to think that he made my 1820 bassoon for himself to play in the opera because it pre-dates his next surviving instrument by almost five years (it has a confidently clear stamp on the bottom joint which declares that it is made by 'Savary jeune', à Paris, 1820). His later instruments were very highly prized, a fact confirmed when I showed my early example to my old teacher, Cecil James. Cecil's father, Fred, had been the very first principal bassoonist of the newly formed London Symphony Orchestra in the 1890s and, at that time, he was still playing a Savary. Cecil told me that this was always his father's favourite bassoon, and he only abandoned it when the

---

[40] Jean Nicolas Savary (1786 – 1853), the most influential maker of his day, described by his contemporaries as the Stradivari of the bassoon.

decision was taken in 1896 to raise the pitch at which the orchestra played, a decision which forced the wind players to buy newer more modern instruments.

My speculations about previous owners of my Savary bassoon led me along some curious investigative byways. There was a fine tradition of eccentricity amongst nineteenth-century bassoonists, amongst whose number (and here's a little known fact) was Charles Darwin's son. This lad, with his bassoon, features in Darwin's sadly neglected study of the habits (to borrow Darwin's own terminology) of earthworms with the catchy title (I am not making this up) of 'The Formation of Vegetable Mould Through the Action of Worms with Observations of their Habits'. I've no idea how Darwin carried out his research but he claims to have counted the number of worms in his garden, arriving at the improbably precise figure of 53,767 per acre. Having counted them he then piled them all onto his billiard table and pressed his son into service to play the bassoon to them. Here is the relevant passage, in case the reader should be unfamiliar with the original text:

"Worms do not possess a sense of hearing. They took not the least notice of the shrill notes from a metal whistle, which was repeatedly sounded near them; nor did they of the deepest and loudest tones of the bassoon. They were indifferent to shouts, if care was taken that the breath did not strike them. When placed on a table close to the keys of a piano, which was played as loudly as possible, they remained perfectly quiet. Although they are indifferent to undulations in the air audible by us, they are extremely sensitive to vibrations in any solid object. When the pots containing two worms, which had remained quite indifferent to the sound of the piano, were placed on this instrument, and the note C in the bass was struck, both instantly retreated into their burrows. After a time they emerged, and when G above the line in the treble clef was struck they again retreated..." Darwin continues in this vein for some time, but I think this passage gives the gist. Later, the bassoon was once again pressed into the service of science, this time to demonstrate that plants are deaf (at least deaf to seduction by low-pitched music).

There we shall leave our lugubrious Victorians to their earnest scientific enquiries, returning to my lovely Savary: one issue on which Darwinian experiments could cast no reliable light was to establish what pitch it was designed to play at. This is not quite as obvious as it might seem, for in common with almost all these antique instruments the original crook, or bocal (that is to say the curved metal piece connecting the body of the instrument to the reed) was missing. The length of this piece, plus the length and width of the reed itself (the most perishable of all the bassoonists' accessories), is a significant determinant of the pitch at which the instrument will play. My experiments suggested that this Savary was most comfortable and settled at a pitch slightly above the modern pitch of a=440'. To explain the importance of this will, I fear, require a detour into a discussion of eighteenth and nineteenth Century pitch; murky waters indeed.

Musicians talk about pitch levels by means of two co-ordinates, a pitch name and a frequency in Hertz, for example a=440'. In this example the 'a' is the a in the middle of the treble stave sounding a sixth above a piano's middle C while the second co-ordinate, Hertz, is a measurement of frequency—cycles per second—that measures the travelling wave or oscillation of pressure caused by vibrations that we hear as sound.

You might think that the pitch at which any particular piece of music is played does not very much matter so long as everyone agrees on what that pitch is, and from the average listener's point of view this is probably true. String players can re-tune within reason to changes of pitch, but for players of fixed pitch instruments such as the woodwind and brass it is not so easy, so the agreed modern standard pitch, which has 'a' at 440', is primarily a convenience for musicians in a world in which you might one day play in Reykjavík and the next in Riyadh.

In order to discover the pitch at which eighteenth-century musicians might have played researchers have focused on the biggest fixed-pitch instruments, organs, of which most of the surviving examples are of course in churches. The physical measurement of the pipes enables an accurate calculation of the pitch, and the conclusions can be checked against other surviving circumstantial evidence, such as correspondence between organ builders and church authorities, and in some cases, composers.

The story that emerges shows that there was no universally recognised pitch standard prior to the mid-nineteenth-century. Not only so, there has always been a tendency for pitch to rise above whatever the starting point might be. There are many reasons, but briefly, the physical fact is that a wind instrument will rise a little in pitch as it gets warmer, so during the course of a musical performance pitch may rise slightly even within that performance. Also, it seems to be a truth that a slightly sharp pitch has a greater brilliance and is more agreeable to the ear than something a little 'below the note.'[41] One additional contributing factor is that church organs were cheaper to build if they were set at a high pitch rather than a low one; the reason being that the lower the pitch the larger the big pipes for the bass notes needed to be, so that a saving both in the space these occupied in the building and in the cost of materials required for their construction was sometimes a significant factor.

By the time of J. S. Bach (the first half of the eighteenth century) several distinctly different pitches were in common use and, for convenience (and because the Hertz frequency measurements were not yet fully understood) these were, and still are, usually discussed in terms of semi-tone differences. Broadly speaking, there were four distinct pitches in more or less common use, each being very roughly a semitone (half tone) different from the others. This meant that in eighteenth-century Europe one might travel from one country to another, or sometimes from one region to another within a country (from a low-pitch Rome to high-pitch Venice, for example), and find music being played at pitches which might differ by as much as a minor third (i.e. four semitones). Pitch levels as high a=465' (in late seventeenth-century Venice) and as low as a=392' (eighteenth-century France) are known to have been in use, a difference of more than a minor third.

Bach would have been familiar with the pitch discrepancies between the organs in the various cities in which he worked. And he arrived at different solutions at different times in his life. The problem so far as modern-day performances are concerned can be illustrated by reference to the oboe writing in his Cantatas (which were of course church pieces so would normally use the organ in that church). The highest-pitch German organs were built in the late seventeenth- and early eighteenth-centuries at a pitch known as 'cornetton', favoured for reasons of economy, as already mentioned. Early in the eighteenth-century there began to be some interest in standardising pitch because musicians were beginning to travel much more widely between cities and countries, and there is also evidence that singers were straining to reach their top notes at the highest pitch. Consequently, pitch was lowered by a semitone, and was called 'Chorton' (choir pitch). This was again lowered and called 'Kammerton', and it was this pitch, approximately equivalent to a=415' (a semitone below modern standard pitch) which was adopted by most woodwind instrument makers. Make

---

[41] One always describes orchestras as 'tuning up'; they never seem to tune down.

an oboe much sharper than this and it will play with a more strident, shawm-like, sound quality.

The upshot, to cut a long story short, was that in Bach's time you might have fixed-pitch instruments within any particular ensemble which were built at different pitches, so, provided the differences were in semitone increments, the solution was for some instruments to transpose, i.e. to play the music in a key a semitone or whole tone higher or lower than written in the score in order to sound at the same pitch. To put it another way, if you have an orchestra playing in D major, an organ pitched half a tone higher would need to play in D flat, half a tone lower, in order to sound the same. And, to return to our oboist in a Bach cantata, this matters a lot because his baroque instrument did not play very successfully in what are called the remote keys, such as D flat minor or F sharp major. Thus in Bach's time it would make most sense for the organist to be the person doing the transposing (their keyboards being, after all, fully chromatic), so that the oboes could play in the simpler keys.

However, when the nineteenth-century revival of interest in Bach's music was sufficiently established for there to be new printed editions of his Cantatas, the editors were not very aware of these issues of pitch and naturally enough transposed the discrepant orchestral parts back to the apparently correct 'home' key, which they usually took to be the key in which the organ part was notated; but this led to a new set of anomalies because the unfortunate result was that the revised oboe parts sometimes now went below the bottom note of the instrument. This editorial decision has led to confusions which persist to this day. To give just one example, Bach's Cantata no. 185 had the oboe part notated a minor third higher than the score (which was set according to organ pitch, or cornetton), so when the 'Bach Gesellschaft' edition transposed everything to 'Chorton' this took the organ (and singers, of course) up a semitone but took the oboe down a whole tone, leaving it with a low B flat, a whole tone below its range. It also gave the oboe a number of C sharps, of which the eighteenth-century oboe knew nothing, which might not matter very much for a modern fully chromatic oboe, but is of course critical when it comes to the use of eighteenth-century instruments which are not.

The pioneers of period instrument performance soon settled on a=415' as the new 'standard' baroque pitch. There was good reason for this: it was after all demonstrably one of the pitches used in the eighteenth-century, and it was very conveniently exactly a semitone below the modern standard a=440[42]. One factor, especially in the early days of the period instrument revival, was that the adoption of a=415' enabled the use of harpsichords which were then being made with keyboards that could slide over one string so that the 'a' key played a string tuned to a=440' in one position and a=415' in its alternative position.

If the choice of a=415' was partly pragmatic and partly based on evidence, the same cannot be said for the choice of the slightly higher pitch, a=430', which is now more or less standard for playing the classical repertoire as opposed to the baroque, that is to say late eighteenth-century and early nineteenth-century music. I am not aware of any historical evidence for this pitch, which sits uncomfortably a quarter-tone above the universally adopted baroque pitch, thereby breaking the rule that pitch variations should be made by semitone increments. So how did this strange pitch come to be chosen?

I was present at the meeting which chose it: the Academy of Ancient Music was about to embark on a massive Decca 'box set' project to record all forty-one of Mozart's symphonies. This was a hugely ambitious plan, and frankly quite scary for some of those involved (including myself) because we had really no idea, as we launched into the youthful (and fairly simple) early symphonies how, and with what equipment, we were going to handle the much more complicated later ones, such as the Jupiter Symphony (no. 41) or the Prague (no. 38). The wind instruments, in particular, were developing constantly in the last years of the eighteenth-century, so the oboes and bassoons on which one might play music written in the 1760s and 70s (i.e. the early Mozart symphonies) would not have the range and keywork to manage music from the next decades. Also, as we have already noted, pitch was gradually rising over these years and the 'new' instruments of the early classical period played at a higher pitch than those used in the earlier period. When it came to the Mozart recording project, the Decca people were adamant that commercial reality dictated that the entire symphony

---

[42] This difference in pitch is still not universally known: Trevor Pinnock tells a touching story of being introduced in Canada to a young jazz keyboard player who had become fascinated by the famous harpsichord cadenza in Bach's 5th Brandenburg Concerto. She was unable to read music so that, amazingly, she had learned this extremely demanding 'riff' entirely by ear from his Deutsche Gramophon recording. Even more remarkable, though, was that, unaware that baroque pitch was a semitone below what she was used to, she had learned to play it in D flat, a much tougher feat than its original key of D major.

cycle must be recorded at the same pitch. That they were never seriously challenged on exactly why they thought this shows where the power lay in the musician/record company relationship, but the assumption was, I suppose, that a box set containing the whole symphony cycle should be consistent (but what is the likelihood of someone sitting down and listening to all the symphonies in sequence, and, even in the unlikely event that they did, would it matter that the pitch changed slightly at some point in the 'box'?). Be that as it may, the Decca insistence caused a problem: this was a ten-year recording project, and, for reasons just described, at its start it should have been clear to record at the pitch which was in common use at the time, i.e. a=415', one semitone below modern standard pitch, but none of the later instruments, required for the later symphonies, played at the lower pitch, so it appeared that a higher pitch would be required from the start. A meeting was held to settle the matter, or at least try to, but it ended in deadlock, with the oboists conceding that only a small rise from baroque pitch (as far as, but no further than, a=421') could be considered and the brass players (and clarinettists, who were not involved in the early works) refusing to contemplate anything lower than a=435'. To break the deadlock some bright Decca spark proposed to split the difference, and a compromise of a=430' was eventually agreed. The irony was that this is a pitch which no one had advocated (and, incidentally, a pitch at which I never found a bassoon of this period to be comfortable). Bizarrely, this is the pitch which has now become the standard all over the world for period instrument orchestras playing music from the classical period. So much for authenticity and for musicological integrity.

~~~

These years, the early 1980s, were something of a golden age for London's freelance musicians. The old-style LP was being quickly superseded by the new CD format and, with breath-taking optimism, the recording moguls were racing to re-record everything. The Academy of St Martin in the Fields and the English Chamber Orchestra were early leaders in the race but the new period instrument orchestras, with projects such as the Mozart symphonies recording, were not far behind. The demand of the record industry for new product to satisfy the burgeoning CD market was apparently insatiable.

There was also a parallel recording world provided by the film industry. When it came to recording the sound-tracks for their movies the major film-makers had been largely driven out of the US by the greed of the US musicians' union,[43] and many of big Hollywood blockbusters had their music recorded in London (for example, the Star Wars soundtrack by the London Symphony Orchestra). Playing for 'film sessions' was a valuable source of additional income for London's orchestral players.

The third ingredient in this comparative boom decade was that the 1980s was also a time of rapid expansion in affordable air travel. This made orchestral touring a more manageable and, at least from the players' position, profitable occupation. All in all, it was a period when a busy freelance musician could make a reasonable living.

No one leading this kind of freelance life should complain about being too busy, and I don't think I often did, but even at the age of thirty it was clear that this was a young person's profession. Look at an orchestra next time you see one and count the number of its members over the age of, say, forty-five. As my 30th birthday approached, I was already beginning to puzzle about what happens to musicians when they grow old (or when they grow up), and to ask myself what I would be doing when I reached my 50s and 60s. Sadly, the only answer I could come up with was, "The same as now, but only if you are very lucky." For this reason, while not exactly discontented with things as they were, I was nevertheless restless. I knew that I did not want to be leading this same life forever, so I was keen to take on any new assignment even if I had no clear idea of where it might lead.

∼∼∼

One of my first glimpses of a life outside my immediate experience came with an unexpected appointment, for reasons never fathomed nor explained, to the Music Advisory Panel of the Arts Council. This group of selected volunteers, supposedly a representative cross-section of the professional music world, was charged with the difficult task of making recommendations to the main Arts Council board on how the Council should allocate its music budget. The Council

---

[43] London's musicians proved not much less grasping than their LA colleagues and it was not long before they too had priced themselves out of this market. The newly accessible East European cities, many of which had excellent orchestral traditions, were soon becoming irresistibly (to the Hollywood mogul) competitive. Many major movies of the 1990s had their music recorded in Budapest, Prague or Warsaw.

was responsible for policy and the Panel was supposed to advise on implementation. The Panel's membership actually comprised a rather quirky cross-section of professional music. There were no discernible criteria for selection (curious this, given the time and effort the Council spent imposing just this kind of 'transparency' on its client organisations) and incredibly I was, so far as I could discover, the very first 'real' working musician ever permitted to join these august discussions. Consequently, much as I was puzzled as to how I came to be a part of this unfamiliar world, so I was also treated by other panel members and council officers with a mixture of curiosity and fear; to have a person who actually played the notes sitting at the advisory table was regarded by some as a dangerous experiment, a kind of 'worker' representation. My co-panelists comprised composers, journalists, educationalists, academics and a number of representatives of assorted minorities (both ethnic minorities and non-traditional music minorities such as jazz and world music, but so far as I can recall, and this would be quite impossible nowadays, no women). This was a period in which regional devolution was on the broad political agenda, so the advisory panel had more than its fair share of regional arts bureaucrats who invariably and relentlessly ground their regional axes to the great detriment of any sensible discussion of issues. Axe grinding was a problem, too, with the 'single-issue' advisers although, to be fair to them, their *raison d'être* on the panel was entirely to represent their particular axe and grind it. Amazingly, there was no equivalent voice on the Panel to speak for the London-based or any other symphony orchestras, nor for opera as an art form, nor for the chamber orchestras, nor for chamber music and certainly not for period instrument performance, of which the majority of the Arts Council Music Panel had, I suspect, not yet heard. And as for singers, I could imagine an argument amongst these panellists, whether they 'counted' as musicians at all. By some bizarre quirk, I seemed to have become a most unlikely, and very singular, spokesman for an enormous chunk of, in fact almost the entirety of, the classical music profession.

This seemed ludicrous at the time, and with hindsight even more so, and the lack of well-informed advice in some of the key areas of the Council's responsibility caused it a catalogue of high-profile problems which could have easily been avoided. A prime example had arisen just before I joined the Panel and concerned the future funding of London's numerous symphony orchestras (a perennial Arts Council puzzle). The issue is easily described: London has five full-time symphony orchestras (the London Symphony Orchestra, London Philharmonic, Royal Philharmonic, Philharmonia and the BBC Symphony Orchestra) plus the opera orchestras of English National Opera and the Royal Opera, as well as other salaried BBC orchestras such as the BBC Concert Orchestra. Of the five main symphony orchestras, three had no home base, a fourth, the BBC orchestra, had only a rehearsal and recording home, not a concert venue, so the London Symphony Orchestra was unique in having a 'home' at the Barbican Centre (and even this had been a relatively recent development). Obviously, if starting again with a blank slate, no one would design such a state of affairs. Most great cities focus their music on one orchestra in one purpose-built hall; for example the New York Philharmonic, the Leipzig Gewandhaus, the Berlin Philharmonic, the Orchestre de Paris, the Boston Symphony, Philadelphia, Los Angeles, and so on. Vienna is an exception with two major halls and two orchestras, the Vienna Philharmonic in the Musikverein and the Vienna Symphony in the Konzerthaus. London has no great concert halls (neither architecturally, unless you count the extraordinary Royal Albert Hall, nor acoustically distinguished) and at least one, possibly two, too many major orchestras. There had recently been an Arts Council report,[44] greeted with ridicule within the profession, which proposed moving the Royal Philharmonic Orchestra (RPO) to Nottingham, a 'solution' on which neither the RPO nor the City of Nottingham appeared to have been asked to express a view. This was a knotty problem indeed, which made it especially ridiculous to ask our part-time committee, comprising a mixture of well-intentioned amateurs and ruthlessly single-minded lobbyists, many of whom were essentially hostile to Western art music, and most also politically fiercely anti-London, to reach any defensible, or even reasoned, recommendations.

Another problem for the Panel was the extent to which it was steered (or you might say manipulated) by the full-time executives who, naturally enough, had their own agenda and opinions. In true 'Yes Minister' fashion, these civil servants were committed to ensuring that their own, or departmental, views would prevail, and their preferred method was to ensure that their views would ultimately emerge as 'advice' from the advisory panel. However, if for some reason the Music Panel was uncooperative its advice could be ignored or overruled.

---

[44] Issued under the rather poetic title 'The Glory of the Garden'. In reality, this was a garden in which substantial hard pruning was recommended.

A prime example of the weakness of the advisory system arose when we came to consider a hot issue of the moment (and a hot potato still), the disproportionate size of the annual grant to the Royal Opera House, Covent Garden. The ROH was then, as it often seems to be, in the middle of a sequence of hugely expensive and controversial productions and amongst certain members of the Panel, a hatred of the 'elitist' ROH ran deep; the size of the ROH grant was a rare issue which united the special-interest axe-grinders (who hated opera on principle), the regional representatives (who hated London), and a few, such as myself, who wanted value judgements about artistic standards to be given greater weight when assessing grants. But opera also had its supporters on the Panel, too, so the debate over the size of its subsidies was both lively and lengthy, but, unusually, fair and honest. Eventually we made a rare show of resistance to the guidance we were being given by our oleaginous executive. Our long-debated conclusion was that we would continue to disagree on the 'politics' of whether the scale of grants to opera was right or wrong or disproportionate, but that consistently poor artistic quality over several years should at last be reflected in an actual cut in the grant (the executive was proposing an increase) and we duly recommended accordingly. The very next morning there was a hurriedly assembled press conference at which the Arts Council chairman, with the then chief executive of the ROH, Jeremy Isaacs, sitting alongside him, announced an increased grant. The ROH undoubtedly had (and no doubt still has) influential friends in the corridors of power, who had moved with impressive speed to dismiss our pinprick attempt to deflate the royal operatic balloon. It was extraordinarily frustrating for those Panel members who had bravely pushed back against official advice to see not only that our advice would not be followed, but also how seamlessly we had been outmanoeuvred; the speedy announcement of the new (higher) grant ensured that the full Council would never get to consider its own advisers' recommendations.

The advisers were, in truth, being asked to do an impossible job, and in an atmosphere of unremitting negativity: usually we were told that the overall music budget had to be cut (or increased below inflation), so the panel's discussions were most often about how to slice an already small pie more thinly. I can remember only two occasions when there was an above inflation increase in the music budget, and both times this came to us with an instruction, already agreed by our ultimate masters, the Council, to extend funding to new areas of music.

Thus, even in the good years we were forced into slicing pie more thinly in order to find space for new areas of grant support.

One of our tasks as individual members of the committee, was to report on the performance of Arts Council clients in our particular field. Thus, for example, I was dispatched to Liverpool to attend, incognito, a Liverpool Philharmonic concert and submit a written report. I found this a surprisingly demanding exercise: because all the symphony orchestras, both London-based and regionally based, were without friends on the committee I was most reluctant to write anything other than a positive account of what was, to be honest, a rather below-average concert. Thus, even when operating, for once, within my area of expertise I did exactly what I criticised my co-panellists of doing, that is to say putting my actual opinions to one side in order to defend my specialist corner. For if I was lukewarm about the Liverpool Phil it was quite possible to imagine some of its already limited grant being diverted to spend on jazz or brass bands or indeed anything deemed at that moment to have greater 'relevance'.

I am inclined, now, to forgive the single-issue corner-fighters on our committee. After all, if you are, say, a brass bandsman[45] and find yourself on an advisory board, surely you must fight for the very thing which caused you to be appointed in the first place. I am much less forgiving of the narrow-minded *apparatchik* representatives from the regions (Regional Arts Boards I think they were called at that time). The problem with these people was that they were relatively numerous (the Council had to have all the regions represented, or none), so were able to gang up to become a strong anti-London lobby. Whatever differences they might have had amongst themselves were overwhelmingly trumped by their shared and passionately held belief that London sucked in a disproportionate share of total available funding. Of course most of the national companies are based in London, as are the great majority of organisations which take their work on tour, so of course London attracts more subsidy than other UK cities. But there was enough truth in the charge of a London-centric funding bias to ensure that those panellists who lived and worked in London were generally on the defensive, arguing rather awkwardly to preserve a less-than-perfect status quo. So how had these regional representatives become so dominant?

---

[45] Thomas Beecham, eminent conductor and purveyor of one-liners, was once asked if he liked brass bands. "They have their place, which is out of doors and at least a mile distant."

When the Arts Council was established, in 1946, it was answerable to the Treasury but given the freedom to award its grants according to its own judgement; this was the much-vaunted 'arm's' length' principle, and was a very British, and honourable, achievement. However in the late 1970s responsibility for the Council was transferred from the Treasury to the Department of Education and Science (as it then was) which took a very different approach. Until this point it might have been credible to argue that the role of the Arts Council was as an advocate for public subsidy of the arts, but as soon as the DES took over, the famous arm's length was greatly shortened—indeed the arm would now firmly control that which it held. Political interference in the arts became normal and arts spending would become just another lever for implementing government social policies. I do not suppose that the Treasury ever had a policy for the Arts, but, henceforth, grants were to be distributed with conditions, and clients (as we learned to call them) became subject to evaluation according to the criteria flowing from the Policy. Everything had to be measured, and, inexorably, politics began to assert its supremacy.

And there was worse: the constant search for measurement of the extent to which any particular art form, or company or institution, contributed to arts policy goals became a smokescreen concealing an alarming loss of nerve about making value judgements. Almost any subjective judgement was to be avoided if possible, and one of the many avoidance devices was to concede a greater role to the regions, which should now be allowed to make decisions for themselves. The rise of the regions against a London-centred system of decision-making was very much a part of the wider political *zeitgeist*, and was itself a government policy. It was replicated in many other contexts, but in the world of the Arts Council, it was justified using the entirely specious argument that arts policies would thereby be rendered more 'democratic'.

This must also have been the time that that dread word 'accessibility' became one of the policy conditions. Insistence on accessibility is also something of a smokescreen: the real fear amongst our pusillanimous bureaucrats was that they might be accused of elitism. The charge of elitism is so terrifying to the arts bureaucrat because it introduces into the debate such frightening (although interesting) issues as the distinction between high art and culture, subjective judgements about quality and, of course, whether art <u>should</u> have social purposes. Accessibility became a kind of code word for populism or dumbing down: after all, access, unless it is literally about ramps for wheelchairs and lifts rather than stairs, is already available for almost all art forms: museums are mostly free, concerts are public, libraries are full of freely lendable books, the internet is freely available to all. So strictures about 'accessibility' are really just another means of policy-based interference in artistic content.

It was disturbing to feel the enthusiasm with which the supposedly 'arm's-length' agencies embraced the new thinking. For example, the Council would regularly issue more or less strangulating reports, with names such as 'Cultural Diversity Action Plan', with stated aims such as, "Ensuring the arts recreate the sense of community, identity and civic pride which should define our nation." The problem with this kind of political rhetoric is that it is insidious: most people would hope to live in a society which is tolerant and reasonably egalitarian, certainly in the sense of equality of opportunity. The trouble is that the arts are not a very effective policy instrument for achieving these social goals; but, and this is where it was so difficult on the Advisory Panel, to argue this exposed one to accusations of being negative and defeatist, and even worse, old-fashioned and, sin of sins, elitist.

There was also a paradox that, amidst all the admonitions to promote 'accessibility' there were some pressures pulling the bureaucrat in the opposite direction, away from the 'popular': the Arts Council exists to subsidise those artists, musicians and writers whose work is important. But how are our arts' bureaucrats to decide that something *is* important? This is a nice puzzle; one criterion for judging the importance of a work is that it is original, and history suggests that if a work is original the public will probably not much like it. Indeed, if the public *did* like it, it probably would not need subsidy at all. By this convoluted reasoning, official patronage can favour work which is arcane or meaningless over that which has real appeal, the very opposite of the 'democratisation' which our poor confused administrators claim to be aiming for.

The dire consequences of the rise and rise of the cultural bureaucrat were many: one example from my brief time as an adviser was the announcement that henceforth each Regional Arts Board would be required to spend a defined proportion of its devolved budget on ethnic minority music and a fixed percentage (it might have been 3%) on commissioning new works. It was well-intentioned (I think) but while some regions (London and the West Midlands, for instance) easily met their quotas, there were others which struggled: the West Country, at least at that time, had a tiny ethnic minority population, so their South

West Arts Board was inevitably scraping a barrel to find suitable projects to hit their targets. There was evidence, too, that some composers were researching the geographic distribution of their colleagues and moving to parts of the country where composers were thin on the ground, in order to improve their chances of commissioned work. This may have been enterprising and ingenious but it was hard to feel that it would result in better quality work.

Thirty years on and it is still all too easy to find examples of the collective timidity which characterised the 1980s. Almost every arts organisation nowadays will have its more or less ghastly mission statement which will be couched in a peculiarly vacuous language. My bet is that this generic mission statement will still make reference to 'accessibility', and probably also to 'social inclusion', 'diversity' and 'community', and will very likely also plan 'to put people first' and possibly even 'empower learning in the creative society'. The meaninglessness of these phrases was nicely captured in a spoof funding application which was circulating some years ago amongst dissident 'elitists' in those years of cultural oppression. It was entitled, 'I ate Prunella Clough'[46] and went something along these lines:

'Project Aim:

'To increase access to the arts by feeding artists to the masses. By eating the body parts of artists the public will develop a better understanding of contemporary art…the process is one of assimilation whereby artistic sensibility will be consumed by members of the public, especially those with limited knowledge of art or opportunity for participation. The benefit of this approach lies in the fact that no mental effort is required to attempt to understand art. In other words, a direct hands-on approach with quantifiable outcomes.

'Project Delivery:

'Artists approaching the end of their lives naturally wish to give something back to the community. They are invited to donate their body parts to our organisation whose remit is to advance public understanding. Criteria for selection of artists for the project will be based on their ability to transmit artistic ideas organically and with good taste. Body density and ease of digestion are the

---

[46] Prunella Clough (1919 – 99), an artist known for a multi-layered painting technique in which she would use a variety of tools and materials to apply paint (which itself was sometimes mixed with sand) to her canvas, including sandpaper, wire wool, rollers, wallpaper scrapers and pieces of wire mesh. She also made 'assemblages' from found objects gathered from industrial sites.

prime considerations; artistic merit may be used as a 'tie-breaker' in borderline cases. Selected artists will be given the comforts required to live out their final days and, importantly, will be well fed. Upon their death, body parts will be distributed to those most in need, with special focus on ethnic minorities living in deprived areas who have never previously expressed any interest in the arts.'

The rather desperate irony of this mock application captures something of the brutality which prevailed in what became known as the Thatcher years. To take just one other example, following that most terrible IRA outrage, the murder of the MP Ian Gow, the *Sun* newspaper was prompted to conduct a telephone poll on the restoration of the death penalty which purported to reveal that 21,928 of those questioned were in favour, and only 432 against. Simultaneously the same newspaper was expressing outrage that the jury system was 'broken'. One of their staff journalists had described his own recent experience of jury service in an unidentified drugs trial; how the jury divided into two warring groups, those who would believe *anything* the police prosecution said, and those who would believe *nothing* the police prosecution said; how, after five hours of heated and shambolic arguments which had little to do with the evidence, and much more to do with prejudice, emotion and simple stupidity, the jury failed to agree, thus necessitating an acquittal, almost certainly the wrong verdict.

The absurdity of running simultaneous campaigns, to restore the death penalty and to emasculate the jury system, was picked up by Auberon Waugh, writing in *Private Eye*. The *Sun,* he wrote, had expressed outrage on behalf of its readers at the number of unjustified acquittals, but never any fear over unjustified convictions which would, of course, have fatal consequences if their bring-back-hanging campaign were to succeed. In a spirit of fairness and everyday utilitarianism, our columnist pointed out that one lesson of history was that it is not the typical middle class reader who is most in danger of being hanged in error. "Victims are usually working class, and of below average intelligence. It would save time and trouble if we abandon the jury system altogether and randomly select 20 or so *Sun* readers to be hanged every year. This will satisfy their low taste for drastic punishment while convincing the rest of us that something useful is being done to make the world a better place."

But I digress. There was another new phrase of dubious merit in the cultural discourse of the Thatcher years which was to describe organised artistic activities as "the creative industries." Its origin was, I suppose, to be found in the view, fashionable amongst dismal economists and enthusiastically adopted by arts administrators tasked with persuading their political masters to support a regime of arts subsidy, that everything, especially those things benefiting from government subsidy, should have an economic value. The attempt to introduce a kind of pseudo-scientific measurement of the value of arts expenditure prompted a widening of the definition of 'the arts', which duly became, "the arts and creative industries", an approach which became enshrined in the very title of the responsible minister whose department would thenceforth be known as the Department for Culture, Media and Sport. The expression 'creative industries' has now become so commonplace that discussion of which so-called 'industries' are to be included is rarely heard. The measurement of their economic contribution includes, it seems, such unlikely activities as advertising, the antiques trade, computer games and fashion. Within music, grunge is measured alongside opera, while *Hello!* and Jane Austen are equals in the publishing industry. In other words, critical judgement is absent. There are, too, some notable absentees in types of activity. For example, I wonder why gardening, a defining British activity, is excluded from a 'creativity' list. Garden Centres, or 'cheque-book gardening' as the late Sir Christopher Bland was once heard to describe them, would surely contribute usefully to the bottom line of the 'cultural and creative industries', and surely the bottom line is the only purpose of this value-neutral way of looking at things.

But rather than quibble about the details, we should keep in sight our deeper objections to evaluation of artistic activity exclusively by economic results. To treat heritage and the arts as no more than saleable goods strips them of their real value. Further, this economic approach is meaningless to ordinary common-sense people, with the consequence that arts bureaucrats end up talking their own language, comprehensible only amongst themselves. The result is the imposition of an ever more flabby and unproductive political correctness on a diminishing number of recipients of grants. The pettiness of this is particularly striking when looked at alongside some of the real-world themes of our time in which asylum-seekers are abandoned, the internet drowns in pornography, religious wars rage in the Middle East and so on. And in the face of these horrors, our benighted arts administrators, continue to insist that public funds should only be used to support work which reflects the cultural mix of today's society (or some such nonsense).

The confused thinking about the so-called creative industries continued long after my brief time as an Arts Council adviser, culminating, some years later, in the shambolic mess known as the Dome. This government-created project, supposed to draw millions to gaze in wonder at the cultural miracles about to unfold in the new millennium, turned out, of course, to be empty and vulgar; in the end fit only for the worst examples of popular culture, such as, to give but one example, the Miss World contest, for which it proved an ideal venue.

With hindsight, I made no useful contribution at the Arts Council and it was a relief when my involvement in the formation of the Orchestra of the Age of Enlightenment meant that I had become a potential supplicant at the court of arts funding, a conflict of interest which gave me a welcome pretext for resignation. Frustrating as these tentative steps into a musical world outside the orchestral 'rank and file' undoubtedly were, they did provide some modest intellectual stimulation which was otherwise in short supply, and hinted, no more at this stage, that there could be careers in music capable of development alongside a linear playing career.

~~~

A second source of frustration, as my 30th birthday loomed was the absence of children. Julie had had a traumatic late-term miscarriage a few years earlier and in 1981 we decided to try to adopt a child. This entailed embarking on a rather gruelling process of winning, or at least being placed in, a hotly contested 'beauty contest' for selection as one of our local authority's list of approved adopters. In the world, as viewed through the microscope lens of the typical social worker, our lives must have seemed irregular and unreliable: we were both self-employed, which meant that work was uncertain, we both travelled a fair amount and kept strange hours even when working in London, we were unable to be sure from one year to the next what our income would be. All in all, we felt we were quite likely to fail in this invidious competition in which couples were to be judged against a template deemed 'normal', and most would be found wanting. And it was competitive: almost the first thing we were told, as one white couple in a room of about fifty hopeful candidates for selection as adopting families, most of whom were also white, was that the local authority policy was to place children in ethnically matching families and that in the previous twelve months in our London borough of Kensington and Chelsea, there had been only six babies available for adoption who were not mixed race, four white, two black. And they ran these adoption recruitment contests several times a year.

Despite this, we were, as it turned out, very lucky with the individuals who ran our local adoption and fostering team. They were led by a remarkable and rather unlikely figure, Laura Sprohl, one of whose many great characteristics was a healthy scepticism of the political correctness which was even then such a defining feature of public and political life, and especially amongst social workers (even more so than my unloved arts bureaucrats). Nevertheless, even in our enlightened borough, surviving the adoption approval process was challenging. There were six (or was it eight) more or less public meetings including all the applicant couples. Of course, attendance was compulsory—at least, non-attendance would undoubtedly have been interpreted as a fatal lack of commitment—and those who survived this preliminary process were then required to submit to a series of private interviews, both as a couple and individually. This was the point at which the process became more rigorous, while at the same time, strangely reliant on guesswork: the questions were of course carefully designed to challenge attitudes to politics, social issues, race, disability, drugs, alcohol, smoking, sex (straight and gay) and in truth more or less everything, and it was in practice impossible not to try to frame one's answers so as to meet one's interrogator's supposed expectations. For instance, the question might be, "Thinking about the child you might adopt, do you hope this will be a white baby?" Well, you have been told in the meetings that this is highly improbable, so it is easy to answer that mixed race would be OK, but there is still a calculation to be made: do you say that you hope for a white child but any race will be considered (this is probably nearest to the truth), or do you express a positive enthusiasm for creating an ethnically diverse family; but to do this might be seen as questioning the policy of finding racial 'matches' for children. And then there come the questions about disability and the inevitable follow-ups to test your limits: it might be all very well to welcome a mixed race child, but what if your new baby were also to be blind, deaf or Downs Syndrome or otherwise impaired? Once you answer the first question dishonestly it becomes harder to draw a clear line. And then, if there are no babies, would you accept an older child? And if so, how old is the oldest that you would take on? What about an older child with a traumatic history and unresolved emotional behavioural issues? What about a disabled child? And if yes, how seriously disabled? And so on. At each question, whether about how many marital arguments you had last week, or your excessive drinking habits, or whatever else you might be threatened with, you have to fashion some kind of answer which is neither completely untruthful, nor so damned honest as to eliminate you forthwith from the contest. It is a fine line to tread.

Having made it through this stage onto a short-list, would-be adopters are next subjected to a further series of interviews, this time by an independent social worker from outside their own local authority area. In our case this was even more demanding, because our man (well, he was not much more than a boy really, and certainly had no more experience as a parent than Julie and I had) came from the neighbouring borough, the Peoples' Republic of Brent (prop. Ken Livingstone) and was from a much more politicised school of social work, who would, I strongly felt, thoroughly disapprove of the kind of middle-class aspirational parents that Julie and I, despite our efforts to disguise it, were obviously destined to become. Many of his questions simply repeated the ground we had already covered but I do remember being struck more or less dumb by this one, "Now, Felix," leaning keenly forward and fixing me with a beady eye, "What is your concept of parenting?" I fell at this hurdle and, despite my determination always to remain calm and rational in the face of such provocation, confessed, rather tetchily, that I simply did not understand the question. I knew that the last thing I could afford was to be judged quick-tempered, opinionated, self-regarding, superior and, in a word, middle class, and equally clear was that I had just given the game away. Some energetic back-pedalling was required in order to minister to my interrogator's desire for the warm bath of his soft-focus aspirational abstractions, but I remember thinking I had blown it, and could only reflect, with some bitterness, that if every parent who conceived a child by conventional methods were subjected to such intense vetting before pregnancy, the human race would be an endangered species within a couple of generations. And so it was with some surprise and relief that we found ourselves eventually on the council's list of approved adopters. Of course this was not a guarantee of an actual adoption but at least we didn't have to go to any more of those dismal meetings.

Despite its rather obvious foreseeability I felt ambushed by my 30th birthday, unable to escape the knowledge that I had not achieved anything very solid as my twenties drew to a close. I had not been enthused by the glimpse I had been given, thanks to the Arts Council, of the world of music 'politics', and, as just described, Julie and I were hoping to adopt but without any certainty about whether, or when, this might happen. My real trouble, it seemed clear, was that I did not know anything other than music (and little enough of that, looking back). The famous chess champion, Lasker[47], when once asked how many moves ahead do you have to see in order to become a top player, replied "One; if you always make the strongest move you cannot be defeated." True enough, even if rather obviously avoiding the real question of how to identify the strongest move. I was in the awkward position of doubting if I would recognise my 'strongest move' if it jumped up and biffed me on the nose, but I nevertheless needed to do something, so, *pace* Lasker, perhaps it did not matter too much what that something was. Reasoning thus (if it can properly be described as reasoning) I enrolled in a correspondence law course (it seems an extraordinarily strange thing to do, looking back on it) with an outfit based in Oxford which taught a four-year course in law for external candidates for a University of London degree.

Although finding the time for textbooks and re-discovering the discipline of regular essay writing was challenging, I enjoyed my return to the admittedly very shallow waters of academia. The academic level of this course was scarcely demanding: the first two years concentrated on four broad legal areas, with an examination in each at the end of Year 2 that had to be passed if you were to progress to the next stage. The four subjects were Constitutional Law, English Legal History, Contract and Crime, and I found that the first two demanded little more than a broad knowledge of English History (which I was pleased to re-visit), a working familiarity with current affairs and a basic training in essay writing. It seemed that my brief education at Winchester was coming into its own.

If Constitution and English Legal History required little more than a re-visiting of my Wykehamical education, the Law of Contract and Crime required some new learning, a little of which was theoretical but mostly consisting of cases. Many of these were no more than dull exemplars of important points of law, but, just as one might be nodding off to yet another learned judicial exposition of legal principle, one would come fizzing back to life with a case so bizarre that all such tedium was at once forgotten. Crime, especially, could be tremendous fun.

---

[47] Emmanuel Lasker (1868 – 1941) World Chess Champion for an amazing 27 years from 1894 to 1921.

All of life was here, of course, from the villainous to the tragic but also the 'best' cases could provide wonderfully vivid vignettes of the absurdity of people and events. It is impossible to capture much of this in just a few examples but I can perhaps give a flavour of the fascination, and the ludicrousness, of what are ultimately matters which the courts have to take seriously.

The very first thing that a new student learns about the criminal law is that an offence can only be committed when there exist, combined in one event, an *actus reus* (the action itself[48]) and at the same time *mens rea* (the intention to do it). One nicety about this definition is that the act and the intention need to exist simultaneously, a point neatly illustrated in R v Murphy, the circumstances of which probably gave pleasure to everyone except the unfortunate policeman at the centre of the drama who was attempting, at least initially, no more than to administer a caution for a minor traffic violation. The facts of the case were not in dispute: a constable on foot patrol had indicated to our ignoble defendant, Murphy, to pull in to the roadside to be questioned about a defective light on his vehicle. Murphy drew to a halt on, or close to, a pedestrian crossing, so our constable invited him to move his car back some yards. Complying, Murphy put the car into reverse and it duly came to rest not only a safer distance from the crossing but also on the officer's right foot. Our constable, thus pinned to the tarmac, now urged Murphy to move his car again which, after some pause for reflection, Murphy refused to do. So, after some further negotiations it came to pass that Murphy was charged with assaulting a police officer in the pursuance of his duty, and was acquitted at first instance on the grounds of impossibility. No assault had occurred because, at the moment the car mounted the constabular foot (the *actus* of the alleged offence) there was no intention to commit the offence. The *mens rea* developed only after the event, thus failing the simultaneity test.

And the pleasure to be had from reading such cases was not always confined to the oddity of the facts themselves; sometimes the judges, no doubt aware that their words on a particular point of law will be disseminated, can find an elegance of expression more memorable than the rather sordid facts of the case alone would merit. Take R v Collins, a 'burglary with intent to rape' case the outcome of which also turned, at least in part, on a question of intention, the essential facts

---

[48] The law has difficulty when there is no *actus*: failing to do something, such as not rescuing someone from drowning, only very rarely can be prosecuted as a crime.

not being in dispute. The appeal was heard by Lord Edmund Davies[49] whose judgement in the House of Lords began as follows:

"This is about as extraordinary a case as my brethren and I have ever heard either on the Bench or while at the Bar. Stephen William George Collins was convicted on 29 October 1971 at Essex Assizes of burglary with intent to commit rape and he was sentenced to 21 months imprisonment. He is a 19-year-old youth, and he appeals against that conviction by the certificate of the trial judge. The terms in which that certificate is expressed reveal that the judge was clearly troubled about the case and the conviction.

Let me relate the facts. Were they put into a novel or portrayed on the stage, they would be regarded as so implausible as to be unworthy of serious consideration and as verging at times on farce. At about 2 o'clock in the early morning of Saturday, 24 July 1971, a young lady of 18 went to bed at her mother's home in Colchester. She had spent the evening with her boyfriend. She had taken a certain amount of drink, and it may be that this fact affords some explanation of her inability to answer satisfactorily certain crucial questions put to her. She has the habit of sleeping without wearing night apparel in a bed which is very near the lattice-type window of her room. At one stage in her evidence, she seemed to be saying that the bed was close up against the window which, in accordance with her practice, was wide open. In the photographs which we have before us, however, there appears to be a gap between the two, but the bed was clearly quite near the window. At about 3.30 to 4.00 a.m. she awoke and she then saw in the moonlight a vague form crouched in the open window. She was unable to remember, and this is important, whether the form in the window was on the outside of the window sill or on that part of the sill which was inside the room, and for reasons which will later become clear, that seemingly narrow point is of crucial importance. The young lady then realised several things: first of all that the form in the window was that of a male; secondly that he was a naked male; and thirdly that he was a naked male with an erect penis. She also saw in the moonlight that his hair was blond. She thereupon leapt to the conclusion that her boyfriend, with whom for some time she had been on terms of regular and frequent intimacy, was paying her an ardent nocturnal visit. She promptly sat up in bed, and the man descended from the sill and joined her in bed and they had full sexual intercourse. But there was something about him which made her think

---

[49] Lord Edmund Davies was the uncle of an occasional colleague at the time, the flautist Paul Edmund Davies who later became the principal flautist in the LSO.

that things were not as they usually were between her and her boyfriend. The length of his hair, his voice as they had exchanged what was described as 'love talk', and other features led her to the conclusion that somehow there was something different. So she turned on the bedside light, saw that her companion was not her boyfriend and slapped the face of the intruder, who was none other than the appellant. He said to her, "Give me a good time tonight," and got hold of her arm, but she bit him and told him to go. She then went into the bathroom and he promptly vanished.

The complainant said that she would not have agreed to intercourse if she had known that the person entering her room was not her boyfriend. But there was no suggestion of any force having been used on her, and the intercourse which took place was undoubtedly effected with no resistance on her part.

The appellant was seen by the police at about 10.30 a.m. later the same morning. According to the police, the conversation which took place elicited these points: he was very lustful the previous night. He had taken a lot of drink, and we may here note that drink (which to him is a very real problem) had brought this young man into trouble several times before, but never for an offence of this kind. He went on to say that he knew the complainant because he had worked around her house. On this occasion, desiring sexual intercourse—and according to the police evidence he had added that he was determined to have a girl, by force if necessary, although that part of the evidence he later challenged—he went on to say that he walked around the house, saw a light in an upstairs bedroom, and he knew that this was the girl's bedroom. He found a stepladder, leaned it against the wall and climbed up and looked into the bedroom. What he could see inside through the open window was a girl who was naked and asleep. So he descended the ladder and stripped off all his clothes with the exception of his socks, because apparently he took the view that if the girl's mother entered the bedroom it would be easier to effect a rapid escape if he had socks on than if he was in bare feet. That is a matter about which we are not called upon to express any view, and would in any event find ourselves unable to express one. Having undressed, he then climbed the ladder and pulled himself up on the windowsill. His version of the matter is that he was pulling himself in when she awoke. She then got up and knelt on the bed, she put her arm around his neck and body, and she seemed to pull him into the bed."

So, you might ask, what did the distinguished judges conclude? And the answer is itself a nicely narrow point, as narrow indeed as the width of a windowsill.

To explain this without over-complication requires taking a step back, to look at the nature of the charge. Collins was charged with the offence of 'burglary'. Burglary, as defined in the Theft Act 1969 Section 9, may be committed when a person enters any building or part of a building as a trespasser with the intention of committing theft, criminal damage or rape. So what it came down to was this: when the complainant invited Collins to have intercourse, was he on the outside window ledge, in which case he had not entered the building, and only did so when invited in, or was he on the inside window sill, having entered the building with intent.

Edmund Davies continued thus, "…what the appellant had said was, 'She knelt on the bed, put her arm around me, and I went in.'" If the jury thought he might be truthful in this assertion, they would need to consider whether or not, although entirely surprised by such a reception being accorded to him, this young man might not have been entitled reasonably to regard her action as amounting to an invitation to him to enter. If she in fact appeared to be welcoming him, the crown do not suggest that he should have realised or even suspected that she was so behaving because, despite the moonlight, she thought he was someone else. Unless the jury were entirely satisfied that the appellant made an effective and substantial entry into the bedroom without the complainant doing or saying anything to cause him to believe that she was consenting to his entering it, he ought not to be convicted of the offence charged…and even though one may suspect that his *intention* was to commit the offence charged, unless the facts show with clarity that he in fact committed it he ought not to remain convicted."

Of course, there is a large element of the ridiculous in this regrettable story, but it is very appealing, if one can use this word in its non-legal sense, that the niceties of legal argument can have such real-life applications. One regret about Collins is that the law lords, having once touched upon the matter, did not go on to decide whether, in their learned opinion, Collins was, or was not, justified in keeping his socks on. Their wisdom on this point, while of no great practical use, would surely have been worth reading. And with that question, suspended, as it were, in time, I suggest we leave the law, just as I did nearly forty years ago, and return to the world of orchestras.

Chapter 5
Inventing the Orchestra of the Age of Enlightenment

The concert which took place in the church of St Margaret, Westminster in December 1985 would have been a routine affair but for one unusual feature. The orchestra was the Academy of Ancient Music, whose founder Christopher Hogwood was its invariable director from his seat at the harpsichord. Tonight, though, we were in the hands of Sigiswald Kuijken, a much-respected violinist with his own orchestra[50] based in Belgium, and a rare visitor to London. The very novelty of working with a guest director made this a concert of special interest for the musicians in the orchestra, even if the circumstances which had brought it about owed more to accident than to strategy. Hogwood had originally planned to direct the concert himself, as usual, but a more attractive overseas engagement intervened. So Kuijken was hired, and although the orchestral players, excited by the novelty of working with a rare visitor, contrived to deliver a fine enough performance, the concert would have made no more than a transient impact had it not been for the events which followed.

The concert was sponsored by a US investment bank, the Bankers' Trust Company, and I was one of a few of the players invited to dinner afterwards with the sponsor's party. I found one of my neighbours at dinner to be surprisingly well-informed about music as well as being a pleasingly attentive listener, and so it was, in response to some forensic questioning, that I found myself expounding on some issues which had been troubling me for some time which I had hitherto kept substantially to myself. The gist was that London's freelance musicians had achieved a remarkably dominant international position in period instrument performance but were now in danger of becoming stuck at their

---

[50] La Petite Bande

current level of (relative) mediocrity. A survey of the London period instrument scene at this time would show a plethora of orchestras, all of which operated on the same business model and were, consequently, producing substantially the same results. This model was exemplified by tonight's orchestra, the Academy of Ancient Music, of which Christopher Hogwood was owner and proprietor, and was replicated by all the other leading groups. For example there was The English Concert (prop. Trevor Pinnock), John Eliot Gardiner and the Monteverdi Orchestra, Roger Norrington and the London Classical Players, Harry Christophers and The Sixteen, Andrew Parrot and the Taverner Consort and Players, and many other more ad hoc ensembles, too. That these groups were so strongly identified with their founders was a gift to the recording companies which were now so eagerly boarding, and in some cases driving, the bandwagon, allowing them to focus their marketing and promotion on the person of the founder, thereby creating a strong brand and a pleasingly steeply rising sales graph. But a significant weakness was that these orchestras had become dangerously complacent career vehicles for their founders and there were no longer sufficient incentives to raise standards or look for new challenges.

There was a second weakness which could have longer term implications: as a result of their freelance, project-based evolution, none of these orchestras, even the most successful, were providing full time employment, or anything near it, for their members, so a 'pool' of musicians had grown in London who between them supplied the membership of all of the various orchestras. A frequent criticism of the period instrument orchestras at this time, and there was some justice in it, was that their membership comprised no more than a shuffled pack of a small group of freelance musicians. In effect, therefore, if you were to scratch their surfaces, they were indistinguishable. For those swimming in this freelance pool, of whom I was one small fish, our situation was curiously similar to that of London's freelance musicians a century earlier: in the absence of any public funding, orchestras then were assembled at the whim of conductors and it was not until the last years of the nineteenth-century that a group of players came together to turn the tables. They formed themselves into the London Symphony Orchestra, established their own administration and thenceforth would engage their choice of conductor, rather than the other way around. I outlined this historical parallel to my attentive neighbour and, warming to my theme, went on to explain that our situation now was actually worse than that of our predecessors: our owner/proprietors had, by 1985, been in this field for ten years or more and were building international reputations based on the numerous recordings which we, the humble workers, had been making for them. And as conventional orchestras around the world belatedly awakened to the challenge of the new period instrument upstarts and began to fashion some response, it was 'our' conductors, the likes of Gardiner, Hogwood, Pinnock, Norrington et al, who were now receiving attractive invitations to appear as guest conductors (and in some cases appointments as music directors) with orchestras and opera houses around the world. The consequence of this new celebrity was that our conductors' commitment to and, crucially, their availability for, work with their own orchestras at home was declining as a direct and unforeseen (at least by their orchestral players) consequence of the very success of their enterprises. These overseas offers were doubly irresistible because not only were they much better paid but also in some important respects they came with fewer responsibilities and much less financial risk: as a guest conductor you are not responsible for the administrative and financial health of your host organisation; you are relieved of having to make unwelcome 'domestic' decisions of the who-should-play-at-back-of-the-second-violins kind, and the considerable financial risk of promoting concerts in London or elsewhere was now someone else's headache. From the point of view of the orchestral players in London, our current situation was highly troubling, or should have been if its weakness had even been recognised. But no one had yet acknowledged the dangers, and there was a complacent assumption that the status quo was fine and secure. In any case, no alternative model had been suggested. We appeared to be trapped in a system which was actually damaging to our long-term employment prospects. This may have sounded too much like a self-serving complaint from someone whose main concern was to protect his own employment (and to some extent it was), but there were also two other, more strategic, factors at work which offered a glimpse of a possible escape route from the cul-de-sac we seemed to have created for ourselves.

As previously mentioned, the pioneers of our kind of music-making were not based in London. My own triumvirate of heroes comprised Nicholas Harnoncourt, Gustav Leonhardt and Frans Brüggen, but there were other leaders too: Sigiswald Kuijken, our director that evening, was one of course; a few of our string players were now commuting across the Channel to work with Ton Koopman's Amsterdam Baroque Orchestra; the American William Christie, was making a name for himself in France. All were top class musicians whom

London audiences ought to be able to hear if London was to make a sustainable claim to be a centre of excellence. None of these important artists, I continued, appeared in London because there was no platform for them; none of the orchestras invited guests (except by mistake, as tonight) and there was no concert series in which they could appear. London at this time was often rather unthinkingly described as the musical capital of the world but this was based, it seemed to me, rather on the quantity of musical activity than on its quality. Far from being the best, music in London was somewhat parochial and uncompetitive. This evening's concert, the Academy of Ancient Music with Kuijken, had shown how a new ingredient in orchestral leadership could transform what would have been a good concert into a special occasion, so there was surely an opportunity here if we could just devise a way to bring the acknowledged international leaders in our field to London.

A second kind of opportunity was also coming into view. There was beginning to be interest in working with period instruments from 'real' conductors, by which I meant those who worked in the traditional, modern-instrument orchestral world. These mainstream *maestri* were held back from dipping their toes in the water by the very same problem I had just outlined: our period instrument orchestras consisted exclusively of the owner/proprietor model and no proprietor had any incentive to offer his orchestra as a gift to someone else, especially if that someone else might very well turn out to be technically better-equipped, and possibly more interesting, than the said proprietor. The first 'real' conductor to take an open-minded interest in our new way of doing things was Charles Mackerras, but the most significant for our story was undoubtedly Simon Rattle.

Rattle's influence on British music has been phenomenal, and even then, when in his early thirties, his name had resonance well beyond the parochial boundaries of the professional music world and could open doors normally firmly closed. I had been aware of the precocious Simon since he was about ten years old. This had been a time when my mother was involved in local authority music provision in Oxfordshire and she had got to know Simon's father who was the music adviser for the City of Liverpool. He was clearly proud (and why not?) of his remarkable son, and his youthful doings were assiduously reported. Thus, when this paragon appeared in the National Youth Orchestra when I was a (slightly older) member, his reputation went before him. Our paths continued in a curious way to run in parallel without often crossing. When I was studying at the Royal College of Music he was at the Royal Academy of Music. My first orchestral job after College was in the Bournemouth Sinfonietta and just after I left to return to London, Simon won a conducting competition for which the main prize was a position for a year in Bournemouth. This had proved to be something of a poisoned chalice for Simon. He was ruthlessly over-worked by the Bournemouth orchestra managers: since his post was largely funded by the sponsorship, he was a provider of irresistibly cheap labour to a cash-strapped (and lazy) management, who gave him an impossible workload which involved learning a huge amount of music which was unfamiliar to him. His preparation was inevitably sometimes sketchy, and he was often given a rough ride by the orchestra as a result. Consequently, as his year as a work-horse conductor drew to a close, he had become so disenchanted with the music business that he was seriously considering turning his back on his burgeoning conducting career. To buy a little time, he applied to, and was accepted by, Oxford University to read English. My father at this time was Principal of Hertford College and my mother was still much involved in the encouragement of all things musical, especially within the college, so there was a kind of inevitability that Simon would be pressed into some involvement. There was a series of memorable concerts in Hertford College, with Simon at the helm, in a few of which my services were enlisted. My cellist colleague, Tim Mason, knew Simon better than I did at this point, but we both had the key information that Simon wanted to try his hand in this new period instrument world and, since he unquestionably had, despite temporary setbacks, star quality, his interest in our work had huge potential. However, as just outlined, there was no orchestral vehicle for him to work with, nor concert series to provide a platform.

My long-suffering dinner companion, Michael Rose (I had paused for breath long enough to learn his name) now began asking about potential solutions. The conclusion was in one sense obvious: a completely new orchestra should be formed with a mission to address all the failings of the existing structures. The new enterprise could build on the strengths of the existing orchestras (which contained a number of highly skilled and intelligent musicians whose potential was not being fully exploited) while avoiding at least the worst of their weaknesses (primarily that they had become career vehicles for their owners). It would turn on its head, just as the London Symphony Orchestra had done a century earlier, the existing business model, so that it would in future be the players who would engage their conductors, not the other way around. With renewed energy and creativity it would provide the platform for guest conductors to re-invigorate, even revolutionise, the too-cosy world in which we were currently plying our trade. At the stroke of baton, as it were, our problems would dissolve, at least in principle…with one bound, in other words, we would be free. But, needless to say, this 'one bound' would be extremely hard to take: however irrefutable the logic for its creation, starting a new orchestra in a field which, as described above, was already overcrowded, would require an imaginative vision and a mighty (and financially reckless) leap which I could not imagine how to take. Nevertheless, coffee having been and gone, Michael and I parted with the mutual satisfaction, as I thought, of having righted some of the world's wrongs, at least in theory.

I am embarrassed, now, to recall how innocent it all was; this was just talk…and so far as I had any thought that it could become real it would have been on the assumption that someone more experienced than I would arrive at the same obvious (once you'd thought of it) conclusion and would find a way to do something about it. So I was astonished when Michael called the very next morning, and even more so when that call revealed what an experienced listener he was: it was only now he revealed that he was not merely a banker enjoying an evening out at his firm's expense; he was himself responsible for the Bankers' Trust sponsorship programme (he had decided not to tell me this the previous evening, he said, because he didn't want to inhibit the freedom with which we were talking) and furthermore, one of the bank's special interests (or Unique Selling Points in the clunky corporate jargon) was investment in start-up ventures. To cut to the chase, Michael asked if I would come to his office, bringing some like-minded colleagues, to discuss how we might pursue the ideas we had so recently been discussing. Thus was the Orchestra of the Age of Enlightenment born, or perhaps I should say, more accurately, conceived.

As events unfolded, the depths, or perhaps better described as shallows, of my naïveté and innocence were never quite believed, especially by Christopher Hogwood, and it is a source of sadness to me that I never fully persuaded him that I had not deliberately set out, as he naturally assumed, to steal a sponsor from under his nose. From his point of view the saga and aftermath of the Kuijken concert looked very different. He told me, some years later, that as soon as he had realised he would no longer be available to direct that fateful St Margaret's concert he instructed his orchestra manager, Judith Hendershott, to cancel unless she could find a sponsor who would underwrite the anticipated loss of around £5,000. As no sponsor was found and the date was fast approaching he repeated his instruction to cancel, but, at the last minute, she told him that the Bankers' Trust[51] had stepped in to save the day. Only after the event did he learn (and this shows that naïveté was not mine alone) that the sponsorship amounted to a mere £500, one tenth of the sum required, and Christopher found himself personally liable for the balance. Even this might have been an acceptable 'investment' if it ensured that the sponsor became a longer-term supporter of the orchestra. This did not happen, of course, and Hogwood famously dubbed our new venture the 'Age of Embezzlement', a name which stuck for some considerable time. Not only so; Judith Hendershott, summarily dismissed from her post as manager of the Academy of Ancient Music following her wilful concealment of the true financial position, was to become the first manager of the Orchestra of the Age of Enlightenment for the very good reason that she was willing to work, initially, for nothing and we, the Board of this embryonic enterprise, were penniless.

The next, more formal meeting with Michael Rose took place a few days later in his Liverpool Street office and, as with so many other aspects of this story, I was extraordinarily lucky to find, at very short notice, a strong group of colleagues available and willing to come with me and lend credibility to my idea. I have no written record of who was there, but I do remember that our group included the cellist Tim Mason, who later became the orchestra's first chairman, and his wife, the viola player Jan Schlapp. Also present were the two Tonys, Pay and Halstead, representing the woodwind and brass departments, who were not only outstandingly articulate but also were 'grown-ups', that is to say players with substantial experience in modern instrument orchestras. Tony Pay had been for many years the principal clarinet in the Royal Philharmonic Orchestra and Tony Halstead was principal horn in the English Chamber Orchestra. The violinist (and leader of AAM) Catherine Mackintosh was there, as was, I think, Marshall Marcus, who was to become, some years later, one of a succession of chief executives of the OAE. Of course it was a matter of chance which players were available, so, to that extent, they were a random selection; but in truth these

---

[51] I believe the original connection with the Bankers' Trust was made by the violinist Catherine Mackintosh, via a friend, or perhaps relative of her husband's who worked at the company. 'Cat' became one of the remarkable quadrivirate of OAE leaders, the others being Elizabeth Wallfisch, Alison Bury and Margaret Faultless, who, by some gravity defying balancing act, managed a kind of four-way job share in those early years.

were all excellent people with an articulate and persuasive passion for their work, and all were apparently willing to commit to a first concert to launch our new venture. For his part, Rose outlined a proposal: Bankers' Trust was to be the lead sponsor of a short festival at the South Bank Centre in summer 1986 and he offered to engineer an invitation for our new orchestra. Thus it came about that the OAE's very first London concert was at the Queen Elizabeth Hall at the extraordinarily improbable invitation of André Previn, the artistic director of the Bankers' Trust summer festival. He would have been as surprised as anyone to find that he unwittingly played such a seminal role. Previn knew many things about music in many genres, but period instrument performance was something in which he had neither experience, nor, so far as anyone knew, interest.

At this first meeting, the next steps were identified. These were, in themselves, routine but at the time seemed immensely exciting. We had, almost by accident, embarked on an adventure, and were to be guided by the experience of the Bankers' Trust. However, there were constraints. We had no money, and the bank would do no more than meet the most essential initial costs beyond underwriting the first concert. We had no management and no means to pay for even the most minimal administrative services. We had no office, of course, and no publicity material, no orchestra photograph (there was not yet an orchestra after all) for the concert programme, press releases and so on. And there were questions of governance: we needed to register as a charity before we could raise any money, and charities need trustees. Whom could we ask? And above all these difficulties, there loomed what was perhaps the biggest question of all: we were talking about an orchestra which did not exist, so who would play in it? And how would they be selected? Who would be our first conductor and who would lead the concert? And, having decided these questions, which of us would do which tasks and how would we monitor progress?

We also discussed a name. Somehow we contrived to emerge from our first meeting having settled on the Age of Enlightenment. I think that Michael Rose himself was promoting this name but I can't be sure. It certainly was not my choice. Of course there was no certainty that AoE (as it was at first known) would survive beyond its first concert, but of course we needed to work on the assumption that it would. In the event we turned to Sigiswald Kuijken once more, hoping to maintain some of the momentum which his Academy of Ancient Music concert had given us and he came up with an eclectic (or perhaps I mean bizarre) programme which somehow encapsulated in music the statement we were trying to make as an orchestra. Unusually, this first concert combined baroque and classical repertoire (unusual because baroque and classical works were generally played at different pitches, and it was rightly thought that period instrument performance was hard enough already without compounding the difficulties by insisting that players switch instruments between pieces), and presented rarities too: we began with Telemann and Rameau, and the second half had a symphony by Haydn and another by that giant of Belgian musical history, Francois-Joseph Gossec.[52]

The closeness of the date of the first concert gave us a very tricky problem, so far as engaging players was concerned. Many of the best of them, having diaries which were filled for many months ahead, would be unlikely to be available, so we were inevitably going to be unable to field our very best team. And of course we had no one, nor any process, to decide which players should be in this notional first team. One of the great weaknesses in the existing orchestral structure, and one we were specifically trying to overcome, was that such personnel decisions (who is a member of your orchestra and how are they chosen?) were taken behind closed doors by the orchestral founder, sometimes with advice from whichever sycophantic clique he had at the time assembled around him, sometimes on a whim. The last thing we wanted was that our new venture be perceived as just another unaccountable clique, but we were undeniably an entirely self-appointed group at this stage (for how could it have been otherwise?). Our self-selection in what was supposedly a 'democracy' was a tricky issue from the outset, and made more so because we needed to ensure that the players in our launch event would not acquire 'sitting tenant' status, acquiring the right to be asked in future simply by virtue of being the first, or only, available cab on the rank today. We would need to keep membership fluid so that when our first-choice players became available (assuming the orchestra survived so long) we would still be in a position to invite them. So, for these highly pragmatic reasons, we came up with a solution which could be justified

---

[52] Gossec's name brings to mind a cruel remark made by Denis Healey when he heard that Dan Quayle had been nominated as George Bush's 1988 vice-presidential running mate, "Mr Quayle's is scarcely a household name … even in his own household." As for poor Gossec (1734 – 1829), his main, perhaps only, claim to fame is that he lived to the enormous (for that time) age of 95, being born when Handel was at the height of his operatic powers in London (*Alcina* and *Ariodante* both premiered in 1735), studying in Paris with Rameau and outliving both Beethoven and Schubert.

as a matter of principle: membership of the orchestra would be open to everyone. The broad church membership would then be asked to elect an artistic planning committee from amongst their numbers, who would be responsible not only for the detailed personnel questions but also for the wider artistic policies (what the orchestra should play and who should conduct it). This plan, born of a worthy attempt at accountability, made the orchestra vulnerable to the criticism, in which there was enough truth for it to be uncomfortable, that such a committee would fail to create as clear an identity for the orchestra as a single artistic director or music director would achieve. And it also put a significant burden on the management to create a coherent agenda which would enable the committee to ask itself the right questions and reach sensible and clear conclusions.

All this structural stuff needed organisation and here again we suffered from having no money. We were fortunate, in a sense, that Judith Hendershott had been fired by Christopher Hogwood so was available and willing to work for little or no money at the outset. She thus became, more or less by default, the first manager, and although her time with the Orchestra of the Age of Enlightenment (OAE as it had now become) was short, her contribution was vital in the first year of the orchestra's life. Two achievements in particular stand out. The first was to arrange Simon Rattle's first appearance with the orchestra, a groundbreaking performance (an overused expression, of course, but in this case true) of Mozart's 'difficult' opera *Idomeneo*.

As already noted, Rattle's potential involvement had been one of the key drivers for the idea of the OAE, but his star had risen so rapidly since his return from self-imposed exile in Oxford that by 1986, OAE's first year, his diary was full for the next two years at least. However, when Tim Mason and I met him to talk about our new venture he was immediately with us, but, characteristically, with conditions. Or rather a single condition, namely that we had to do *Idomeneo*, and not only so but with an international cast of his choosing. Judith did a remarkable job of assembling a fabulous cast;[53] the Queen Elizabeth Hall was hired and the concert performance announced to great anticipation but there was one big problem. We had no money to pay for it. We were still in the process of building a board of trustees for the orchestra to develop a sustainable fundraising strategy, but it was too soon, early in 1987, for them to have delivered. But we had made a start, and one of the newly appointed trustees was the redoubtable Martin Smith, who was introduced, I think, by Michael Rose. Martin had worked

---

[53] Including Arleen Auger, Philip Langridge and Carol Vaness as a magnificent *Elektra*.

at Banker's Trust but had subsequently set up Phoenix Securities as a 'boutique' financial services operation. So far as *Idomeneo* was concerned the key date at which we had to make an irrevocable commitment to go ahead was a mere six weeks before the concert; this was the date after which all the musicians would have to be paid (according to Musicians' Union rules) regardless of whether the event took place or not. The OAE Board met exactly seven weeks before the concert date and took the inevitable, but nevertheless painful decision to cancel *Idomeneo*, unless a miracle happened and we raised an additional £20,000 before the end of the week. Smith and other trustees undertook to work through their address books to contact friends and colleagues in a final fundraising push, right up to the eve of cancellation. And, not for the first time in the OAE story, the miracle happened—one of Martin Smith's elegantly phrased, but nevertheless rather desperate appeals landed on the desk of one of the most successful (although ultimately doomed) City take-over kings of the 1980s, John Gunn, who had that very week taken up a new position as chairman and chief executive of a huge conglomerate empire called British and Commonwealth. Not only so, he told us later that he had just decided to confront his Board with an ultimatum…the old (smaller) B&C had since time immemorial been making an annual donation of £25,000 to the Conservative Party; Gunn's decision was that this should be cancelled, or, if it were not to be cancelled, it must be matched by an equivalent arts sponsorship. And no sooner had he decided on this course than Martin's letter dropped smoothly on to his desk, asking him to step in to save our day.[54] John Gunn's support, as it turned out, went far beyond saving our day—it opened the second chapter of the OAE story. For Simon Rattle's insistence on *Idomeneo* had not been mere wilfulness: he had been approached (indeed had been assiduously wooed) by Glyndebourne Opera, for whom Mozart opera was historically at the very heart of their repertoire, with an invitation to conduct a series of Mozart operas. Simon was now in a position to make another of his famous conditions: he would accept provided that Glyndebourne engage the

---

[54] John Gunn's fall was a cautionary tale of City life in the Thatcher years: one of the many companies which had been bundled up into the new British and Commonwealth empire was a computer services company, Atlantic Computers. This company's business model involved leasing computers under contracts which guaranteed generous upgrades, open-ended contractual commitments which were not properly quantified, let alone accounted for. Atlantic Computers turned out to be a black hole; it was in administration within ten years and was to take Gunn's entire B&C empire down with it.

OAE as their orchestra. This was an enormous ask: not only was the OAE an unproven quantity, but Glyndebourne had a longstanding contract with one of London's very best orchestras, the London Philharmonic Orchestra, who had played in the pit for the Glyndedourne summer season for the last fifty years. To lose a key part of the season would put the financial viability of their summer activities into question, so they could be expected to mount a titanic struggle to cling on to the status quo. Nevertheless, despite the problems which a decision to switch allegiance from one orchestra to another would inevitably cause, Rattle succeeded in persuading a no doubt highly sceptical Glyndebourne administrative team to come to our concert performance of *Idomeneo*. Of course, it was a thrilling success (otherwise there would be no story), and there followed the momentous invitation for Rattle and OAE to present, over a six-year period, new productions (plus a revival the following year) of the three great Mozart / da Ponte[55] operas, 'Marriage of Figaro', 'Cosi fan Tutte' and 'Don Giovanni', starting with a new Peter Hall production of Figaro in 1989.

The second of Judith Hendershott's achievements was to secure a recording contract with the new Virgin Classics label, recently launched under the experienced eye of Simon Foster, who had made his name with the mid-price EMI 'Classics for Pleasure' label. The very first Virgin/OAE project was to record the same Haydn symphonies, directed by Kuijken, which had been included in our opening concerts. With a Glyndebourne contract in the bag and now with a recording contract on the table, OAE had made a dizzyingly fast start. But the truth is we were travelling at a dangerously high speed: the orchestra was still a tiny start-up operation run from the Hendershott bedroom without an office and without any support staff. And it was the next recording project, vastly ambitious in hindsight, which triggered the first major crisis and almost caused our rickety runaway train to jump the tracks altogether. In the end, though, we survived, but I'm afraid Judith herself was the primary casualty.

The ambitious plan which triggered the crisis was for a ten-day recording project at the EMI Abbey Road studio (famously the location for another new recording venture, The Beatles) making two orchestral CD's with Charles

---

[55] Luigi da Ponte, the librettist for what are arguably the three greatest operas ever written, led a life which, were it the plot of a novel would be dismissed as too absurd to be believed: he was a Jewish Roman Catholic priest who married an English woman, was on intimate terms with Casanova and the Holy Roman Emperor, ending his days as a greengrocer in Philadelphia. He is buried beneath a freeway in the Bronx.

Mackerras, the first being Mendelssohn's Italian Symphony and the complete Midsummer Night's Dream incidental music (including, at some risk of farce, an exceptionally recalcitrant nineteenth-century ophicleide) and the second, most challenging of all, was Schubert's monumental ninth symphony, the 'Great' C Major. Only about three weeks before the first recording day we (we being at this time the elected player members of the Board, Tim Mason, Marshall Marcus and myself) discovered the shocking truth that almost no players had been engaged. The reasons were never entirely clear, but I believe that Judith was so overwhelmed by the range and scale of the management tasks she had to deal with that when, very late in the day, she finally got around to starting to book the orchestral musicians she found, not surprisingly, that almost none of players we wanted were available for such an extended period at such short notice. Unfortunately, but perhaps not so surprisingly, she froze, a rabbit in the headlights, rather than seek help: it was the responsibility of the orchestra's artistic committee to monitor and approve the lists of players engaged; Tim Mason and I had tried our best to extract information from her but had been repeatedly fobbed off with vague assurances and it was not until the eleventh hour that such prevarication was no longer sustainable. There was a fraught meeting to discuss the dire and, from our young orchestra's point of view, life-threatening situation in which we found ourselves, namely we had a contract for ten days of recording and no players. There could be no doubt that Hendershott had concealed from us the true state of affairs, and there now fell to Tim and myself the unwelcome task of delivering the news to Judith that her services were to be dispensed with forthwith. Less personally painful, but nevertheless exceedingly challenging, I took on the task, a potentially poisoned chalice, of trying to fix a band in a matter of days for what was supposed to be a definitive statement of our new orchestra's quality and aspirations. And, of course, when I set about it, I found exactly what Judith had found—no one was available for ten consecutive days in three weeks' time.

Charles Mackerras had a reputation for intolerance of incompetence, so I had good reason to be nervous when I invited myself over to his house to break the news, not only of the circumstances of Hendershott's abrupt withdrawal from the fray but also that it had fallen to me to try to clear up the mess we were now in. Expecting a full-scale row, probably followed by a conductorial resignation, I laid the situation out in all its horrid detail. Charles remained extraordinarily calm and heard me out without interruption. When he did respond it was with a pragmatism which, in the circumstances, I scarcely deserved and for which I was immensely grateful. I suppose that had our straits been slightly less dire he might well have reacted with a 'conventional' temper tantrum, but the position was in truth so bleak that it must have been obvious that rage would achieve nothing. As we contemplated the situation, we quickly concluded that the choices were limited: either walk away immediately, or roll up our sleeves and make the best of things. Having opted for the latter course, Charles was clear that I should abandon any idea of trying to engage only those who were available for the full ten day period…we already knew this would be impossible, or at least would not deliver results of a high enough standard. So I was to book the very best players I could find on a session-by-session basis: if the best player was available for one session only, that is what he or she should be asked to do. This meant, of course, that the personnel in the orchestra would be a kaleidoscope, ever changing from one day (indeed each morning and afternoon) to the next, and there would be scarcely anyone, and as it turned out no-one amongst the violins, who played in every one of those sessions. Charles opted to trust me on the choice of players and all he asked in return was that I provide him a list (and a seating order for the string players) at the start of each day so that he could learn each person's name. In those pre-email days this meant sending an early morning fax each day, which Charles usually replied to with hand-written comments. In one of these exchanges, he decided that the plural of 'fax' should be 'faeces,'[56] and later, as I came to know him better, he would often refer to our matinal exchange of faeces during these highly intense few days. And as for the recordings, especially the Schubert, they were, in the circumstances, miraculous and I was extraordinarily impressed at the outstanding, and consistent, results Charles achieved with his kaleidoscopic orchestra. Indeed, I have sometimes wondered whether Mackerras did not quite achieve the musical reputation he deserved precisely because he was such a consummate professional that people overlooked his wonderful musicianship. It should be noted, too, that the remarkable success of these

---

[56] I only know one other joke about the fax machine which I include because at least some readers will still know what a fax machine is. In a few years it will be utterly forgotten. So here is a 'period' joke for the delectation of the over 50s and puzzlement of the young: a judge comes into court confessing he has left the judgement he is meant to read in his country cottage. Counsel, a northerner, suggests 'Fax it up, m'lud' to which the learned judge, not a northerner, replies, 'Yes, it does rather.'

recordings[57] was a tribute to the resilience and adaptability of the players themselves, who were coming in and out of the studio seldom knowing after each session who their colleagues were going to be for the next.

~~~

With the abrupt departure of Judith Hendershott in 1988 it was decided to advertise the managerial position, and I was a member of the interview panel in the summer of that year. The surprisingly large number of applicants confirmed the remarkable impact OAE had already made, and we spent an entire day interviewing short-listed candidates before retiring to the pub afterwards to recover and reflect. The consensus was that none of the people we had seen had convincingly met our (probably unrealistically high) expectations and that we should try again and re-advertise after the summer holidays. During this post-mortem, possibly over the second pint, I had ventured that I could do a better job than any of the people we had just interviewed. When baldly written down this of course sounds unattractively boastful, but it was intended merely as a justification for rejecting all that day's candidates and re-advertising the post. Up until this point it had simply not occurred to me that I might do the job myself, and, had I thought about it at all, I would have dismissed the idea as absurd. And, since it was absurd to think of appointing someone as unqualified as myself to be the new manager it would surely be even more so to appoint someone perceived as even less equipped for the task. I think this was understood by my colleagues; at least no one immediately responded with a job offer, and we went on a family holiday immediately afterwards. While away I found myself, for the first time, thinking seriously of the possibility of a career change. The idea was growing on me.

Try as I might I could not help but think of this orchestra, rather proprietorially, as my brainchild, and consequently I had a big emotional investment in helping it succeed. Surely it would be an act of cowardice not to try to play a central role in determining its fate which was, right now, hanging by a thread. Here was a great opportunity if I had the courage to grasp it.

---

[57] It gave me particular pleasure, and some amusement, years after I had left the OAE, when the Schubert Great C Major symphony was picked as best available version (from a large field including many of the world's most famous orchestras and conductors) in the BBC Radio 3's respected 'Building a Library' feature.

There were other, more domestic, reasons why a change from a purely freelance existence was beginning to appear attractive. Julie and I had adopted a child, Eleanor, in 1983, and another, Daniel, in 1985. We were both still working in freelance orchestras which seemed to be continuously expanding their international touring.

I had reached a point, in 1986, when I was out of the country on tour for almost six months of the year with the Albion Ensemble, Academy of St Martin in the Fields, The English Chamber Orchestra or Academy of Ancient Music, and this was making it particularly hard for Julie to manage her own professional career while simultaneously bearing the brunt of the children duties. Matters came to a head sometime in 1987 when my precarious freelance balancing act—trying to be a member of four separate orchestras as well as several chamber music groups—became simply unsustainable. I was too often in the awkward position of having to choose whom to play for when schedules clashed and I was in truth giving satisfaction to no one. The solution had to be to resign from two of my regular orchestras in order to give fuller attention to the others, and, having reached this painful, if honourable, conclusion, I duly penned two letters of resignation, eventually dropping them determinedly into the post box with some sense of relief. To my considerable distress, in the next three days I had calls from the two orchestras with whom I had planned to continue (I had not yet said anything to them of my plan to favour them with a bit more of my presence) to let me know that, with regret, they had decided that I should be replaced with someone whose availability would be more assured. So in the space of three days I had resigned from two positions and been fired from the other two, leaving me with rather more 'time to spend with my family' than I had anticipated. If I had felt relief when I originally posted my two resignations, it was with much more urgent relief that I managed to withdraw them before they had been acted on, and to reach a realistic accommodation with the two organisations which planned to dispense with my services, thus restoring most of the *status quo ante*, but without solving the fundamental diary management problem. And then, quite out of the blue, came a further, though welcome, new twist.

Daniel was one year old in 1986 and the formalities of his adoption had been delayed because his birth mother had disappeared. Almost the only thing that was known about her was that she had come to England on a one-year student visa from Venezuela and had overstayed (partly, no doubt, because of her pregnancy). She had now disappeared, and was on the official missing persons list, both of the police and of the Venezuelan authorities. One consequence of her disappearance was that we could not proceed with the adoption by consent (the birth mother has to sign a consent form), so had to seek a court order to complete the process which, although unlikely to fail (in the absence of a parental or local authority challenge) was a cumbersome and time-consuming business. Then, while these formalities meandered along their legal path, we had a phone call from our local authority adoption unit to let us know that, totally unexpectedly, Daniel had been found to have a sister and, in short, would we take her as well? The circumstances were amazing: our excellent social worker, John Parker, who had helped us with both Eleanor and Daniel, the two adoptions we had already completed (or nearly so in Daniel's case), had taken a call, one day, from Charing Cross Hospital where they had a young woman, who was saying that she did not want to keep the baby to which she had just given birth. He was called in to talk to her, as was normal in such circumstances. She said that this was her first child; he did not recognise her name and her appearance was unfamiliar, but nevertheless he had a strong sense that he had in fact met her somewhere before. He left her bedside to think this over, and eventually he came to wonder if this could be Daniel's missing mother whom he had met briefly the previous year when Daniel had been taken into care. When challenged she denied it but he persisted, and finally she reluctantly admitted that she had given a false name, had changed her appearance and had claimed that this was her first child. She had done it, she said, because she was afraid that the hospital, "Would not help her for a second time." As her story emerged it seemed that she had made mistakes at every turn…the father of her first child had left her when she became pregnant, and she had told the social services when Daniel was born that she never wanted to see the father again, and would give up the child for adoption. Then, once free of the new baby, she went straight back to him, but this time <u>she</u> left <u>him</u> within a few weeks, only to discover after doing so that she was pregnant for the second time. The outcome of this sorry chapter of errors was that Daniel was found to have a full sister whose discovery was truly a miracle. Out of all the social workers in London, her mother had unwittingly contrived to pick the very same one she had dealt with before. Had anyone else been called to her bedside the two siblings would surely have led their entire lives unaware of each other's existence. Thus did Julie and I achieve the impossible, an unplanned adoption. Polly, our surprise new arrival, was only ten months younger than her brother, so we had two-and-a-half year old Eleanor and a pair of almost-twins, and it goes without saying that the strain on domestic arrangements, already severe enough for me to be trying (and failing) to find some more or less drastic solutions, intensified. This was the state of affairs when we set off on our brief holiday in Wales in summer 1988 and soon after our return to London I duly submitted my application for the Orchestra of the Age of Enlightenment's re-advertised management position.

Knowing, as I did, how little I fitted the 'person profile' the OAE was seeking in its search I was in truth surprised eventually to be offered the post, and shamefully unprepared for my new role. Of course I understood better than anyone how and why the orchestra had come into being, the aspirations of the players and the personalities of the key people in its story thus far, but nevertheless, my total lack of management experience, and the errors this led me into, is painful now to look back on. Because of the very democratic principles we had, for good if pragmatic reasons, committed to at the outset, OAE was also a uniquely tough managerial challenge. The first of these dratted principles[58] was that there was no artistic director to take responsibility (and blame) for the artistic programme and, importantly, for the many thorny personnel decisions within the orchestra. So it fell to the manager to formulate and implement an artistic programme[59] while simultaneously being in charge of the money. And as for sales and marketing, these were mere words to me at this point, devoid of meaning.

The very first concert of my tenure (plans for which were naturally initiated some time before I began) exemplified all the organisational weaknesses (and more) and was a searingly unforgettable experience. The work was an operatic rarity, Luigi Cherubini's *Medée*, in which the *tour de force* title role was sung by the formidable mezzosoprano Lisa Connell. I was still playing in the orchestra at this point and I learned there and then that the multi-tasking required if I was to continue to play in the orchestra was actually impossible (*Medée* includes an aria, "*Solo un pianto*", with a horridly intimidating bassoon *obbligato* ending on

---

[58] I should perhaps have learned from Groucho Marx, "I've got my principles… but if you don't like 'em I have plenty others"

[59] Technically this was the responsibility of the Artistic Direction Committee, but committees are never much good without agendas, so setting the agenda went much of the way towards creating an artistic policy.

a sustained high C optimistically marked *diminuendo a niente*[60]) if only because of the need to run (literally) to the front of house receptions before the concert and in the interval in order to fulfil (at least partially) my managerial role with sponsors and other supporters. One particular issue with *Medée* haunts me to this day: with so many new tasks to deal with I had overlooked the fact that this opera, very unusually, includes a substantial quantity of dialogue; not recitative, but actual speech. And in French. We had an entirely English cast, as I recall, whose command of French was pitiful and whose accents were on a narrow spectrum ranging from terrible to comically execrable. No one had insisted that they should at the very least learn their lines, and I was so ignorant that I had no idea that engaging a language coach was absolutely essential. So our soloists, who were (mostly) excellent singers, simply stood on the stage (this was a concert performance) of the Royal Festival Hall and read their lines without any sense of meaning and with positively Churchillian French accents. It is hard to imagine anything more embarrassing. I have a shameful feeling that it was broadcast on Radio 3 and have never forgotten the virulent hostility of the review by the eminent music critic of *The Observer*, Hugh Canning, who was a friend of my predecessor. Sadly, although his personal attacks were ill-informed and uncalled for, his devastating judgement on the concert itself was painfully accurate.

As a member of the Board and the so-called Artistic Development Committee I had played a small part in early discussions about the next big project, but, with so many other pressing issues crowding in, I had in truth been happy to leave much of this to others. The reality of dealing with it now was a shock. The South Bank Centre (SBC), the umbrella organisation responsible for the Royal Festival Hall, Queen Elizabeth Hall and the small Purcell Room, had invited us to deliver an eight-concert series, each to feature one of the late Haydn Masses and the two late oratorios, The Creation and The Seasons. These eight large concerts were to be given over a nine-week period from mid-October to early December 1989. The all-Haydn programmes had been devised by Sir William Glock. We could scarcely decline such an offer, but it was indeed a monster of a project, which would be a daunting enough challenge even today, but back then it was almost overwhelming: the programmes looked nice enough

---

[60] This is the same high C on which the famous bassoon solo which opens Stravinsky's *The Rite of Spring* begins. In the Charpentier context '*niente*' was all too easy to achieve, the '*diminuendo a niente*' less so.

on paper, but I knew that one of the few certainties in an uncertain world is that Haydn is death at the box office. A series of eight all-Haydn concerts in as many weeks was therefore a heroic, but scarcely advisable, artistic statement. It was no great surprise, given recent upheavals, to discover that no detailed planning had been done. The challenge was daunting: there appeared to have been no discussions with the SBC about the cost of all this, and when I was finally able to present a preliminary costing (largely based on guesswork) to Graham Sheffield, head of artistic planning for the SBC, he turned an alarming shade of grey. The concerts were so tightly scheduled (one a week, more or less) and were to happen so soon that there was no chance of sharing costs with any other promoters, so the South Bank were obliged to foot the total bill for their spectacularly over-optimistic brainchild. While Sheffield and Nicholas Snowman were considering their response I had no choice but to set about constructing our huge edifice because the whole project represented the OAE's entire concert output for the coming Autumn. We needed, to start with, eight conductors and thirty-two solo singers, a chorus for all eight concerts, a number of instrumental soloists, and, of course, a budget, which required a rehearsal plan for each concert. In its history thus far the orchestra had not used as many as eight conductors, nor anything like thirty-two soloists, and we had never played a choral work (so had no pre-existing chorus to call on). With each concert having a different conductor, there could be no continuity of approach across the whole series. My blood runs cold, still, when I remember the amateurish randomness of the choices of soloists. I had no experience and minimal understanding of voices (it was not until I began working with Trevor Pinnock a few years later that my education, so far as voices are concerned, properly began) and this was also my first experience of dealing with London's notoriously grasping concert agents who represented the singers. These parasites (I would say vultures, but I was not yet, quite, carrion) were soon at work, in a ghastly feeding frenzy, to suck the blood of the callow novice who was in such desperate need of their clients. And when it came to the choir, when it was eventually engaged, it consisted of an ill-matched assortment of freelancers chosen more for their availability than for their skills. The truth is that even the most battle-hardened veteran would not have had time properly to plan and implement this monumental project. The result, eventually, was shockingly second rate. The orchestra's reputation should have suffered terrible and perhaps permanent damage but somehow the goodwill and optimism which surrounded our early efforts allowed us to ride out our embarrassing failures; and, to be fair, there were a few successes, notably Charles Mackerras's 'Creation' and Mark Elder's account of the rarely (in the UK, at any rate) performed 'Seasons.'[61]

The conductors were intended to represent the wide range of *maestri* this still-young orchestra would work with. This meant that some came from a background of period instruments (for example, Ton Koopman and Sigiswald Kuijken) while others came from a modern orchestra background. Charles Mackerras was one of these, but others, Ivan Fischer, Gustav Kuhn and Mark Elder, I was meeting here for the first time. Some but not all would re-appear in future seasons.

The most difficult conductors to re-engage for future projects were Ton Koopman and Sigiswald Kuijken. Koopman's diary was completely full for years to come, mostly with projects with his own Amsterdam Baroque Orchestra (ABO), and when we eventually located a few available days, it was impossible to agree on repertoire: very reasonably he refused to conduct repertoire with OAE which duplicated what he did with his own orchestra. This meant that he would only offer baroque music of exceptional obscurity (and hence unmarketable and already rejected by ABO), or repertoire on a big scale (e.g. operas and oratorios) which had been deemed too expensive even for his own generously subsidised organisation.

Kuijken, too, began to be troubled by an incipient 'identity crisis': he had suffered criticism at home from his own musicians in La Petite Bande who perceived him as giving OAE, the new kids on the block, repertoire which they felt he should be doing with them. So Kuijken, too, reached a point at which he would only agree to discuss 'great music' in future. Needless to say, just as with Koopman, by 'great' he really meant large scale and expensive. This was utterly impractical…not only did we want to reserve our most high-profile projects for those of our conductors who were, genuinely, conductors, such as Simon Rattle, Charles Mackerras, Ivan Fischer, Mark Elder and the like, but also wanted Kuijken to appear as a violinist rather than a conductor. So it was that Kuijken,

---

[61] The performance survived the very best efforts of fate to deal a killer blow: the concert day began with an early morning call to tell me that our soprano (Joan Rodgers, I think it was) was cancelling because of flu. By mid-morning I had replaced her, but later that afternoon the new soprano also pulled out, for the same reason. It was not until two hours before the concert was due to begin that Ann Dawson bravely agreed to step in to a role she had not sung for many years.

having launched OAE on its path, was never again to appear with the orchestra after our bizarrely exclusive Haydn-only season.

On a personal level, I was sorry about this because I enjoyed his company. One skill which Kuijken shared with our other period instrument specialist conductors, Leonhardt and Brüggen, was a remarkable command of English as well as other languages, although they were all outdone in this regard by Carmen Prieto, our Spanish agent, who had had the great good fortune, though she may not have fully appreciated it at the time, to be educated at the English School in Madrid. This meant that all her classes were conducted in English and she was taught, mainly, by two Edinburgh spinsters who sounded exceedingly fierce but of whom Carmen always spoke with affection. The legacy of these Morningside matrons is that Carmen's English is remarkable, and exceptionally correct, and she was a great connoisseur of the quirks of the English language. I can recall repeating to her a slightly risqué joke which Kuijken had told me. This appealed to Carmen partly because it demanded a fine understanding of English (as well as of ancient Greek) and partly because, being told by Kuijken, it had great rarity value, a Belgian joke: Boston has a particular kind of fish, called scrod, which is much prized locally. A gentleman, flying to Boston on a mission to buy this local delicacy, climbs into a cab and addresses the driver, "Please, take me somewhere I can get scrod."

"Many people ask me this," replies his driver, "but you're the first to have used the pluperfect subjunctive." Carmen evidently recounted this to Leonhardt, and the 'scrod joke' thus acquired a kind of currency among these English language connoisseurs. Years later, when recalling this fishy joke, she reminded me, because she had recently come across it again, carefully recorded in an old notebook, that I had followed it up with the observation often attributed to George Bernard Shaw that the word FISH itself might possibly be spelled G-H-O-T-I: GH as in enough, O as in women and TI as in nation.

Gustav Leonhardt's command of English was almost as perfect as Carmen's, and equally old school. Mr Leonhardt, as I always thought of him, was one of the last to succumb to the modern insistence on instant communication and, when we began working together in the late 80s and early 90s he would write me the most elegant letters in his distinctive script. The telephone was for emergencies, and as for the fax machine, he only began to use it after that technology had already been overtaken by email.

It was one Christmas Eve in the early 1990s that I received one of Mr Leonhardt's emergency calls. The background was a kind of grumbling trench warfare he was engaged in with the Philips record label. He and Nikolaus Harnoncourt had, long before, made a groundbreaking series of recordings of Bach Cantatas and had had to haggle over which of the two hundred or so cantatas each would record. There were a few which Leonhardt regretted 'losing' to Harnoncourt, and he had persuaded Philips to allow him to record some of these with OAE. The contentious issue for Mr Leonhardt and the Philips team concerned the choice of soloists: Leonhardt had a particular antipathy towards the style of singing church music which can be broadly categorised as the English cathedral tradition. This has developed over several centuries and is characterised by a focus on beauty of tone at the expense, critics argue, of clarity of diction (a failing which might be thought the natural outcome of a life spent singing in cavernous cathedrals in which the acoustics defeat any attempt at clarity). Leonhardt always wanted singers whom he trusted to sing with the clearest possible words, while Philips, or rather their marketing people, always insisted on well-known names to sell the discs, regardless of their style of delivery. I was caught in the middle of these disagreements, a case in point being the choice of the soprano Barbara Bonney for our recording. Bonney was at that time one of the world's leading singers in this kind of repertoire but, remarkably (considering her fame), Leonhardt did not know her work and asked me to advise. I was naturally delighted for OAE to appear with one of the top soloists of the day, so reassured him that all would be well.

We had given two concerts shortly before Christmas with the recording scheduled for the week between Christmas and New Year, beginning on 27th December. Mr Leonhardt called me on Christmas Eve, and after characteristically polite preliminaries about my health and happiness, gently dropped his bombshell that he found Miss Bonney, as he called her, to be an 'ice-maiden' and, in short, he would be unable to proceed with the recording unless she was replaced. In order to play for time while trying to work out how to persuade him that it would be quite impossible to sack 'Miss Bonney' and even less possible to imagine finding a replacement on Christmas Day, I enquired whether he had a soprano in mind for the role whom I might contact to check availability and explore options. His reply was immediate, "My favourite soprano, of course," (I loved that 'of course') "is Mrs Thatcher, but perhaps not suited to this repertoire."[62]

This was classic Leonhardt. Behind the austere, and rather intimidating, exterior was a quite different man. He lived with his wife Marie (a violinist and herself an important figure in the period instrument world) in a museum in Amsterdam; the museum was an unmodernised eighteenth-century canal-side house owned by the Dutch government. The top floor was let at a peppercorn rent to the museum 'curators', Mr and Mrs Leonhardt, who had lived there with minimal electricity and no hot water since, it seemed, time immemorial. The 'museum' was not open to the public and I once asked Mr Leonhardt about his curatorial duties. He told me he was obliged to give a tour to anyone who should ask. When I had the temerity to ask how onerous this obligation was he simply pointed out that he very rarely answered the telephone ("Perhaps you have noticed?"). The austerity of his top floor accommodation was in some contrast to that of the basement. This was converted into a garage, and on one of my visits he had just taken delivery of a brand new bright red Alfa Romeo. A few months later I was to travel in this magnificent specimen of Italian engineering machismo on the German autobahn, and to this day I wonder how we escaped with our lives. The weather was appalling and we were utterly lost, looking for a hotel somewhere between Bonn and Cologne in which we were supposed to be staying. As Mr Leonhardt explained, in such circumstances his usual solution was to point the car in the general direction of The Netherlands and hope. This he did, at top speed in virtually zero visibility. My tentative enquiry that perhaps he might have a map somewhere in the car was greeted with the smallest acknowledgement, but he leaned over to the glove compartment, taking his eye completely off the road, and said, "I do have a map," then, "Do you want to read it?" in a surprised tone which suggested I had just revealed an exotic taste in rare literature, possibly in an ancient dead language.

In complete contrast to our flirtation with a very modern kind of death by Alfa Romeo, was something which turned the clock back almost three hundred years. OAE had an Amsterdam concert and Leonhardt and his wife, Marie, invited a number of players back to their canalside home afterwards. He showed

---

[62] Mrs Thatcher certainly was a soprano, rather a shrill one, in her early days as prime minister. Her image-makers, however, decided that she would sound more authoritative as a mezzo-soprano, so she was coached to lower her register. In her last years as PM she had almost turned herself into an alto.

us some of the keyboard instruments in the collection downstairs and, in almost total darkness, gave an impromptu improvisation on a clavichord (the softest, most intimate keyboard instrument from J. S. Bach's time), with his guests crowded attentively around. It was a magical moment, for it took only the smallest imaginative leap to feel, in the darkness, that we had stepped back into the eighteenth century, perhaps to gather round Johann Sebastian Bach himself as he played for his children.

When I went across to Amsterdam to see Mr Leonhardt (when needing answers faster than the old-fashioned post could cope with) I would, whenever possible, also call on another Amsterdam resident, Frans Brüggen. Working with Frans was one of the great musical experiences in those early OAE years.

The first time that Frans joined OAE he had conducted Beethoven's *Eroica* symphony. I was still playing in the orchestra in those days and it was an extraordinary experience for everyone, especially, perhaps, for those amongst us who had experience of ordinary, as opposed to period instrument, orchestras for whom the *Eroica* was such standard repertoire. With Frans we discovered it afresh, partly because of his total commitment and understanding of the work but also because, using our early nineteenth century (or in some cases eighteenth century) instruments we discovered that the work is at the very limit of what these instruments can do; and somehow the sheer difficulty made it an enormously intense experience. The concerts were a huge success, and when that success was so hard-earned it felt like an even greater triumph.

Brüggen's extraordinary gift was to conduct Beethoven as though the music had been written only yesterday. And it brought to mind, for me, the shattering impact this music had had when it really was new, described with characteristically vivid drama by the composer Hector Berlioz, in his diary. Berlioz was at the time still a student at the Paris Conservatoire where all the Beethoven symphonies were then receiving their Paris premières in the celebrated Conservatoire concert series. "In an artist's life," Berlioz writes, "one thunderclap sometimes follows swiftly on another, as in those outsize storms in which the clouds, charged to bursting with electric energy, seem to be hurling the lightning back and forth and blowing the whirlwind. I had just had successive revelations of Shakespeare and Weber. Now at another point on the horizon I saw the giant form of Beethoven rear up. The shock was almost as great as that of Shakespeare had been. Beethoven opened before me a new world of music, as Shakespeare had revealed a new universe of poetry."[63]

Berlioz was determined to share his discovery of Beethoven with his own composition teacher at the Conservatoire, Jean-Francois Lesueur.[64] In truth, Berlioz had a low opinion of Lesueur, finding him a rather conventional and formulaic composer who should be challenged by exposure to the force of nature which was Beethoven, "In this connection…Lesueur, an honest man without envy in his nature and devoted to his art, but the prisoner of musical dogma which I must be allowed to describe as sheer delusion, let slip a significant remark…confronted with the immense enthusiasm of musicians in general and of me in particular, he shut his ears and carefully avoided the Conservatoire concerts. To have gone would have meant committing himself to a personal opinion of Beethoven; it would have meant being physically involved in the tremendous excitement which Beethoven aroused. This was just what Lesueur, without admitting it, did not wish to happen. However, I kept on at him, solemnly pointing out that when something as important as this occurred in our art—a completely new style on an unprecedented scale—it was his duty to find out about it and judge for himself; and in the end he yielded and let himself be dragged to the Conservatoire one day when the C Minor Symphony[65] was being performed. He wanted to give it an unbiased hearing, without distractions of any kind, so he dismissed me and sat himself at the back of one of the ground-floor boxes, among people he did not know. When it was over I came down from the floor above, eager to know what effect this extraordinary work had had on him and what he thought of it."

"I found him in the corridor, striding along with flushed face. 'Well, master?'"

"'Ouf! Let me get out. I must have some air! It's amazing! Wonderful! I was so moved and disturbed that when I emerged from the box and attempted to put on my hat, I couldn't find my head. Now please leave me be. We'll meet tomorrow.'"

"I was triumphant. The next day I hurried round to see him. The conversation at once turned to the masterpiece which had stirred us so profoundly. Lesueur let

---

[63] 'The Memoirs of Berlioz' translated by David Cairns
[64] Jean-François Lesueur (1760 – 1837), professor of composition at the Paris Conservatoire from 1818.
[65] Beethoven Symphony no. 5 in C minor.

me talk for some time, assenting in a rather constrained manner to my exclamations of enthusiasm. But it was easy to see that my companion was no longer the man who had spoken to me the day before, and that he found the subject painful. I persisted, however, until I had from him a further acknowledgement of how deeply Beethoven's symphony had moved him; at which he suddenly shook his head and smiled in a curious way and said, 'All the same, music like that ought not to be written.'"

The Beethoven experience, and the response of the Paris music establishment to it, was a turning point for Berlioz and, later in the diary, he records with a characteristic flourish, "Lesueur's dogged refusal to accept the evidence of his senses finally convinced me of the hollowness of the theories he had been striving to instil in me; and from that moment I abandoned the old high road and made my own way across country, over hills and valleys and through woods and fields."

It was probably one of Frans Brüggen's *Eroica* concerts which persuaded John Drummond, then director of the Proms, to abandon the old high road and invite us (OAE with Brüggen) to perform Beethoven's Ninth Symphony, the famous Choral Symphony, on the penultimate night of the Proms (Henry Wood always programmed Beethoven 9 on the night before the last night extravaganza, so this had become an important Proms tradition). This invitation was a huge feather in the cap for a still young orchestra, and just the kind of establishment endorsement we needed. Of course, for the 9th Symphony we had to expand our numbers enormously, and especially so as to cope with the sheer scale of the 5,000-seat Royal Albert Hall. Our orchestra and chorus together numbered 160 people.

A Brüggen Beethoven 9 was itself a rare and important musical event and, despite its size and expense, I sold it to a number of European promoters, one of which was the Théâtre de la Monnaie in Brussels. In those pre-Eurostar days the logistics of transporting a group of 160 musicians to Brussels and back within a 24-hour period was itself a challenge and I did something which was, for us at that time, a rare step: I chartered a plane. We flew from Stansted one Saturday morning, gave a fine concert that evening and returned at a leisurely mid-morning hour on Sunday. Brussels airport seemed strangely festive that morning, with flags and bunting much in evidence, and it turned out that they were opening a new terminal that very day, presumably choosing a Sunday as the quietest day of the week. The departure of our little flight coincided with the opening ceremony and consequent celebrations. Our group, needless to say, shared in the festive spirit, encouraged by the champagne service on our aeroplane (we were of course the only passengers, so I had been able to add this little celebratory flourish into our charter contract), and we reached Stansted in good humour. As our happy group gathered in the baggage hall, there was an announcement inviting Mr Warnock to identify himself, and within moments I found myself being escorted back airside where our plane's pilot was waiting, looking troubled. He greeted me with, "Mr Warnock, I owe you an apology. We've left your luggage in Brussels." I was puzzled, of course. How could they know that my bag was missing when our luggage had not yet even been unloaded from the plane which I could see was sitting unattended on the tarmac. So, "How do you know that it is my bag?" I asked.

"No, you don't understand, it's not just yours. We've left all the baggage in Brussels."

I was astounded. How could such a thing happen? The story gradually began to emerge. On any passenger flight there are two things which require personal visual checks by the flight captain: one is that the fuel tanks have been correctly filled and the other is a visual inspection that any cargo is properly distributed and secured in the hold. Our pilot confessed that he was facing a suspension of his licence because he had failed to carry out the visual check of our bags, instead accepting assurances from the senior Brussels baggage handler that all was well. With hindsight I suppose this gentleman (if such he was) had been partying with the rest of the ground staff. The pilot then continued his story: during take-off the autopilot setting was indicating that the plane was too light and he and his co-pilot had concluded that there must be an instrument malfunction. So they switched the autopilot off and had flown the plane home manually. He was distraught…although, it seemed to me, a good deal less because of the loss of his entire cargo of luggage than because of the likely disciplinary consequences to himself. His problems were of course not mine. I had 160 musicians at Stansted at lunchtime on a Sunday who needed to be re-united with their bags (and in the case of the double basses, with their instruments). My first thought was that the plane should simply turn round and fly back to Brussels but unfortunately this wasn't possible, and it was becoming clear that there was actually no way that the missing luggage could be brought to Stansted that day…there were too few flights and too little spare capacity in those that there were. Very soon, for the troops were growing restive, I had to break the baleful news that they would have to return home without luggage and that I would let them know when I had further information. It was amazing how many people had problems with this…an absurdly high number had packed either their car keys or their house keys in their suitcases, but it was our timpanist and double bassists who had come off worst of all, for they had lost their instruments and all, it emerged, had engagements the next day. I had to leave people to solve their own, mostly self-inflicted, problems and try to establish the fate of our bags and missing instruments. I eventually left Stansted, some hours later, having located the missing cargo in Brussels (grateful, at least, that it hadn't all been dispatched to Hong Kong or some such alternative destination) and arranged for it to arrive on various scheduled British Airways flights (at considerable cost to our charter company of course) to different airports over a time period determined by the extent of spare capacity on these flights. Because I could not be certain that all the lost cases carried the home addresses of their owners it was decided that everything should be delivered as it arrived to the orchestra's office, located at that time at an address in London's Soho district.[66] So, on my return to London and after the briefest appearance at home, I settled in the office for an indefinite stay, to take delivery of assorted suitcases, calling the musicians to collect their property as it arrived and was identified. As matters turned out it was another great party…and probably the longest weekend of my life, stretching from Sunday afternoon until sometime around Tuesday lunchtime, but a regular parade of (mostly) sympathetic musicians, often armed with a consoling bottle, did much to alleviate the strain.

---

[66] I have fond memories of that little office in St Anne's Villas, Soho: the building was one of a short terrace of early nineteenth century 'cottages', a rare survival from an earlier age, surrounded by modern offices and other commercial enterprises, some of dubious repute, from subsequent times. The tenancy of the building had been donated as a form of sponsorship, the only drawback being that it was registered for domestic, as opposed to business use. That it had previously been occupied as a private residence I discovered when I came across a clipping from The Evening Standard, used as lining paper for a desk draw. The previous tenant had reportedly kept a pet tiger which he was in the habit of exercising, during the hours of darkness, in Soho Square. The beast's owner had, it seemed, disappeared in mysterious and still unexplained circumstances, abandoning everything including his bizarre pet which had been discovered, according to the 'Standard' story, by a visiting electricity meter reader who, descending in the dark into the property's basement, had been confronted by a starving tiger, somewhat enlivened at the prospect of its next meal.

And as for the hapless pilot, he was indeed suspended for several weeks, but a few weeks later the importance of the visual check regulation was brought home when another plane, flying from Bilbao to Exeter airport, crashed a few miles short of its destination, apparently having run out of fuel. The accident enquiry eventually established that it had left Bilbao with only half the fuel on board that it should have had, and that the pilot had failed to carry out his visual check. Had our pilot checked his fuel, I wondered?

~~~

Another of the conductors to re-appear regularly following that nail-bitingly seat-of-the-pants series of Haydn Masses was Mark Elder. Elder did not bring the kind of total immersion in the music of earlier times as Brüggen or Leonhardt offered, but his enthusiasm, bravery and technical skill in tackling repertoire of which others might not see the value opened up another strand of programming with long-term implications for the development of the orchestra: unusual operas in concert performance. A case in point was Giacomo Rossini's *Ermione*. It was rather late in the year 1991 that I realised that the following year was the bicentenary of the birth of Rossini. Startled at having failed to spot this potentially useful programming 'peg', I did a little research into what others were doing to mark the Rossini anniversary and was surprised to find that it was being allowed to pass almost unnoticed. Was there an opportunity here? And if so, what to choose? My thought was to find an unusual scene to extract from one of the operas (there is almost no purely orchestral music by Rossini) to make the second half of one our Queen Elizabeth Hall concerts.

Enquiries soon led me to a leading Rossini scholar, a Canadian musicologist, Philip Gossett. I found his phone number in Toronto and called him one afternoon. He was in the midst of shaving and apparently had to be out of his apartment in five minutes, so I had time to ask just one question: what is the best act from any Rossini opera which could be suitable for concert performance. Philip didn't hesitate, "Act II of *Ermione*, no question." I was rather stunned, mainly because I had never even heard of the opera let alone heard it.

Ermione, it turned out, was one of Rossini's relatively neglected *opera seria*. It had been a failure when first staged (in Naples) and had had only two revivals, both fairly recent, one at the Pesaro Rossini festival and the other in the beautiful Teatro Real in Buenos Aires. Fortunately for me, the Pesaro performance had been recorded and within a few days of my Canadian phone call I had the CD. Listening to the work for the first time was unforgettable: the opera is a Greek tragedy and the music totally extraordinary, incredibly hard for the singers and with a major role, as befits a Greek tragedy, for the chorus (which even sings during the overture). Another unusual thing about the work is that it is surprisingly short (by operatic standards), with less than two hours of music, and I decided there and then that we must do the whole piece. In truth I thought Act I more immediately appealing than the Act II which had so excited Philip Gossett. It had the most terrific (or perhaps I mean terrifying) arias for three high Rossini tenors and for Ermione, while Act II was more of an ensemble piece (hence Gossett's recommendation for concert performance), including the operatically unusual feature that Ermione herself is on stage throughout the act.

As for casting, it was obvious that there would be only a handful of singers in the world who knew this work, so tracking down the Pesaro cast was the sensible starting point. I was very lucky to find that the intensely dramatic young soprano Ana-Caterina Antonacci, who had sung the title role, was available for a few dates in 1992. Not only so, she was thrilled to sing the role again[67] and had never, at that point, sung in England, so it was inevitable that we should build everything around the dates she could offer. At this point I took the idea to Mark Elder who was then the music director at English National Opera. He did not know *Ermione* either and, despite my own confidence, it was a great relief when he expressed his excitement at the discovery. With Mark's enthusiastic support we pressed on, and had the good fortune to find that two of the three tenors from the Pesaro cast were also available; and what tenors they were: the American, Bruce Ford, agreed to sing the technically fearsome role of *Pirro*, while the almost equally challenging *Oreste* would be sung by Keith Lewis. These were two of the world's leading Rossini tenors at the time, so, with Antonacci already on board, we had a powerful cast.

In the forefront of my mind, at this time, was to find a logical continuation of Simon Rattle's Mozart opera series at Glyndebourne. So, I justified (to my own satisfaction at least) the enormous cost of assembling this international cast to give just two performances, by thinking of it as an investment to persuade the Glydebourne management team to engage the OAE in this kind of repertoire. Nineteenth-century *bel canto* opera was very much new territory so far as period

---

[67] I met her some years later by chance in a café in Amsterdam; when I reminded her of our *Ermione*, she described it as her 'death role'.

instruments were concerned so, as often seemed to be the case, we were taking big risks. The most scary of these (leaving aside the eye-watering cost of the venture) was the possibility that one of our star singers would be ill when the concert days arrived. Since this was virtually unknown repertoire, and ridiculously hard to sing even with plenty of learning time, the chance of finding a replacement singer on the day would be zero, so this was an exceedingly high wire with no safety net. I did take the precaution of identifying the cast from the Buenos Aires performance (which included two US-domiciled Vietnamese tenors) and I let them know the dates of our performances, but I couldn't afford the luxury of paying them to be on standby, and certainly not to fly them across the Atlantic on the off-chance that we might need them. Despite this ever-present risk of catastrophe I invited the Glyndebourne team to attend our concert and was thrilled when the General Director, the Casting Director and the Music Director all accepted the invitation.

The concert performances were amongst the highlights of my time with OAE. Mark Elder brilliantly conveyed his enthusiasm to the entire company and, despite cruelly little (for such an unknown work) rehearsal time, everyone rose to the occasion. It was the start of an important relationship with Elder, who went on to do other unfairly neglected operas[68], so it was with bitter disappointment that I discovered, only a year later, that Glyndebourne were to stage *Ermione* in the following season with Andrew Davis (who had come to our concert) and the London Philharmonic Orchestra; not only so, but they had Antonacci and Bruce Ford in their cast. Although this was a bitter pill, it was sweetened somewhat by Glyndebourne's offer of baroque opera to OAE. So whether or not it was by way of apology, the orchestra did emerge with a continuation of the Glyndebourne projects.

Now, 25 years after the *Ermione* adventure, I see that there was a kind of nerveless self-confidence about it which becomes more difficult to sustain with every year of additional experience. I am not sure if I would be brave enough to take the same risks today, and wonder if, to borrow the title of John Drummond's entertaining autobiography, I have been 'tainted by experience.'[69]

---

[68] His next project was Weber's *Euryanthe* which is neglected by opera houses because it is so impossible to stage (too many magical transformations) but for which the music is simply wonderful.

[69] The circumstances in which this accusation was levelled at Drummond were in truth very different: while Head of Radio 3, Drummond learned that his masters at the BBC

My departure from the Orchestra of the Age of Enlightenment was painful to me personally, but the reason I find it hard to write about, even after so many years, is not the hurt to my vanity (although this was undeniable) but because the Board's reasons for tipping me out of the managerial chair were never fully explained. My problems came to a head in 1993: our previous three summers had revolved around the Glyndebourne Mozart operas with Rattle, which always happened in the school holidays, but this year, 1993, there was to be no Glyndebourne season at all for the first time since the 1930s, to allow for the building, in rapid time, of the exceptional new, Michael Hopkins designed, opera house. Julie and I (with the three children of course) decided to take advantage of this once-only freedom during the summer holiday period to make a three-week visit to her family who were distributed along the west coast of America from Seattle (or rather Orcas Island where Julie had spent her childhood summers) down through Oregon.

My relationship with the OAE Board had been difficult since, at least, the start of the year, in part because I had become convinced that some of the high principles with which OAE had started now needed to be leavened with a dose of pragmatism. The particular issue was the question of membership of the orchestra: as mentioned earlier, the original decision had been to have a rotating membership which meant, as applied to the wind and brass sections, that we had co-principals who were supposed to divide the available work between them (with my role as manager being a kind of moderator and, ultimately, judge in the event of non-agreement between parties). I had a long-held rule of thumb that no orchestra can ever achieve greatness without certain key positions being occupied by top class players; in particular the first oboe and first horn (and of course orchestra leader) are the most vital positions, and the sharing arrangement between our two first oboes was simply not working often enough for me to feel truly secure in this department. The reason was not that our two principal players were not good enough, nor that they were unable to reach agreements about who did what (although this was sometimes the case); no, the trouble was that all too often neither was available and neither was willing to prioritise OAE

---

were undertaking a review of Radio 3 to which he had not been invited to contribute. When he complained (vigorously) he received a memo explaining that, as Radio 3's director his views would be considered "tainted by experience"!

engagements over their other work: Paul Goodwin was an indispensable member of, and frequent soloist with, The English Concert, while Tony Robson was the regular oboist with John Eliot Gardiner's orchestras and was afraid, and with good reason, that he might lose this position if he was not always available for them. Our position was also weakened by the fact that there were no other strong candidates for this most essential position in the orchestra. This situation was beginning to compromise quality; too often we were undertaking important engagements with guest oboists who were not really on top of the job and I felt that this simply could not continue. My analysis of the problem was undeniably correct, but the solution was mishandled: in discussion with Tony Robson it became clear that the only basis on which he could abandon his John Eliot Gardiner position was if he were to be offered all the OAE oboe work. Otherwise he would simply not earn enough. And he was willing to commit, subject to this condition. Paul Goodwin, by contrast, made no secret that he had a much greater ambition as a soloist and conductor, and it was obvious that he would continue to give these roles priority over orchestral commitments. He had, in fact, only appeared twice with the orchestra in the previous twelve months. My discussions with Robson had had to be conducted in some secrecy because we did not want to jeopardise his current work in the event that we failed to come up with a position for him. And I had to know that he would accept if I was to sacrifice the OAE's democratic principles in this case and to absorb the resultant flak. While these negotiations were continuing I had felt unable to take Goodwin into my confidence because premature publicity could have been fatal for a successful agreement, but I should have sought some way to secure his agreement to the proposed change before implementing it. In due course, though, Robson became the first exception to the co-principal policy in circumstances which appeared to have been, and indeed were, the result of whisperings in corners rather than properly open discussion. The unfortunate outcome was that, during my extended absence in the USA, Goodwin started a campaign against this decision, characterising it as a conspiracy to oust him, which clearly achieved some traction with the Board who duly added it to their growing charge sheet against my name. This 'charge sheet' was in truth never revealed to me but the general sense was, I believe, that I was showing insufficient respect for the orchestra's governance and procedures.

 Another misunderstanding concerned a role which I had inadvisedly, but almost accidentally, taken on as Head of Early Music at the Royal Academy of

Music (RAM). I had a call one day from Sir David Lumsden, then Principal of the RAM, whom I had known slightly from his days as organist of New College, Oxford. He invited me to visit him in his RAM office and our discussion was extraordinarily frank, mainly because, as he told me at the outset, he was retiring the very next day. He went on to say that his greatest regret was that he had failed successfully to bring 'early music' and period instrument performance into the regular life of the Academy, and, in short, he asked if I would 'take on' the early music department on a part-time basis. Lumsden's vision was grand (though there was scarcely time for it to be fully articulated): the big prize, now long forgotten, was that the Higher Education Funding Council (HEFC), which holds the purse-strings for all higher education institutions, was actively pushing for a merger of the RAM with the Royal College of Music. Neither, it was felt, had the scale as a stand-alone institution to achieve the kind of critical mass which would enable them to compete internationally. A merged single institution would bring significant economies of scale. This was certainly true of the two institutions' early music departments, neither of which had sufficient student numbers to offer the kind of practical and academic training which was available at, say, the Utrecht conservatoire which was specifically focused on early music. Lumsden's motive for talking to me about this was to raise the possibility that the Orchestra of the Age of Enlightenment might become an integral part of the newly merged departments: the principal players would take on the one-to-one teaching, and they could also begin to develop student orchestras and chamber music coaching which the step change in numbers would for the first time allow. HEFC was offering a significant one-off financial bonus, as well as ongoing improved funding support, to oil the wheels for the proposed merger. The tantalising prospect was that an OAE collaboration with a new conservatoire, running alongside the orchestra's residencies at the South Bank Centre and, in summer time, at Glyndebourne, would give the orchestra a permanence, an established status, which, in due course, could become the basis for seeking annual Arts Council core funding on a par with existing Arts Council clients such as the London Symphony Orchestra, the Philharmonia and others. This seemed a tremendous opportunity, and I left the principal's office that day having, totally out of the blue, been appointed Head of Early Music with a one-day-a-week commitment to help deliver the vision.

Needless to say, the reality was substantially at odds with the vision: following Lumsden's retirement there was no one to steer his bold plan through the institutional bureaucratic maze, and it quickly became clear that the enthusiasm of the RCM was lukewarm at best. Soon, too, there were drastic cuts in the HEFC's own funding which meant that they would be unable to deliver the carrot of an improved financial settlement which had undoubtedly been the main driver for the project. Meanwhile, as the prospects of actually landing the prize of an exclusive relationship with a completely new educational institution rapidly receded, the OAE board took my day-a-week absence simply as a sign of lack of commitment to my 'day job'.

On our return from our long-awaited US holiday I felt as a third-world dictator must feel when he has rashly left his country briefly, only to return to find a coup in full swing. The very next day following our return, a Board meeting had been arranged at which I was asked to resign as Chief Executive and was offered a part-time position as Artistic Adviser, a completely new position. It was obvious that the Board had taken the opportunity of my three-week absence to prepare their position quite carefully and, for my part, I was quite unprepared and also somewhat jet-lagged. I tried to argue my case, but it was soon clear that a decision had been taken and the Board, marshalled by the non-playing members and led by Martin Smith, were not in listening mode. Eventually, because I could not afford to be completely unemployed I accepted the new position, and was soon to be found working alongside my successor, David Pickard. It is greatly to David's credit that he managed to make this strange partnership work (it was clearly at least as awkward for him as for me), but it did not alter the fact that it was time for me to seek employment elsewhere.

Chapter 6
Re-Inventing the English Concert

Moving to The English Concert in 1995 was a relief after six intense years with the Orchestra of the Age of Enlightenment. I had always admired Trevor Pinnock, its artistic director, but had only once played in his orchestra, and that on one of the very rare occasions when he was not at the helm,[70] so I knew less about it, really, than any of the other orchestras of its kind. Amongst the few things I did know was that The English Concert enjoyed a wonderful recording relationship with Deutsche Grammophon (DG) *Archiv* and that most of their schedule of work in the 1980s and 90s had been shaped to meet the record company's needs—the need to prepare the recording repertoire in concerts and the need to sell the records around the world through international touring. The English Concert was recording five or six CDs each year, so the cycle of preparation/studio recording/touring kept the orchestra's diary healthily full.

It seemed self-evident that this artistically secure operation needed no more than an invigorating injection of energy, especially in fundraising, to thrive: Pinnock, as artistic director, would be responsible for the programme planning and for personnel decisions, freeing the executive to focus on, well, executing. At the OAE, by contrast, the chief executive had to spend an inordinate amount of time on the cumbersome processes by which decisions on all artistic matters were laboriously, if democratically, reached, then take personal responsibility if criticism resulted. In truth, I had always believed (despite founding OAE on different principles) that a benevolent dictatorship was the most efficient form of government for an orchestra, and Trevor was certainly more benevolent than

---

[70] It was a recording of Handel op.7 organ concertos played, and directed, by Simon Preston.

the other orchestral owner/proprietors who, it must be said, did not set a high bar in this respect.

My complacency was to be exceedingly short-lived. The very first meeting in my role as the orchestra's new manager was with Roger Wright, then DG's head of A&R (Artists and Repertoire) who delivered a serious shock. DG had decided not to renew the recording contract, due to expire in twelve months' time. It was a brutal decision, although not without a certain logic: the strengths of this group had originally been in the mainstream late baroque repertoire, typically the music of Purcell, Corelli, Handel and Bach. Then, in the mid-1980s, Trevor Pinnock, with DG support, had taken on a New York-based classical-instrument orchestra with a view to recording all the Mozart symphonies with this US ensemble. When the New York enterprise acrimoniously failed, the recording contract was transferred back to The English Concert which rapidly had to transform itself from a baroque specialist ensemble into a classical chamber orchestra. The orchestral membership changed, with baroque specialists giving way to players with more solid orchestral experience, including a change of leader from Simon Standage to Peter Hanson. Now, with the completion of the Mozart project, The English Concert needed to decide whether to move, in repertoire terms, forward or back. Most of the competitor orchestras were embarking on a relentless march into later Classical and early Romantic repertoire: Beethoven cycles abounded, as did other new explorations (such as the epic Mackerras Mendelssohn and Schubert recordings referred to in the previous chapter). As for Deutsche Grammophon, Roger Wright did not think Pinnock the best conductor for nineteenth-century repertoire (he was, after all, first and foremost a harpsichordist) but neither did he want to re-record standard baroque repertoire already in the catalogue. This left choral music or lesser-known instrumental works, and for these the DG marketing men felt that they wanted to bring on some of the younger talent. The truth is that DG's decision to favour new ensembles was prompted by marketing concerns more than any artistic considerations, but whatever the rights and wrongs of the case, Trevor Pinnock found himself at an awkward crossroads: as a harpsichordist his instinct was to return to an earlier musical period, but he found himself (or rather his orchestra) curiously ill-equipped to do so, with a group of musicians around him who were less fluent in the seventeenth and eighteenth-century repertoire than those with whom he had started the long journey back in the early 1970s. As a result of this first meeting, I found that my second was a meeting at Trevor's kitchen table in which he proposed closing The English Concert. And all this, before I had even got my feet under my new desk.

Shocking though this was, it nevertheless felt strangely familiar to find myself in charge of an orchestra suffering from an existential crisis. The OAE had, up to this point, existed in a permanent state of financial insecurity in which every ambitious project might turn out to be its last, and the challenge had been to create a clear and sustainable identity after a frenetic start-up. With The English Concert the issue was almost the mirror image: how to create a new and exciting identity for an already-successful organisation in danger of being overtaken by younger competitors. One thing, though, the two orchestras did have in common: neither had any money.

We came to two conclusions while debating around the kitchen table which, when baldly recorded here, may seem blindingly obvious but which were nevertheless hard to address head-on. The first concerned people: Trevor had said, with characteristic honesty, that with his current group of players he could not confidently programme Bach's Brandenburg Concertos. These magnificent works should be at the very heart of the repertoire of a specialist baroque orchestra (or, put another way, it would be hard to call yourself a specialist baroque orchestra if you do not have the wherewithal to programme them), but they make great demands on the players' solo and chamber music skills in a number of key instrumental positions. For example, the first concerto is a violin concerto, the second has four soloists—violin, oboe, recorder and trumpet. The fourth concerto is another violin concerto with the addition of two solo recorders, number five is for solo flute and includes the famous harpsichord cadenza, while concerto number six has two solo violas and two violas da gamba. So we decided to set a target: we would programme all six Brandenburg Concertos in three years' time and would use the intervening years to make whatever new appointments were needed with this repertoire always in mind. If, after three years, Trevor was still not confident in his players' abilities in this repertoire the orchestra would be closed.

The second decision concerned short-term planning: the orchestral personnel changes would evolve over our three-year time frame, but we would in the meantime need to find some bold programming ideas to give a new sense of purpose. Once again I found myself in familiar territory: I had expected to have an artistic programme more or less imposed by artistic director and record company, yet here we were again staring at a blank piece of paper, trying to fill it with attractive programmes. My fear was that most of my best ideas had already been given to OAE (and Trevor's was that he would simply be repeating programme ideas from ten years earlier), but I did mention one project that had not yet seen the light of day, and was delighted to find that Trevor was enthusiastic: Haydn's *Philemon und Baucis* is an opera for puppets, and unsurprisingly is a great rarity, both in concerts and, even more so, on stage. We decided to stage it.

England has no tradition of marionettes beyond those ancient knockabout fairground characters, Punch and Judy. And although puppet theatre enjoyed a brief popularity during the Commonwealth interregnum in the mid-seventeenth-century (after the conventional theatres were closed by the Puritans) its ascendancy did not survive the resumption of normal theatrical service under the restored king, Charles II. Puppets thereafter had no real place in popular culture, at least until the televisual adventures of Sooty and Basil Brush and, more recently, the cinematic exploits of Wallace and Grommet and the political satire that was Spitting Image.

In Continental Europe, by contrast, marionettes have had a more continuous history: Aristotle describes their use in story-telling and, centuries later, the early Christians were using them in versions of morality plays designed to convert the ignorant heathen. Eventually, as these puppet representations became more ribald and scurrilous, they were banned by the Church, but this in turn had the unexpected consequence of stimulating the creation of the Italian *Commedia dell'Arte* (including Pulcinella, a prototype for Mr Punch), probably the earliest form of professional theatre.

Haydn's *Philemon* shows that the central European marionette tradition was alive and well in eighteenth-century Austria. The composer spent his best creative years in the service of Nikolaus Prince Esterhazy in Eisenstadt, to the east of Vienna, and the palace grounds included a marionette theatre for which, from the mid-1750s onwards, Haydn had to produce entertainments as part of his duties as court composer. Sadly, all of the music for the Eisenstadt puppets was destroyed in a fire in the nineteenth-century and the only works which now survive are those few which had been copied for performances in Vienna. *Philemon und Baucis* was one such and survives as a complete libretto and some incomplete orchestral parts.

So, when we began considering what needed to be done, the first issue was to complete the score by searching out music from other Haydn operas to fill the missing spaces where there were arias in the libretto but no original music. Adding alternative arias was a common enough practice in the eighteenth-century: for example, some of Mozart's most wonderful arias, now usually known as 'concert arias', were written either as 'insertion arias' to be added into works by other composers, or as substitute arias in his own operas, usually written when a particular star singer was engaged for whom the original arias were unsuitable in terms of vocal range or, commonly, not deemed by the diva to be sufficiently florid to show off his or her skills to best advantage[71].

The second issue with *Philemon*, overlapping with a third, was who could provide the puppets? And where could we perform a marionette opera? The fourth, and biggest question, from which I averted my gaze for the time being, was how much would it cost and how could we find the money?

Our plans eventually began to take shape following a meeting with Walter Reicher, director of the annual Haydn Festival in Eisenstadt, Haydn's home for most of his career. Dr Reicher's mission was to present in his Festival everything Haydn ever wrote, and *Philemon* had apparently been on his wish list for some time. So it was his enthusiasm (backed by a budget) which gave the project a real chance, even though by presenting the work in Austria we were adding considerably to the costs and the complexity. To describe *Philemon* simply as an opera for puppets, may give the impression that we are talking of a grand kind of Punch and Judy show. In reality, our puppets would need to be at least two-thirds human size, large enough to command attention on a crowded stage, as well as to be sufficiently visible from the back of a concert hall. The stage would inevitably be crowded because each puppet figure would be operated by its own on-stage puppeteer and each character in the opera would also be represented by a singer (naturally enough) and an actor (because the piece contained extensive dialogue). Thus, in *Philemon* each character would be represented by four different 'people' (the puppet itself, puppeteer, singer and actor), the stuff of nightmares for a director trying to make sense of the action to his audience. Happily, not all of the potential complexities were immediately obvious as we sat at Pinnock's kitchen table, and in any case the great thing about the project was that it changed the conversation from one of negativity, decline and possible

---

[71] These divas could be demanding: when the teenage Mozart first travelled to Milan for the première of *Mitridate, re di Ponte* no fewer than nine numbers had to be re-written at the insistence of the singers.

closure to an upbeat and positive plan. Such a plan was full of risks, as ever, but it was with a new sense of purpose that we set about it.

Pinnock's work on the restoration/completion of the music was a great example of his strengths. He has always been the most practical of musicians in the sense that his performance decisions are invariably driven by his instinctive feel for the demands of the music rather than by any slavish pursuit of academic correctness. He regarded any claims to 'authenticity' in performance with suspicion, recalling with approval, for example, how he had first been inspired, in the 1960s, by a fine recording of Telemann's Paris Quartets on which Gustav Leonhardt played an unhistorical Neupert harpsichord, while Frans Brüggen, Jaap Schröder and Anner Bylsma, all of whom were later at the cutting edge of the historical revival, all played on modern instruments. Also, as he sometimes reminded me (knowing that I had spent fifteen years as a member of the Academy of St Martin in the Fields), Brüggen and Leonhardt had appeared as concerto soloists with the modern-instrument Academy in the 1960s, a thoroughly hybrid musical experience.

During my time as a member of the Academy I had occasionally discussed the historical revival with Neville Marriner whose views were in fact surprisingly close to Pinnock's. Marriner regarded any claim to performance 'authenticity' with the deepest suspicion, but he did not dismiss the period instrument fashion (as he saw it) out of hand. On the whole, his view was that period instrument orchestras were to be admired for discovering a new (and commercial) performance idiom but that they would come to be seen in the same tradition as his Academy, that is to say innovators in terms of style, but not as the musical revolutionaries which they sometimes claimed to be. At first I rather dismissed Marriner's view, thinking that he was on the defensive, fearing that his beloved Academy was being made to look out-of-date. But over time I have become more open to his suggestion that our appreciation of performance styles is much more governed by fashion than we like to admit. For example, we are now completely accustomed to the convention that the string sections in orchestras must all use the same bowings, for to do otherwise would look chaotic and amateurish (as well as risking violinists crashing into each other in constricted spaces on stage); but it is, in truth, only relatively recently that such uniformity has been universally adopted. The great conductor Leopold Stokowski[72] insisted that his

---

[72] Leopold Stokowski (1882 – 1977), Polish-born British conductor most strongly associated with the Philadelphia Orchestra, and Disney's *Fantasia*.

string players should not bow in unison, and there is a review, written in about 1930, of a concert in the Free Trade Hall in Manchester by the visiting Berlin Philharmonic Orchestra, in which the author complains that his enjoyment of their playing was spoiled by the parade-ground unanimity of the bowing. According to this view, which now seems utterly bizarre, such rigid uniformity deprived the performance of expression and spontaneity.

It is deeply frustrating, of course, that we shall never see an eighteenth-century orchestra in real time, nor hear what it actually sounded like. The famous Mannheim orchestra, so much admired by the English traveller and musicologist Charles Burney in the 1770s, was generally agreed to have set new standards, but its celebrated qualities of refinement and discipline were by no means universal. Consider this management report, quoted by Neal Zaslaw,[73] of the orchestra at the *Opéra de Lyons* in 1786 listing some issues which were surely not unique to that city, "The leader has neither great intelligence nor an accurate style of performance; among the second violins one has no tone and another is incapable of improvement due to nonchalance and little intelligence; the first oboist, who is also the first flautist, takes it upon himself to be absent for the overture and often for the entr'actes; three players, including the principal cellist, never attend rehearsals, and the cellist attends only performances of opera and major ballets; the first bassoonist appears only when he likes his part, often staying away for a week at a time, and the second bassoonist follows his lead; and some members of the orchestra are in the habit of leaving after the overture in order to give lessons to their pupils."

Returning (with a sigh of relief) to the present day, the success of *Philemon und Baucis* proved something of a turning point in re-establishing self-belief, but Pinnock never lost sight of the goal we had set, back in 1996, to schedule the Brandenburg Concertos as a kind of viability test and, four years on, that moment arrived: a ten-concert US tour with programmes to include all six concertos. During the intervening four years by far the most significant personnel change was that the wonderfully engaging violinist Rachel Podger had taken over the leadership of the orchestra from Peter Hanson,[74] and this so revolutionised the

---

[73] In a small pamphlet entitled, 'Toward the revival of the classical orchestra.'

[74] Peter was an excellent orchestral leader but suffered from a curious inhibition and expressive deficit when cast as a soloist. He reminded me of the actor in *King Lear* who

level of performance, indeed the whole approach to the music, that other changes, which had seemed so necessary a few years before, could now be allowed to evolve more gently. Rachel's arrival in our little world also re-energised Pinnock to recapture his natural enthusiasm at the harpsichord which had been flagging in the absence of the exhilarating musical sparks which she so instinctively provided.

So we embarked on our US tour of the Brandenburg Concertos with great confidence and my pleasure at its success (and of course the consequential continued existence of The English Concert on our return to the UK) was only (and only briefly) marred by a little incident of which my vanity was the only casualty: one of the unusual (and for a cost-conscious manager irritating) characteristics of this great sequence of concertos is that each is scored for a different instrumentation, with the result that on a long tour there are some players who are seriously underemployed and consequently, in the view of this particular cost-conscious manager, excessively expensive: when on tour, freelance musicians of course have to be compensated for their inability to take on any other engagements, so must be paid on their free days as well as for the days when the concert requires their presence. On the Brandenburg tour, for example, the horn players are only called for in the first concerto, a trumpet only in the second, a second recorder only in the fourth and so on. Concerto no. 6 features two violas da gamba who do not figure in any of the other five, and our solution for this tour was to ask one of our two cellists to 'double' on gamba and to hire an American gamba player who would join us only when that work was on the programme (concerto no. 6 also calls for a cello, so we could not ask both cellists to double). Our choice of gamba player fell on Susanne Heinrich, a distinguished exponent of that rare instrument, and it was one of my first tasks on arrival in the US to meet her at the airport in New York (she was flying in from Canada) and deliver her to a rehearsal with my musicians who had themselves just arrived from England.

Once I had successfully identified her at the gate, I introduced myself and she immediately exclaimed, with pleasing enthusiasm, "You don't mean to say you are the Felix Warnock, the bassoonist?" and declared herself absolutely thrilled to meet me. Well, I must confess that my chest puffed ever so slightly

---

was described by a sharp-tongued critic as "playing the King as though afraid someone was about to play the ace."

out as I, with such false modesty as I could muster, admitted I was indeed one and the same. How fortunate, I thought, to be greeted with such generous enthusiasm by a colleague from the other side of the world who is so pleasingly well-informed and musically discriminating; what an excellent choice we had clearly made to invite so fine an artiste to join our little group…and so on for some time in a similarly vain vein, her evident delight in my company apparently undimmed. But it couldn't last. As we eventually departed the airport and settled comfortably into our waiting car, she explained that she had for years been retelling a story about me which had been recounted to her by an English musician, and she was now pleased to have the chance to confirm its truth. "The story goes," she said, "that you were once stopped by the police while driving a group of musicians home after a concert. Your car evidently suffered from numerous defects and, after listing them all, the police officer asked if you had anything to say.

"To which you answered, 'I think I should say it after you've gone.'" Such was the origin of my transatlantic fame. I was downcast. Years of toil in the orchestral trenches counted for nothing against an off-the-cuff remark which had, in a pre-internet age, somehow gone viral. Actually I remember the occasion quite clearly. I was at that time the not-especially-proud owner of a 20-year-old Morris Minor (according to its log book the car had rolled off the production line in April 1952, just as I had done in January the same year) which was heavily over-loaded just then with four passengers in addition to myself as the driver, plus their instruments and cases of concert clothes. The result was that my poor little Morris was proving unequal to the task of climbing the long hill just beyond Henley, an unavoidable obstacle on the drive from Oxford back to London in those pre-motorway days. My rather tetchy reaction to the policeman's surprisingly polite cataloguing of my car's mechanical defects arose more from anxiety about whether we would make it to the top than from any pangs of conscience about the undeniably parlous state of our lights and tyres. And the finger of suspicion, in terms of who might have told this tale, points not to an English musician, but to an amiable Scot, Steve Tees, whose ample frame was weighing heavily on the back seat of the Morris and whom I therefore blame not only for telling the tale but also, at least to some extent, for being the cause of the original laboured hill-climb.

As has been noted in a previous chapter, the Americans are always reliably generous hosts to visiting musicians, and we had numerous post-concert receptions on our Brandenburg tour. One conspicuous difference between this and earlier US tours was that my role had changed. I was no longer amongst the 'other ranks', looking for free drinks and the avoidance of the intense attentions of the post-concert gripper (see Chapter 1), but was now a grown-up, responsible for the behaviour of my younger charges and, based on my own experience, nervously aware of the dangers. Musicians on tour can be something of liability—when on stage, of course, they can't so much as open their mouths, but when they do get a chance to speak they sometimes appear to feel there is some catching up to do.

An illustration of the dangers was provided by the BBC Symphony Orchestra which employed, for a time, a percussionist blessed with the splendidly percussive name of Kettle (although he did not, in my time at any rate, play the kettle drums), who was noted for his often dramatic and invariably inappropriate interventions. A memorable instance occurred when the self-important wife of one of the orchestra's sponsors, seeking to assert her superiority over the humble orchestral artisans with whom she was obliged to engage in social discourse, observed in condescending tones, "My husband's in oil, y'know." Whereupon fate intervened, the large reception room suddenly falling momentarily quiet, just long enough for Kettle's unforgettable riposte to echo startlingly in the still silence, "My God, she's married a sardine."

The conversation-stopping boot was on the other foot when one of my occasional charges, tired of constantly being asked, on such meet-the-musicians occasions, what he did in his day job, would routinely answer, delivered as a throwaway line, that he was a brain surgeon. This would usually have the desired effect until the day when his interlocutor, far from being non-plussed, exclaimed, "Good heavens, so am I. Where do you practice?" Not so much a conversation stopper as a conversational knock-out.

And the selfless spirit of social engagement which makes the company of orchestral musicians so enriching does not always shine through when more selfish gratifications are more immediately available: a bassoonist colleague, at one of these post-concert receptions, was spotted stuffing himself with strawberries; and when I say stuffing, he was not simply eating them, he was none-too-furtively filling his coat pockets until they bulged conspicuously on both sides. A public-spirited colleague took matters in hand in a novel way by hailing our frugivorous pilferer as though greeting a long-lost friend, first by clapping him heartily on the back, then, as though to re-emphasise his enthusiasm, gripping him firmly with both hands at the waist, and squeezing. Overripe pockets oozed unattractively, in due course giving every appearance of blood on the carpet.

A similarly distressing inclination towards selfishness may also occasionally be expressed in writing: a noticeboard near the stage door of the Royal Festival Hall was for a time requisitioned by the local authority (the old GLC) for the display of earnest 'public awareness' posters. One such, addressing the risk of flooding, consisted of a map of London under the headline, "What would you do if London flooded tomorrow?" beneath which a helpful colleague had written the single word 'breaststroke'.

~~~

Returning to Europe from the American tour, and happily still in employment, the next big project was a European tour of Bach's great masterpiece, *St Matthew Passion*. At the heart of the tour was a pair of concerts in Spain, or more particularly, Barcelona. The Barcelona deal had been clinched by my long-standing friendship with Maricarmen Palma, the circumstances of which require a short historical detour: Maricarmen, when I first knew her, was running a small concert agency, Trio Concerts, based in Barcelona promoting overseas chamber music groups around the Catalan region. She it was who had first introduced us (us in this case being the Albion Ensemble) to the wonderful artistic programme sponsored by the biggest regional bank, the Caixa de Barcelona, and she herself, in a kind of poacher turned gamekeeper move, was now running the bank's extensive musical programme.

In the Albion days, we would make an annual trip to Barcelona, playing mainly children's concerts. These visits usually involved establishing a base in the city for ten days or so whence we would travel to all parts of the region, playing three one-hour-long schools concerts per day (with accompanying scripted commentary delivered in Catalan by a local teacher). This daily routine would usually finish in early afternoon. Given that we had most evenings free to explore Barcelona's nightlife, especially its restaurants, and that our schools routine would begin again with early starts next morning, our Barcelona lifestyle was a serious test of stamina.[75]

Following Maricarmen's elevation from concert agent to central player in the bank's huge sponsorship programme, one of her great projects was an annual community Messiah: absolutely not a 'scratch', turn-up-and-sing Messiah as sometimes happens here in the UK. No, for the Barcelona Messiah Maricarmen hired a professional orchestra, soloists and chorus. The choral forces were expanded to include four local amateur choirs plus, and this was the unique feature, up to two hundred additional volunteers for whom the only selection criterion was that they should have previously done no choral singing (or none since childhood). This army of novices was recruited via advertisements in the local press during the summer months and those selected, by interview and audition (which must have been a nerve-shredding experience for non-singers), were required to commit to a remarkable and arduous twelve weekends of training before rehearsals of the complete work with the professional forces even began. The choruses in the Messiah score were divided into three, with the quiet ones to be sung by the professional singers alone, the moderately large by the professionals plus the four amateur choirs. Only the five or six largest choruses (including the Hallelujah Chorus, of course) were sung by the massed ranks. The performances, when they eventually arrived in December, were electrifying, with at least five hundred performers filling the stage and side galleries of this most fabulous of concert halls, and an audience consisting largely, or so it

---

[75] My own stamina was sorely tested when I returned from one of our debilitating ten-day trips in Barcelona on an early flight in order to go directly from Heathrow to the Abbey Road recording studio. The Academy of St Martin in the Fields was engaged in recording the music for the film *Amadeus*, and we had reached the moment in the movie when Mozart's ageing rival Salieri enters a room in the Hofburg in which is being played the sublime slow movement of the Serenade for 13 Wind Instruments. Any bassoon player will tell you that this long movement is a trial of strength for the bassoons, especially the second bassoon, who has to play continuously from the start until the finish in an endless long legato line without any real pause for breath. In those days, the early days of the new digital recording era, producers were very reluctant to make edits (the editing technology being both somewhat primitive and costly), so the solution was to do nothing but complete takes. We thus played the slow movement from start to finish over and over again for something like three hours, and I can only describe this as a near-death experience which I recall, without pleasure, whenever I hear the (admittedly sublime) sequence in the film.

seemed, of the enthusiastic friends and relations of the two hundred volunteers. All of this was funded entirely by the bank and administered by Maricarmen and her team. Maricarmen herself was a fiery character, one of those who saw the world in black and white; you were either her greatest friend or her bitterest enemy, and I am sad to say that I moved, during the course of a few days, from being amongst the former to a position amongst the latter (admittedly numerous) group.

The English Concert and Trevor Pinnock had twice been engaged for the great Messiah project and our position in Maricarmen's firmament was sufficiently high for her to have invited us to give two performances of J.S. Bach's majestic St Matthew Passion, and, importantly in the context of this story, at a majestic fee. These concerts were at the heart of a tour which comprised two performances in France, three in Spain (the two for Maricarmen in Palma, Majorca and Barcelona plus one for a different presenter in Valencia) and a concert in Munich on the way home. We were to fly to Barcelona from Paris on a Saturday, travel to Majorca on Sunday morning, with a performance there that evening. On Monday, we would return to Barcelona to rehearse with the massed choirs, play the concert on Tuesday, drive to Valencia for their concert the next day, and finally take a flight to Munich on Thursday with a concert that same evening. This was a tough but workable schedule: the main difficulty was that some of the solo singers were reluctant to sing on two successive nights, because of the length of the work, and especially so if there was travel on the concert day, but they had all eventually accepted that the financial reality of touring meant that a schedule which included three successive concerts (Barcelona, Valencia, Munich) could reluctantly be tolerated as these were the final three days of the tour and involved only one flight. So, finally all was arranged, with flights and hotels booked accordingly, when I took a call from Maricarmen in which she told me, with some pride, that she had organised an extra concert for the Wednesday in Andorra, the mountaintop mini-state on the French/Spanish border. This was, of course, the day of our concert in Valencia and Maricarmen was not pleased to be told that it was impossible (she seemed to blame me for not telling her that we had concerts after our Barcelona performance), so I promised, without serious hope of success, to enquire in Valencia and Munich if they might change their concert dates. Unsurprisingly both promoters were having none of it, so I had to break the bad news. This time Maricarmen seemed to accept it with better grace, so I was able to breathe a sigh of relief. But some days later she was on the phone again to tell me that she had re-arranged the extra Andorra concert for the 'free' Monday, the day between the Majorca and Barcelona concerts. This may have felt to her like a neat solution but even the most cursory examination of the timings and logistics showed that it was practically impossible, on top of which it seemed quite likely that it would kill my singers stone dead. I had already had some difficulty persuading them to sing on three successive nights, and I was now being told that we had not three but five successive performances (starting in Majorca on the Sunday, and finishing in Munich the following Thursday) in four different countries. However, no situation is so bad that it cannot get worse, and further research revealed that the starting time for the Majorca performance was 9.00 p.m.[76] St Matthew Passion is a three-hour-plus work so my arithmetic suggested that the concert in Majorca would finish sometime after midnight and the check-in time for flight back to Barcelona was 5.30 a.m. (for a 6.30 flight), to be followed by a long and vertiginous coach trip into the mountains north of Catalonia.

This was so clearly an impossible schedule that at first I was confident that common sense must prevail. But it became clear that Maricarmen had already committed to the Andorra adventure and was implacable. Perhaps she was still cross with me for rejecting her previous plan. At any rate, my protests became ever more desperate and the conversation more heated and, at last, Maricarmen delivered her final threat, that if I did not agree she would cancel everything. This was horrible: the cancellation of the middle section of our tour would be a financial disaster (not only were the Barcelona fees subsidising the French and German performances but cancellation would leave a gaping hole mid-tour for which my costs would remain substantially unchanged, but now without income). In short I was faced with calling off the whole tour even though the other, non-Barcelona concerts were already contracted. Our musicians were contracted, too, so that, even if the concerts did not happen, we would be obliged to compensate them for cancellation at such short notice. As for the aggrieved promoters in France, Germany and Valencia, they would at least have grounds to launch actions for breach of contract. To cut a long story short, I caved in and, with a mixture of shame and fear, agreed to Maricarmen's crazy plan. How I

---

[76] Concerts in Spain start notoriously late, most notably in Santander where they begin at 11.00 p.m. There was one occasion in the Santander Festival when we had not yet completed Part 1 of Messiah when the town clock struck midnight, and we had a 5.30 a.m. departure the following (or rather, that same) morning.

persuaded my singers to co-operate I can't now remember but heroically agree they eventually did. Sometimes, of course, such stories have happy endings in which the plucky artists pull bravely together, snatching victory from the jaws of defeat and so on, but sadly not so this time. Our very experienced but rather highly strung Evangelist, who has the crucial role as narrator of the biblical story, was the first casualty. The poor man was sick on the twisting climb by bus to Andorra, and he was not alone for long. Some of our choir had not seen their beds the previous night—faced with a 1.00 a.m. return to the hotel after the previous night's concert and a 5.00 a.m. wake-up call for departure to the island airport some had thought bed scarcely worthwhile—so casualties mounted inexorably as we made for the hills. To give our Evangelist credit, he did attempt the first half of the concert but, come halfway, he clearly could not continue. We had, with reasonable foresight, designated one of the chorus as an understudy for just such an eventuality, but I regret that, being one of the up-all-nighters, our replacement did not shine in Part II, and the concert limped to an unsatisfactory conclusion.

The following night's performance was a great improvement, and was followed by dinner in Barcelona with the sponsors from the Caixa. One of them told us that he had had complaints about the quality of the concert in Andorra, and I'm sorry to say that Maricarmen, instead of drawing a discreet veil over the entirely predictable, indeed predicted, events of the previous day, challenged me to explain. And so it was that I reminded her that the reason we had agreed to the impossible schedule was that she had threatened me with cancellation. Clearly this was not very diplomatic, but the fact is that I was by now beyond caring. After all, my musicians had undoubtedly been taken advantage of, and I had been complicit in this (although under duress), despite having all along thought it utterly outrageous. Maricarmen was herself outraged; she denied everything, whether because she had genuinely forgotten or because she would not admit the truth, I never knew for sure. Nor did I ever discover, because she did not speak to me for the next twelve years, and The English Concert did not appear again in Barcelona until Maricarmen's retirement more than a decade later. And finally, as a coda, when The English Concert did eventually re-visit Barcelona it was to do another of the vast Messiah concerts, this time with our new Music Director Harry Bicket at the helm and a new director of the Caixa's vast music empire. And who should I meet in a box in the Palau de la Musica but the now-retired

Maricarmen Palma herself who greeted me as a long-lost soulmate returning after an apparently inexplicable twelve year absence.

<center>~~~</center>

It was soon after this episode (but not, I think, because of it) that Trevor Pinnock told me of his intention to retire from The English Concert. He had evidently only postponed his bid for freedom following the Deutsche Grammophon crisis of six years earlier but his decision was certainly hastened by the simultaneous news that Rachel Podger, whose inspired playing had so renewed his own enthusiasm, was expecting her second baby. After baby number one she had resumed her leadership role (if on a slightly reduced scale) but baby number two would make the job, with all its travelling demands, impossible. Pinnock, I think, felt that he just didn't have the energy to go through yet another reconstruction process which would (or at least should) involve encouraging the retirement of a number of the longer-serving orchestra members. At the same time he had rediscovered a desire to work at his harpsichord playing which had been somewhat on autopilot for quite some years while he had been preoccupied with other issues (primarily his wider conducting career). He wanted to see what he could do in, "the next ten years or so", as he said, this being the time he felt remained to him before his technical skills might be expected to decline.

Considerate to the last, Trevor promised to soldier on for another two years to fulfil existing engagements and give everyone time to consider the future. His expectation was that The English Concert would wind down over the two years, finish with a big closing event and thereafter maintain a skeleton office for a few months to deal with any final closure issues. The members of the orchestra naturally hoped to carry on, but this was clearly going to be difficult: the departure of the founder after 30 years, the only person ever to have directed the orchestra,[77] was of course an existential crisis on an acute scale, and we were at the same time losing Rachel Podger, our concertmaster, who had brought a new energy to everything the orchestra did. Both would be extraordinarily hard acts to follow, and for a while I doubted the wisdom of attempting to continue.

---

[77] Or almost: Simon Preston had directed the one TEC project in which I had played and, a little before my time Paul Goodwin, for many years the orchestra's principal oboist, had announced his own conducting ambitions with a few concerts with TEC.

I had realised quite early, when thinking about Pinnock's possible successors, that there would need to be real change. To appoint another harpsichordist/director would put the new incumbent in the invidious position of constantly being compared with his predecessor. A possible solution came to me when I heard a recording of the violinist Andrew Manze playing a bizarre set of seventeenth-century Italian sonatas by a composer named Pandolfi. The music was weird, the playing outstandingly inventive and witty, and Manze himself clearly a natural communicator with violin in hand (and, as it turned out, without). He was at the time working with the opposition, as assistant director of The Academy of Ancient Music, and I knew him only by name, but I felt that he might wish to emerge from the shadow of the AAM founder, Christopher Hogwood. The latter still directed the majority of the orchestral concerts and, importantly, their recordings, so there seemed a chance, no more, that he might be attracted by an offer of full artistic control and responsibility. And when he agreed I was delighted to have solved our two problems (finding a new director/conductor and finding a new violinist/leader) with a single appointment, and with the potential to create a wholly new and different musical focus for The English Concert, no longer led from the keyboard and continuo team but directed from the principal violin chair. Swept up in the quasi-improvisational magic of the Pandolfi (did he really exist, or did Manze make him up, I wonder?), I envisaged a return to the original inspiration of The English Concert, with repertoire anchored firmly in the baroque period, with occasional forays into earlier music and perhaps also a few into Mozart/Haydn territory. This was the repertoire where the opportunity for re-invention would lie, for it was a curious fact that many of the period instrument groups which had made their reputations in the music of exactly this high baroque period were now being driven relentlessly into the nineteenth-century. Mozart and Haydn had been flowing off the production lines for some years, but now Beethoven was everywhere, Schubert and Mendelssohn were relatively common, there had been occasional sightings of Verdi and Tchaikovsky, and word had it that there were soon to be 'period' performances of Brahms, Wagner and even Elgar. All this meant that there had quite suddenly opened a surprisingly substantial gap in the very repertoire with which so many of us had all begun. Reclaiming this central ground could be just what The English Concert needed to re-set and clarify its future artistic profile.

Imagine my disappointment, then, when Manze and I began our first detailed discussions about future programmes. He was determined to begin with Mozart and Haydn, and clearly had visions from the outset of moving the repertoire into the nineteenth-century with talk, even at this early stage, of setting Beethoven's monumental *Missa Solemnis* as a medium-term target. This was not at all what I had hoped and it was with the greatest difficulty that I persuaded him to keep at least a foot in baroque territory. Manze had not revealed in the few weeks leading up to his appointment that his ambition was to turn himself into a conductor, rather than 'merely' a violinist/leader, and persuading him to keep playing the violin became a source of friction virtually from the first day of his tenure. An ally in this ongoing struggle was Robina Young, the head of Harmonia Mundi, the California-based recording company with whom Manze was contracted on an exclusive basis. She had a strong interest in keeping him in her artists' list as a highly gifted violinist rather than as a novice conductor of uncertain aptitude.

Manze, at the beginning, was conscientious about building the orchestra. It was agreed that he would not direct everything. We would have guests on a regular basis, and that when available he would lead the orchestra for these guests. One such project, which I had embarked on before Manze's arrival, was a collaboration with the Choir of Westminster Abbey and we had long planned some concerts in Spain, to be conducted by the Abbey organist and director of music, James O'Donnell.

This turned out, for no foreseeable reason, to be the tour from hell even when compared with our previous Spanish adventures with the St Matthew Passion. We were to begin with two concerts in the south of Spain, followed by a huge bus journey to the north (perhaps this aspect of hell should have been foreseeable) with a concert the same day. Things began to go wrong from the very start with James O'Donnell falling ill on the first day. Our wonderfully unflappable (especially in these kinds of situation) concerts manager, Sarah Fenn, medicated him through the first concert, but by day two he was worse, so much so that he was hospitalised in the curiously isolated southern Spanish city of Jaën[78] where a diagnosis of pneumonia meant that he would not be travelling anywhere for some considerable time. Of course I was incredibly grateful to have Manze with us (he was leading the orchestra as per our agreement) because he could step into the conducting breach and save our tour from further

---

[78] Jaën's isolation is a result of its location on a plateau on top of a hill. It is thus a rarity amongst Spanish cities in having no airport.

embarrassment. Indeed his first concert as O'Donnell's replacement was a triumph for him as well as a huge relief to me.

If that concert in Jaën was a nervous business, the next day was simply brutal. Spain, as may be recalled, is a big country and comparatively well-served by regional airports. This is good so far as it goes, but in reality it mostly goes so far as Madrid; the regions do not connect well with each other, and flight schedules are often not conducive to the trouble-free movement of orchestras, especially those which wish to move from one end of the country to the other. In short, there is scarcely a Spanish tour which does not include at least one long bus journey. Our destination, the following day, was León, one of the rather grim cities of the north, a distance of at least six hundred and fifty kilometres. Our three buses set off at 8.00 a.m., braced for a seven-hour journey—we planned a mid-morning coffee stop and lunch somewhere beyond Madrid, aiming for a 3.00 p.m. arrival. As with air travel, there is virtually no way of avoiding Madrid on a drive of this kind, partly because all main roads lead there but in this case also because even the proverbial crow, in the unlikely event that it would choose to fly from Jaën to León, would pass directly over it. So Madrid was our halfway point and yardstick for progress. What we had not been told was that this Saturday was 'fiesta', and that every road within miles of the capital would be grid-locked for the entire weekend. Nothing moved more than a few yards at a time throughout an interminable afternoon. By 4.00 p.m., some time after our projected arrival time, we were still some two hundred kilometres from our destination and still moving at a pace which would have tested the patience even of a snail. The concert was to start at 8.00 p.m., and it was clear that we were now struggling even to arrive by this time, let alone deliver a concert. Also, of course, there was the question of whether the musicians and the choir would be willing to perform. The Abbey Choir had boys as young as nine and to demand a concert from them immediately after a twelve-hour journey would (and perhaps should) qualify as an (admittedly rather niche) form of child abuse. At this point, the gadgets of modern life really came into their own…the boys turned out to be utterly and uncritically content to watch endless movies on their bus, and it was the grown-ups who needed to be coaxed and tenderly cajoled.

Choirs on tour are not always so malleable. There is a fine story of an Australian tour by one of the Cambridge college choirs, St John's I think, for which the men had been specially kitted out in a uniform of blazers sporting their college coat of arms, presumably in the hope of nurturing a sense of corporate togetherness. And the branding exercise succeeded to the extent that the gentlemen of the choir demonstrated, in rather bizarre circumstances, a wish to show off their new kit back home: returning after a concert through some quite remote and rugged Australian country their bus suffered an unfortunate collision with a small kangaroo which now lay stretched out at the roadside. The driver stopped to examine the damage to his bus while some of the singers disembarked in order to observe at closer quarters the damage to the kangaroo. As the group milled around, pending a decision about what should happen next, one of the singers (I assume, for no very good reason other than extensive experience, that it was a tenor) decided that a photograph of the dead animal attired in the corporate colours was an opportunity for a bit of sport not to be missed, so he and a few colleagues propped the poor creature up against the side of the bus, clothed it in his corporate blazer and gathered their remaining colleagues around it for the group photograph that would, he hoped, appear as the front cover of the next college magazine. Unfortunately for our hapless chorister, the kangaroo had not in fact been killed, as had at first been thought, but merely stunned, and the theatrical business in preparation of the photoshoot had restored the creature fully to its senses. Whereupon, naturally, it made a bid for freedom, leaping away into the Australian sunset, still clad, of course, in the team blazer. It was only now, as the liberated beast shrank to a mere hopping dot on the wide horizon, that our protagonist recalled that he had left, in the inside breast pocket, not only his wallet but also his passport.

Meanwhile, back in León, I had made contact with the concert promoter who agreed to delay the concert's starting time by an hour. Arriving eventually at the concert hall at exactly 8.00 p.m. (twelve hours, almost to the minute since departure) I sent everyone off to find what they could to eat while my colleague Sarah and I went into the hall to set about the task of putting the heavy instruments (double basses, timpani and so on) in place, exploring the layout of the backstage area then labelling everything (gents/ladies dressing rooms, soloists, conductor, choir etc.) before checking that the stage was arranged according to Sarah's prior instructions. As often happened, her carefully prepared diagram of the orchestral and choral layout might just as well not have been written and, there being no backstage staff to call on, we began to make the necessary adjustments ourselves, including moving the 'risers' on which the choir were to stand. As I started to shift these, I was brought up short by an enraged bellow from the back of the auditorium. It was our promoter who, in confident but barely comprehensible English, explained that we could not move anything on stage without supervision by his staff. When I enquired of their whereabouts he explained that they had left for the day (having been on call for an earlier arrival), so the stage would have to remain just as they had left it. I explained as best I could that we could not give our concert if the stage was not properly arranged, and we very soon reached a ridiculous impasse. All the while the clock was ticking and it was not long before the diplomatic skills with which I might have begun this frank exchange of views had deserted me and we were shouting at each other in words whose meaning was clear even if the details were not immediately understood by either protagonist. It was the only time I can remember threatening to refuse to give a concert if he didn't concede and eventually, with maximum ill-feeling on all sides, our promoter stormed out leaving Sarah and myself to finish the set-up. The concert was delivered with true British stoicism (which, in the circumstances, amounted to little short of heroism), but there was an unhappy twist in the tail: the promoter didn't pay.

Carmen Prieto, our agent in Spain (not to be confused with Barcelona's Maricarmen), now stepped in with characteristic generosity. It emerged that the non-payment was not specifically related to our late arrival and subsequent shouting match but rather that the entire concert series was bankrupt. We were by no means the only people not to receive our fees, but Carmen paid us (and other of her clients) out of her own pocket and then had to commit further resources and spend years recovering her losses (or at least some of them) through the courts.

~~~

In complete contrast to the nightmare tour of Spain was The English Concert's visit to the United Arab Emirates and Abu Dhabi. The driving force behind this remarkable event was an Iranian businessman of great charm and erudition, as well as energy, Vahid Alaghband, whose Bali Group had extensive property and other business interests in the United Arab Emirates. Vahid had become a sponsor of the orchestra in the UK but his real mission, as it turned out, was to be the catalyst for the transformation of the capital of the UAE, Dubai, from a purely commercial centre into a 'real city'. What he meant by this was a city with a cultural infrastructure of art galleries, museums, concert halls and an opera house. The English Concert's visit to Dubai would, he hoped, add profile and gloss to his biggest speculative building project, the development of a sector of Dubai which was to be grandly, and optimistically, known as the 'Artistic Quarter'. This was 2007, the year before the great financial implosions of 2008/09 and Dubai was riding high as a global marketplace, but it undeniably was a city without public art or music or indeed anything beyond its extraordinarily hubristic architecture.

For a brief moment in this pre-crash year it was possible to imagine that a triangulated project which brought together the political rulers of the emirate states (the Sheikhs) with the commercial oligarchs and entrepreneurs whom Alaghband had assembled to finance the tour, using the good offices of the British diplomatic services to oil the wheels, could be the launch of a long-term development plan for Western, and indeed Islamic, culture in the region. At the time plans to build an opera house were well-advanced; the idea was not that the UAE could sustain its own opera company but that demand for touring opera would continue to grow in Asia (especially amongst the emerging middle classes in China, but also in Japan where there was already an established market for Western classical music but no indigenous Japanese opera companies) and that Dubai's geographic position as a meeting point between East and West would make it a natural stopover for touring companies, in just the same way as it had for many years been a historic hub for East/West trade. All this was shortly after Harry Bicket had joined The English Concert as its music director and we had already been invited by Carnegie Hall in New York to give an annual series of operas in concert performance. The broad plan was to develop a touring circuit for our major large-scale projects which would stretch from London to New York, then across America to the West Coast, returning to Europe by flying West, via Japan and China, to Dubai, Abu Dhabi and possibly Doha. This was a heady vision, probably made more so, almost giddy, by the timing and location of the discussion: it was the end of the first day of my first scoping visit to UAE, at dinner as a guest of Alaghband and other movers and shakers of the business community, including the Chief Executive of the new Dubai Airport (recently opened, and boasting, as she proudly told me, a floor area the size of the City of Cardiff), the Chief Executive of HSBC in the region and others. We dined in a surprising Argentinian restaurant (not great for vegetarians) at the top of a monstrously tall hotel. Perhaps the air was thinner up there, or perhaps our plans for world domination of the baroque opera market (such as it might be) were simply the product of exhaustion. It had been an epically long day. I had flown out from London overnight, to be met at dawn by one of Alaghband's flotilla of elegant and enthusiastic ladies, my first encounter with the energetic Elodie whom Vahid had head-hunted and stolen away from the exclusive George V Hotel in Paris (where one of her duties had been to prevent 'the ladies of the night' from plying their trade too conspicuously in the hotel's bars and restaurants). I had not been given any advance notice of the schedule, only that the main purpose of my trip would be to assess the suitability of the proposed concert venues, there being no purpose-built concert halls in the UAE. On arrival it quickly became clear that something more elaborate was planned than a mere tour of potential concert venues, starting with a drive to Abu Dhabi for a mid-morning meeting at the British Embassy. Shortly before landing, I had turned down a rather unappetising airline breakfast without remembering that I was about to land in a country observing Ramadan, and that this might be my last sight of food for fourteen hours; by 10.00 a.m. I was already regretting my lack of foresight and wondering if I could survive until dusk without so much as a bottle of water, so it was a relief to find myself in the surreal setting of the elegant drawing room of the British ambassador in Abu Dhabi greedily eyeing plates of chocolate Bourbons and an assortment of cakes and sandwiches alongside our coffees.

The discussions here were mainly about sponsorship and the ambassador was generous enough to promise to host a reception for the orchestra's supporters. Armed with this endorsement our next call was upon the manager of the absurdly garish (think Trump Tower bling) Emirates Palace Hotel, built by the Sheikh of Abu Dhabi to host in maximum grandeur a meeting of the G7 (as they then were) economic powers, a meeting which for some reason never took place. It was in this super-luxurious setting that one of our concerts was supposed to take place and Alaghband and the British ambassador did everything, including veiled threats of future withdrawal of business, to persuade our hosts, who included the formidable Zaki Nusseibeh, a Cambridge-educated Lebanese and the Sheikh's principal man of business, to offer us free accommodation in the Emirates Palace Hotel as a form of sponsorship-in-kind for the tour. The 'concert hall' in the Emirates Palace Hotel was in truth entirely unsuitable, being more of a lecture theatre with thick carpets extending not merely wall to wall (damaging enough to the acoustics) but also up the walls and over the ceiling too (fatal). However, in the circumstances, and especially while the prospect of free rooms in such splendour was still a possibility it would have been unhelpful (to use appropriately diplomatic language[79]) to make too many negative comments about the hopelessness of the acoustics. A little judicious sucking of teeth was all I allowed myself, though inwardly my heart was sinking.

Our return through the desert to Dubai was followed by a visit to Alaghband's office to meet his staff and business partners (and, for my benefit, more Ramadan-defying tea and cakes in the privacy of a back office). From there I was to return to my hotel to await a car to take us all to our Argentinian dinner. The heat outdoors was fierce, but, perhaps lulled by air-conditioning indoors and stupefied by cake, I made the novice's error of declining a car back to my hotel which was no more than a short walk away; indeed I could see it through the window of Alaghband's office. I was to learn the hard way that Dubai is not a city designed for the pedestrian. What looked like a simple short walk, with destination in full view at all times, turned out to be a test of nerve and initiative, a kind of urban mountaineering. Walking in the Dubai streets was an adventure, mainly because the 'streets' were, in this part of town at any rate, American-style freeways, and elevated freeways at that. And beneath the elevations was a kind of scrubby wasteland, so the choices, and there were several even over such a short distance, seemed to be to embrace an immediate death by walking amongst the speeding traffic (there were no sidewalks/pavements of course) or risk a more lingering demise by battling the unknowable horrors (do they do snakes in Dubai?) of semi-jungle or sand (quicksand?) below. After one excursion into the undergrowth (dressed in a suit and unsuitably shiny shoes) I chose the high road amongst the limousines whose owners may never have seen a pedestrian before

---

[79] I have always been fond of the exquisite turn of phrase in diplomatic discourse. Consider this virtuoso performance, from amongst documents released by the Public Records Office which include a typewritten letter, written in 1943, from Sir Archibald Kerr, British Ambassador to Moscow, to Lord Pembroke, foreign office minister, "My dear Reggie," wrote HM ambassador, "in these dark days a man tends to look for little shafts of light that spill from Heaven. My days are probably darker than yours, and I need, my God, I do, all the light I can get. But I am a decent fellow and I do not want to be mean and selfish about what little brightness is shed upon me from time to time. So I propose to share with you a tiny flash that has illuminated my sombre life and tell you that God has given me a new Turkish colleague whose card tells me that he is called Mustapha Kunt. We all feel like that, Reggie, now and then," he continued, "especially when spring is upon us, but few of us would care to put it on our cards. It takes a Turk to do that."

that day and appeared to have marked me as an escaped lunatic to be mown down in a spirit of public-spirited ethnic cleansing. I had been concentrating so hard on self-preservation that for a short while I had taken my eyes off my destination, so when I felt sufficiently confident to raise them once more heavenwards I realised that I had twenty-something tall buildings in view, all looking uncomfortably alike. I was suffering in the extreme heat of the afternoon, had not slept for at least thirty-six hours and was now alarmingly disorientated. My only recourse it seemed was to abandon this absurd idea that it was possible to walk to a building that you could actually see from your point of departure, so decided to make for the first building I could reach and take a cab. And it was of course a small, but very bearable, embarrassment to find myself leaning into the open window of a cab, asking, with such British coolness as I could still muster, to be taken to my hotel only to be regarded, not for the first time, as though mad and told that I was already there.

As for the tour itself, a few months later, the venues were as dire as I had feared and the concerts not especially well attended because there was no mechanism for selling tickets. Perhaps for this reason, the most successful events were those which were added at the last minute. The first of these was a concert for a special needs school, unique in Dubai, which had, at first sight, looked as if it would be extremely difficult: the entire school was assembled for our more or less impromptu visit, and the pupils' ages appeared to range from five to eighteen years old. Not only so, but the range of difficulties from which the pupils suffered was equally wide, from minor behavioural issues to serious mental and physical impairment. It was going to be nigh on impossible to find an approach to such an event which would appeal across such a huge spectrum. But I had underestimated our trumpeters, Mark Bennett and Mike Harrison and timpanist, Robert Howes, who rose so brilliantly to the challenge that the more-or-less improvised concert turned out to be a joyous event which achieved the most authentically enthusiastic audience response of the entire tour. Nothing of this kind had ever happened in Dubai before and many of the adults, teachers, carers and, I was opportunistically pleased to note, sponsors, were in tears at the end.

The other last-minute event could scarcely have been more different and, to my regret, can only be written about at second hand. Following our opening concert we received an invitation to play a short concert in the palace of the Sheikh of Abu Dhabi, or, to give him his full title, HH Sheikh Dr Sultan Bin

Khalifa al Nahyan. More exotic still, the invitation was actually from his wife, Sheikha Bint Saif Al Nahyan, the occasion being the launch of a new range of Italian handbags, and the location the palace harem. Given the venue, this invitation could only be extended to the ladies of the orchestra but, since they outnumbered the men on this tour, we were, with some creativity and ingenuity, able to devise a programme (overnight), with odd instrumentation to be sure, which eliminated any requirement for male participation. The ladies were duly bussed off to the palace where their short performance was a mere overture to a substantial lunch party involving a great deal of food accompanied by a show, on temporary catwalks, of the Milanese clothes and, especially, handbags. For those lucky enough to experience it, this was probably the highlight of their week, especially so for one of our viola players who ended the day galloping over the sands on an Arab horse from the stables of the Sheikh in the company of his teenaged daughter.[80]

Despite our best creative efforts, the planning for return visits in future years fell victim to the worldwide financial disasters of 2008 which hit Dubai particularly hard. Amongst other casualties were many of the development projects in which Alaghband had invested, and when the Ruler of Dubai announced a moratorium on all new buildings throughout the Emirates, many who had borrowed heavily to fund their projects were left in serious financial difficulties. Enthusiasm for world tours of rare Handel operas had consequently slipped some distance down the corporate agenda.

~~~

As the first decade of the twenty-first century drew to a close it was becoming clear that my own days with The English Concert were numbered. Since Trevor Pinnock's departure in 2001 the orchestra had shown resilience and imagination

---

[80] It is a reflection on our current sensitivities on sexual equality issues that, although the ladies-only event seemed an agreeable, even amusing, challenge, I had earlier been asked if we would give a concert in Sharjah, the small neighbouring Emirate, the condition being that for religious and cultural reasons no women would be permitted to appear on stage. This offer was indignantly declined amid much huffing about women's rights. An ingenious use of resources would have been to run these two events simultaneously, so that if challenged on the 'no women' stricture we could truthfully say that they all had a prior engagement.

to re-invent itself but, even so, the first years of the new century had thrown up a number of tough challenges. The appointment of Andrew Manze as artistic director had appeared a brilliant stroke at the time, but his peculiarly difficult personality, coupled with his bizarre determination to give up playing the violin, had led to his abrupt departure in 2007. The following two years were exceptionally tough; the process of appointing Harry Bicket as Andrew's successor had taken surprisingly little time to agree in principle, but Harry's existing commitments, mainly in opera, stretched far into the future. The consequence was that, although he made himself available as much as he could (including for the Dubai/Abu Dhabi tour) there were to be two or three years during which I had to find projects for the orchestra led almost entirely by guests. Unfortunately this period coincided with the recession of 2008, the effect of which was to impoverish many of the music festivals around Europe, as well as triggering a crisis of confidence amongst the promoters of the major concert series in Europe and elsewhere. The result of course was that the genuine uncertainty which these promoters had about the size, or even existence, of their future budgets, combined with their uncertainty about the future shape of a leaderless English Concert, gave them a perfectly valid reason to respond to my overtures with a polite request to try again when I could offer the orchestra with its new music director. This is easier to see now, with the benefit of hindsight, but at the time the orchestra's Board responded with something akin to panic, trying to persuade me to turn myself into something of an itinerant salesman, a role which I was never going to be able to fulfil, both because such salesmanship is not in my DNA but also because of a domestic crisis which had been growing slowly but inexorably for several years. Our eldest daughter Eleanor, who continued to live at home, had had problems with obsessive behaviours since her early teens but now, in her twenties, these obsessions had become focused on food and alcohol; by 2010 she was suffering from a toxic combination of alcoholism and bulimia. Julie and I had to manage Eleanor as best we could while also taking over parental responsibility for her daughter Lauren who had been born in 2003. All this meant that I was even more reluctant than I might otherwise have been to spend too much time on the road.

I had also, at last, decided to put the bassoon under the bed forever. I was by now playing so rarely that I knew that whatever skills I might once have had were now fast declining, and I was, in professional terms, skating on the thinnest ice. Having reached the conclusion that I should retire gracefully from the orchestral fray (rather than risk an ungraceful disaster, followed by a disgraceful retirement), I was unexpectedly presented with an opportunity for a final 'date' as a bassoon player in such pleasing circumstances as are worth recounting: it had always been one of my more mischievous ambitions as a player to achieve a tour without concerts, a feat which we almost realised with the Albion Ensemble on our trips to Barcelona, with our schools programmes and successions of free evenings. My swansong as a bassoonist involved appearing in an orchestra without having to play in it. The English Concert had been engaged by the BBC to provide the music for a programme re-enacting George I's famous barge excursion on the River Thames for which Handel provided his Water Music. The TV programme featured a reproduction of the royal barge, populated with be-wigged and costumed musicians, sailing up the Thames accompanied by a flotilla of smaller boats on which the cameras were mounted. All river traffic had been suspended for a few hours, so this extravagant project had to take place exactly as planned, irrespective of the weather. For this reason, mainly because of the danger of inclement weather, the music itself had been pre-recorded in a studio. As it transpired, our fabulously gifted bassoonist, Alberto Grazzi, was available for the sound recording but not for the filming, and so it was that one gorgeous summer's evening in July 2010 I found myself deputising for Alberto aboard a barge on the river, heavily disguised and powdered in eighteenth-century costume and wig, pretending to play a bassoon which had been doctored to produce no sound at all. When I later trousered the not inconsiderable fee for this exercise in mime, it seemed an appropriate conclusion to a playing career which had opened, forty years earlier, with an unforgettable encounter with Pierre Boulez and had continued with modest success, if no great distinction, until this memorably perfect summer evening on the river. The curtain would now fall as I sat, mute and incognito, in circumstances almost as farcical as forty years earlier, but much more fun.

Chapter 7
Double Bar: When the Music Stops

Leaving The English Concert would have been a hard choice had it been voluntarily made, but my Board of Trustees, especially the then chairman, Nigel Carrington, made it inevitable, so in a sense not really a choice at all. By setting some impossible performance targets for 2010, then initiating a process of formal review which could only reach one conclusion when these targets were not met, he left me with little option but to resign. So I duly did so. I had been running orchestras for twenty years and was restless for something else, but my familiar trouble was not knowing quite what it should be. To make a start in a new direction, though, was essential.

My last significant act for The English Concert was to secure its place on a three-year Arts Council funding programme. This was a substantial grant and its timing was perfect. It allowed me to bequeath to my successor a tolerably healthy funding position and, on the music front, the new artistic director was beginning to make an impact. The imminent launch of the long-planned annual opera project at Carnegie Hall in New York meant that alongside the domestic Arts Council-supported programme there was clear potential for further international development on a substantial scale, and the wider economic climate appeared to be recovering, if slowly, from the nadir of 2008/09. The timing of the new grant also sent a welcome message to my trustees that the Carnegie Hall and the Arts Council here at home appeared to have greater confidence in The English Concert than some of its own Board members.

I was no longer a bassoon player in any useful sense, so it was my experience of charitable governance and fundraising which would sustain me in the short term. I knew that I would need to launch my new freelance life in the musical world with which I was most familiar, but also that I wanted, most of all, to look for opportunities which would challenge this musical comfort zone. It was fun, in any case, to be working again with the violinist Elizabeth Wallfisch, on her orchestral training project, the Wallfisch Band. She and I had worked closely together in the 1990s at the OAE, and I had always loved the passion she brought to whatever project she had set her heart on. I was pleased, too, to take on a new assignment with a somewhat wider remit: I had initially approached Classical Opera when they advertised for a fundraiser, inviting them to consider outsourcing some of their fundraising to my small business. It emerged, though, that their Chief Executive, Debbie Coates, was about to take a six-month maternity leave, so they were also looking for someone to step in as a temporary Chief Executive. A specific requirement was that this temporary cover should use his outsider-looking-in point of view to write a business plan for the organisation. So began an association with the Classical Opera company which stretched from the original six-month term to the best part of three years.

Classical Opera had the great good fortune to have an exceptionally generous chairman and principal sponsor, George Koukis, a man who had made his money, initially, in banking software but whose greatest passion is Mozart, and in particular Mozart as interpreted by Ian Page and Classical Opera. The scale of his ambition was impressive: for example, Koukis had spent both time and money, some years previously, on a feasibility study for building a new opera house for Classical Opera on a site in Pimlico, an idea which was both tantalising but at the same time barmy: Pimlico seemed an unlikely enough location, and how on earth was such a project to avoid being the whitest of white elephants if occupied as a 'home' by such a tiny company as Classical Opera, giving only a few shows a year.[81]

Suffice to say that building a home for Classical Opera did not feature large in my business plan, but the idea had nevertheless sown a seed of speculation about whether a less narrowly specialised, independently run music theatre of the right size for eighteenth-century opera (fewer than a thousand seats) could be viable. If there was a gap in the market for such a modest-scale theatre, then a new venture might possibly thrive with the help of some additional fundraising, some institutional backing and with Mr Koukis or some equally committed philanthropic backer.

---

[81] The expression 'white elephant' might have been invented to cover a project such as this. The phrase is supposed to have come from the historic practice of the King of Siam giving rare albino elephants to courtiers who displeased him, so that they would be ruined by the animals' extravagant upkeep costs.

So was there a gap in the market? Surprisingly for a city full of theatres and with numerous medium-scale opera and dance companies, London does not have a small independent 'receiving house' for music theatre. These smaller companies are primarily, though not exclusively, touring operations and they all struggle, for lack of suitable and available venues, to promote their work in London, where their biggest potential audience may be presumed to live. And, in addition to our own homegrown touring companies, there are also overseas companies who might come more often to London if there were a venue to receive them; then there is smaller-scale work by national companies which is unsuitable for their own large venues. Conspicuous amongst these is English National Opera (ENO), whose home, the Coliseum, is actually the largest theatre in London and manifestly too large for it even when it is presenting mainstream repertoire. ENO could greatly benefit from having a regular commitment to a smaller venue which would allow it to show artistically invigorating new work and provide performance opportunities for their excellent youth programmes, while simultaneously renting out its Coliseum home to visiting international companies in the summer months. This would require some heroic management decisions, probably including the disbandment of their full-time salaried orchestra and chorus; but if this hurdle could be cleared (it would need to be part of a comprehensive and persuasive artistic vision) without major strike action or being (further) penalised by the Arts Council, the company could emerge in a stronger, more agile position, able to hire appropriate orchestral and choral services as needed on a production-by-production basis. This could, at a stroke, reduce the annual overhead and enhance the artistic profile.

Apart from the touring operations and national companies, there are also the seasonal opera companies, such as Holland Park Opera, Garsington Opera, Grange Park and even perhaps Glyndebourne, who could be interested in adding some indoor Autumn/Winter performances to their *al fresco* Summer operations. And there might be other possibilities too for a new independent house to take some initiatives: to give just one example, a surprising gap in London's musical theatre scene has been the absence, for several generations, of any high quality presenters of the quintessentially English works of Gilbert and Sullivan. There was a valiant attempt a few years ago to promote a Gilbert and Sullivan season at the Savoy Theatre[82] but the production values were not high enough and the

---

[82] An enterprising joint venture between the music promoter Raymond Gubbay and the theatre (and 'Mousetrap') owner Sir Stephen Waley-Cohen.

quality of singing similarly left too much to be desired. And finally there is a growing market for telecasts of opera and theatre from international houses; the technology for recording these and, most importantly of the sound quality in cinemas, has made the experience of, say, the Metropolitan Opera from New York or the Royal Shakespeare Company in Stratford eminently transferrable to a screen near you. There surely must be other international companies wanting to get into this market. Every one of them is desperate to 'reach new audiences', and the evidence seems to be that there is an audience wanting to be reached.

At this point I found myself thinking about my local cinema, The Coronet in Notting Hill Gate which stands in faded glory at the west end of the main Notting Hill street just before it becomes the tree-lined Holland Park Avenue. Virtually the only thing I was certain I knew about The Coronet was that it had been built as a music hall before being converted to a cinema, so I fell to speculating about how much of its original structure might be left and whether it might be restored to its original purpose as a music theatre.

A Google search revealed that it had been built in 1898 as a top-of-the-range music theatre, one of the last purpose-built music halls. Designed by William Sprague (1863–1933), a protégé of the doyen of theatre building Frank Matcham (1854 – 1920), it had opened to great acclaim but thereafter enjoyed only a short life as a music hall, a form of entertainment which, at the start of the twentieth-century was already past its heyday. Soon cinema was to take over as the most popular mass entertainment and in 1923 The Coronet was one of the earliest of the theatres to be converted to the silver screen.[83] It has had a chequered history since, with numerous changes of ownership, threats of demolition and/or re-development, one such imminent threat being countered in 1989 when the building (or at least parts of it) was granted Grade II listed status.

One lovely summer morning, I was cycling past The Coronet, and, seeing some activity in the front of house area, and acting entirely on impulse, I poked an enquiring nose inside the tiny foyer and asked if the manager was available. This was how I met Rob Syed, who turned out to be no mere cinema manager;

---

[83] The heyday of cinema, the usurper of the popular music hall, was itself surprisingly short-lived, falling victim to the inexorable rise of television in the post-war era. It is hard to believe, now, quite how vast cinema audiences for a brief time were, even in England where there was no large indigenous movie industry to speak of. The largest cinema in London was the 4,004-seat Gaumont State Theatre, Kilburn, in north-west London.

he was, it emerged, a romantic, in love with the 'sleeping beauty' of a building, as he described it, and for ever dreaming of rediscovering glory days which always seemed to be just around an elusive corner.

Having fortuitously happened upon such an engaging and passionate advocate, it was natural to question him about whether anything of the original music hall had survived the many vicissitudes and indignities inflicted upon the building over the years. Rob's enthusiasm was irrepressible, and within minutes of my walking in off the street I was being given a tour: the foyer and auditorium (and the façade fronting on to the main street) were listed, so had survived in a condition close to the original (the auditorium lights looked suspiciously art deco, so I suspect these might have been changed in the 1920s when the building became a cinema, and the seats, as I knew from personal use, were much too comfortable to be original). Hidden behind a crude kind of cladding, the theatre's original boxes survived and it looked to me as if the 'apron' of the original stage might have been cut off so that the current cinema screen sat precisely on what was now the front edge of the stage. Behind this screen, what had been the stage and back-stage area had been converted into a second cinema, with a tiny capacity, above which the original fly tower could still be clearly seen. It had not been in use since 1923, so was in a dreadful state of repair, but, despite that, the essential height was still there. Rob told me that planning permission had been granted for the second cinema on condition that every change made must be reversible. This meant that nothing of the original structure had been demolished, but had simply been left to decay. So, the answer to my as yet un-articulated question was yes, a restoration project was in principle feasible.

I had seen movies at The Coronet many times over the years and had assumed that the theatre consisted only of the main auditorium and the circle above (because this was all that was open to the public and all one can see when the cinema lights are down). This gives a seating capacity of just under four hundred. But Rob Syed's tour revealed that there was a third tier of seating, a huge upper-level Gallery which had been out of use since before 1930 and was now in an utterly derelict state. It had no electric lighting so we went up there with a torch. How amazing to discover such an enormous secret sitting almost, but not quite, in full view. The music hall's original capacity had been thirteen hundred, with most of these seats being the long wooden benches that were now revealed in this derelict Gallery. This extraordinary space was bleakly functional and dizzyingly, vertiginously steep. Needless to say, given that it had not been accessible to the public since the 1920s, it had no kind of safety rail, nor indeed anything to prevent the careless, or drunken punter from pitching head first into the Grand Circle below. It emerged, too, when I began to consider the possibility of conversion to modern use, that the likelihood of tumbling from a great height would be far from the only safety issue: the Gallery was built to accommodate the labouring classes and, in order to protect the more affluent from unwanted exposure to the great unwashed, there was no connecting stair or corridor (apart from the tiny pass door we had used) between the Gallery and other levels of seating. To move from the Gallery to the rest of the building you had (and still have) to exit to the street and re-enter through the main entrance. This was not an uncommon design at the time and is still to be found in some of the more venerable West End theatres. Bringing the Gallery into use in a refurbished theatre would be essential (it could scarcely be called a refurbishment if such a significant part of the building remained abandoned), but it would clearly present a major design and engineering challenge: the narrow benches, which stretched without interruption by intersecting aisles in a curve from one side of the building to the other were steeply tiered. Each step of these tiers was much too shallow to accommodate a conventional theatre seat, so there would need to be a complete re-design of the upper gallery.

We moved next to the back-stage areas but without, on this first tour, exploring every nook and cranny. Just as with the Spartan conditions for audiences in the Gallery, it was startling to see quite how miserable were facilities for the performers when this theatre was designed. Everything was extraordinarily cramped and tiny, but nonetheless, at least to my eyes, fascinating. And when I did eventually explore the surviving dressing rooms and connecting corridors between back and front of house it was wonderfully evocative to find empty milk and beer bottles left there by the last person to leave and turn out the backstage lights in 1923 (I later learned that these were probably the left-behinds of wartime fire wardens). But more startling than all of these delights on this first tour was the news which Rob, with his own inimitable sense of drama, had saved until last: the building was about to go on sale. It was hard not to feel that circumstances were conspiring to draw me in, and however far-fetched a restoration project might be, the series of coincidences which had led me to this point made it irresistible to explore further.

A Land Registry search confirmed that the current owners were, rather surprisingly, the Elim Church, the UK's biggest Pentecostal church, who had acquired a long lease for £3.5 million, some ten years previously. By far the largest Elim congregation in the country was to be found just around the corner at the so-called Kensington Temple near Notting Hill Gate tube station.[84] So large were their Sunday congregations that they had bought the local cinema to use as an overflow meeting space to which they could stream their services but, having secured their own Sunday needs, the new owners were content to allow The Coronet to continue on weekdays as a local independent cinema. The building was returning to the market now because it required very substantial investment just to enable it to continue in this role: this was more than a simple maintenance issue (although this must have been a significant ongoing cost) for, astonishingly, the Coronet still relied on antiquated reel-to-reel projection equipment. The major film distributors had recently decided no longer to supply new films in this old format. Consequently, The Coronet needed at least £750,000 to upgrade to modern digital equipment, an investment the Church was unwilling to make given that the running of cinemas was scarcely part of its core mission.

As for the freehold, this had changed hands more recently. A large North London-based family property empire, the Pears Group, had acquired the freeholds of a very substantial group of buildings in Notting Hill Gate. The Coronet was the end property in the Holland Park direction, while the other properties reached all the way along the block on both sides of the street as far as the corner of Kensington Church Street. The Pears Group had announced soon after their huge acquisition that they planned gradually to shift the entire street upmarket by careful selection of new tenants as the commercial leases expired. I hoped, although without any evidence to support it, that they might look favourably (i.e. provide some financial help) on a plan to develop The Coronet as a modern working theatre, adding some cultural gloss to their ambitious plans for the neighbourhood. Our proposal could contribute significantly to the freeholder's stated aim to make Notting Hill a 'destination' in its own right rather than merely a London Underground interchange and access point for Portobello Road tourists.

---

[84] I have long had a soft spot for the Kensington Temple ever since the day, sometime in the 1970s, when they erected a huge and luminous poster outside the church proclaiming the message, in the boldest caps, "**ARE YOU WEARY OF SIN? IF SO, COME IN AND REST**", beneath which a mischievous free spirit, an orchestral musician perhaps, had added in black marker pen "IF NOT CALL 01 272 5725."

Within a few weeks I had gathered a small team, consisting of a specialist architect, a technical adviser on the requirements of modern theatres and a potential chairman[85] for the board of trustees for the newly created charity, the Coronet Theatre Trust. I had also raised enough money, largely thanks to the generosity of Simon Weil, a longstanding friend and patron of The English Concert, to embark on an initial feasibility study, and thus far, nothing had occurred to dampen my early excitement. However, problems now began to crowd in.

It was clear that my vision for The Coronet as a multi-purpose music theatre was not compatible with any idea that it could be a home for any single company, but nevertheless I hoped that George Koukis could be persuaded to back the project if Ian Page was sufficiently enthusiastic. This was to be the first setback, for Page was wedded to his own vision of a 'home' for Classical Opera, unable to see his company as merely one user amongst many, and The Coronet was in any case too small to offer such luxuries as additional rehearsal spaces. Without Page's backing there was no likelihood that Koukis would become involved.

Soon, there came another setback: the Elim Church wanted a quick sale. We were already well into November of 2013 and they set Christmas as the date for tenders to be submitted. I knew there were other bidders, but my hope was that ours would be the only bid which envisaged restoring The Coronet to its original purpose, and that all the other proposals would run into varying degrees of difficulty with planning permissions given the listed status of the central core of the building. Even with this hope, we were still unable to submit more than a provisional proposal because we had neither the time, nor, in truth, the money, to undertake a full structural survey (including an asbestos assessment of which there was a great deal).

Nevertheless, I remained hopeful. We very quickly had an attractive outline plan for a modern, properly equipped theatre, but the Catch 22 was that we could not raise serious money until we had acquired the building, which we could not acquire without serious money. Our plan, laid out with such eloquence as we could muster, was in truth little more than a plea for additional time and, as such, was no match for any reasonable proposal with financial clout. And there was such a bidder…The Coronet was eventually sold (for over £6 million) to the wealthy owner of the Print Room, an alternative theatre company, just the sort

---

[85] The very same Charles Alexander with whom I had opened the batting for the Dragon School some fifty years earlier.

of backer, with deep pockets, which we had been unable to find in the limited time available. The major surprise, though, was that the new owner only wanted to use the small theatre, the space which was currently the tiny Cinema 2, occupying the original stage and dressing rooms area. So the main cinema use remained unchanged. Which means, of course, that, should The Coronet one day come back to the market, our restoration plan could yet be resurrected.

The failure of this great project was disappointing in the sense that it had been exciting to fantasise (despite all my efforts not to) about creating a new venue in a location with such potential; but it was also a considerable relief not to be committing to a huge and all-consuming project which would inevitably have taken over my life for years to come. Even so, I cannot but speculate, every time I pass the building, about what might have been, and indeed what could, at some point, still be. Rob Syed was right: The Coronet remains a sleeping beauty.

~~~

There were other near misses in my immediate post-English Concert years, the most unexpected of which involved a brief flirtation with that lovely, but underachieving, concert venue, St John's Smith Square. St John's was built in the early Hanoverian years to a most unusual design (with four towers) by Thomas Archer, one of the churches conceived by the 'Commission for Building Fifty New Churches' in 1710. The church was unlucky enough to be gutted by a German incendiary bomb on the very last day of the Blitz in May 1941, and it remained a derelict site for more than twenty years until finally restored to its original glory, re-opening as a concert venue in 1969. In terms of its size (650 seats) and acoustics St John's was a highly attractive venue for small orchestras or larger-scale chamber music, and every musician I have ever asked has loved it. But sadly, the venue consistently failed to attract substantial audiences and had been in a steady and apparently irreversible decline for a number of years.

As a concert venue it certainly suffered from several notable weaknesses. Firstly, despite a stage big enough for an orchestra and space for a choir behind, the back-stage area was woefully inadequate for any ensemble larger than a string quartet. And although the crypt beneath the church had been attractively converted into a restaurant, this too suffered from the weakness that a single narrow spiral staircase connected it with the auditorium. The stairs had to be shared by artists and audience alike, a bottleneck which often led to irritating, and sometimes ill-tempered, queues. Thirdly, and perhaps most serious of all, the venue had failed to develop a distinctive artistic profile. Was St John's a local resource for amateur music-making, debut recitals and the like or did it aspire to be a truly international professional concert venue? The consequence of this confusion was that audiences were offered a peculiar patchwork of amateur and professional events.

Eventually the trustees responsible for the church were persuaded to address some of these issues with a substantial refurbishment: this transferred the back-stage dressing-room areas to a (marginally) more spacious location, opened up a second staircase from the crypt to the church itself and relocated and modernised the box office. Now there was surely a chance to revitalise the artistic 'product'... yet nothing changed. The venue's management seemed unable to raise their game, appearing exhausted and lacking imagination. I would gaze at their relentlessly unchanging brochure of monthly activity, counting how many concerts in any given month I myself might actually go to as a paying customer. Often the answer was none. And now matters were worse than ever because a new concert venue, Cadogan Hall, had recently opened a short distance away in Sloane Square. Following the refurbishment it seemed essential for St John's to re-invent itself quickly while there was still a 'new' story to tell, and failing to do so risked them slipping even further into a decline which could well prove terminal, at least to any aspiration to be an international concert hall.[86]

Some new thinking seemed essential, and quickly, so I contacted the then manager of St John's, Paul Davies, offering to help him seize the time-limited opportunity which the refurbishment had presented. My idea was to set out a much more ambitious and focused artistic programme to position St John's as the venue of choice for small-to-medium size professional ensembles, both orchestras and choirs. We are accustomed to the regular, if infrequent, appearances of international symphony orchestras at the Barbican or at the Royal Festival Hall or at the BBC Proms, but London has never had a comparable, coherently curated, series devoted to the many renowned international and homegrown chamber orchestras. I proposed a research project, involving a survey of all the orchestral and choral groups which fell within this target

---

[86] With the benefit of hindsight, Cadogan Hall seems to have fallen into the same trap as St John's in attempting to be simultaneously an international concert venue and a community hall for local schools and amateur groups. It is an almost impossible combination.

category, to establish whether my hunch that they would welcome such an initiative could be substantiated, and what it would take to transform the prevailing negative views (amongst audiences as well as promoters) of St John's.

It was scarcely a surprise that Paul Davies' response was guarded. However tactfully my approach might be couched, there was bound to be, at the very least, some implied criticism of his management. Nevertheless he must have mentioned our meeting to his Board of Trustees because, not long afterwards, I had a call from the Chairman inviting me to submit a proposal for the initial research with a view to preparing a strategic plan for consideration by the Board. This had begun to feel like a solid and useful project and I was keen to make a start, but, as it turned out, events were moving too fast: the next call from the Chairman informed me that Davies had suddenly resigned and, as a consequence, the Board was now unable to proceed pending the appointment of his successor. My feelings were a mixture of regret for the loss of my project and guilt…I had been looking forward to working with Paul Davies on the attempt to breathe new life into a space which I still believe has considerable potential, and I was uncomfortable, to say the least, to think that my intervention might have been the catalyst to push him into such a drastic step as resignation after more than twenty years in charge. So this was to prove another 'nearly' project…for one could scarcely quarrel with the Board's decision to abandon it pending the appointment of a new Chief Executive who, they might reasonably hope, would prepare his own plan.

Both of these projects, the Coronet and St John's Smith Square, were my own initiatives and I may have become so over-involved in them that I lost sight, for a while, of my determination to find a path away from the world of music. For whatever reason, the project which was eventually to remove me altogether from my musical world crept up on me almost unnoticed while events at St John's were still unfolding. My mother called me one evening to tell me that she had recently given a talk to a small organisation of which she was patron called the Maudsley Philosophy Group (MPG). It had emerged in conversation afterwards that the MPG was in need of a (very) part-time administrator who could also bring some fundraising experience. She wondered if I might be interested. The Maudsley Philosophy Group is a small charity run by academic and clinical psychiatrists based at the Institute of Psychiatry, Psychology and Neuroscience at Denmark Hill in South London, and it was not long before I found myself working a few hours a week for them. The issues with which the

MPG dealt, essentially the ethical and practical issues which commonly arise in mental health contexts, were certainly intriguing, partly because mostly new to me, but also important in clinical practice.

I have to confess that my efforts to raise money for the MPG were almost completely unsuccessful, but nevertheless I found my role gradually expanding to take in the administration of other groups within this academic field. The first of these was a research group called Mental Health, Ethics and Law; and before long I was working on another much larger project, involving the preparation of an application, to the Wellcome Trust, for a five-year research programme called Mental Health and Justice, an exploration, broadly speaking, of the dilemmas arising when clinical practice in mental health contexts collide with the legal system. This was a complex project involving several academic disciplines and numerous institutions, and when our funding bid was eventually successful I was surprised to be asked to stay on to run its administration. So having started with the Philosophy Group (which still continues) I am now fully occupied with mental health research and especially how our highly rational legal system should deal with the sometimes irrational questions which can arise in mental illness. I have the good fortune, now, to be working with some extraordinarily committed academics, lawyers, consultants and PhD students from whom I learn something new every day and who seem to tolerate my ignorance about their subjects, psychiatric and legal, with great good humour.

~~~

Fundraising as a way of life can be wearying. Successes were of course tremendously exciting, but for every success there were numerous cap-in-hand requests which were rejected. I found I could treat these inevitable failures more philosophically, and keep them in proportion, by maintaining an involvement on the other side of the fence; in other words in grant making rather than grant seeking. Soon after resigning as an adviser to the Arts Council, I joined the Music Panel of The Radcliffe Trust, a much more congenial role than the bureaucratically earnest, and politicised, sobriety of our Arts Council committee of the same name. The Radcliffe Trust's six-monthly panel meetings were entertainingly chaired by the then chairman of trustees, Sir Ralph Verney. His meetings, back in the 1980s, could correctly be described as convivial, a rather dated word which captures something rather dated about the occasions. We would assemble at a gentlemanly 10.30 (the committee was overwhelmingly male, though the males were perhaps not all entirely gentlemen) to confer for two hours over coffee and biscuits in the Lincolns Inn offices of an old-school firm of solicitors with the nicely onomatopoeic name of Tweedie and Prideaux. At 12.30 sharp sherry would be served (occasionally champagne if Sir Ralph felt that the Trust's portfolio was bubbling sufficiently) and at 1:00 p.m., preprandially sharpened, we would repair to a nearby restaurant, selected by our chairman, where drink would continue to flow, accompanied by some lunch, until the afternoon was well advanced (and the rest of the day, so far as any prospect of working was concerned, ruined). But despite the undeniable self-indulgence, we took our work seriously and the advisory team was very well marshalled, as it continued to be until her recent retirement, by Sally Carter whose previous career as a schoolteacher meant that she was well-equipped to bring her unruly class to order should it be necessary. Ralph had assembled a motley, and in some instances eminent, collection of musicians from various walks of the profession. There were academics and broadcasters, such as Julian Rushton, Peter Evans and Stephen Plaistow, and the composer Colin Matthews, but for the most part, and this is where we diverged most from the Arts Council approach, we were professional players. The violinist Emanuel Hurwitz was a big figure, as was Thea King, principal clarinet in The English Chamber Orchestra, and the pianist James (Jimmy) Gibb.

I had known of the existence of The Radcliffe Trust since childhood. It had once made an important grant to my father, or rather to his college, to enable him to be relieved of his regular teaching commitments for a term in order to finish his book 'The Object of Morality.' And of course anyone growing up in Oxford could scarcely be unaware of the name of Dr Radcliffe who, it is almost certainly true to say, has more buildings named after him than any other university benefactor anywhere in the world. As an earlier Radcliffe trustee, the late Lord Quinton,[87] elegantly put it in his inaugural Radcliffe Lecture at Green College:

"No human being is more amply commemorated in the buildings of Oxford. Colleges and churches take their names from the divinities of the Christian pantheon, from the Trinity itself and Jesus, down through St Mary's, Christ's body and St John, to such marginally supernatural individuals as St Mary Magdalene and the faithful dead of All Souls. Their names often recur, but

---

[87] Anthony Quinton (1925 – 2010), Master of Trinity College Oxford, and famously described as the funniest philosopher since Hume.

among strictly terrestrial personages the general rule is that there should be only one edifice each…until the great benefactions of Lord Nuffield received physical embodiment the solitary exception was Dr John Radcliffe."

Dr Radcliffe himself was born in the mid-seventeenth-century (about ten years before Henry Purcell) and by the time of his death in 1714 had become one of the leading medical men of his time. Not only so, but he had acquired considerable wealth over the course of his life. He was a plain-speaking Yorkshireman who, by virtue of an extraordinary skill in diagnosis allied to common-sense practical treatments (and a robust scepticism, to put it mildly, of contemporary medical orthodoxies) built a practice which at various times included William III and his Queen Mary, Princess, later Queen, Anne (whose young life he is credited with saving, and whose death he was blamed for failing to prevent[88]), the young Alexander Pope, Jonathan Swift and Isaac Newton amongst many others.

He had been, by his own admission, a man, "over-fond of money," in his own lifetime but it seems to have been generally known that, upon his death, he planned a substantial gift to his *alma mater*, the University of Oxford, which may perhaps explain why his embalmed body lay in state in the Divinity School in early December 1714 before being borne in a grand cortège, accompanied by three choirs, to be buried in the University Church of St Mary the Virgin on the High Street. And when the will was read, the University was not disappointed: his extraordinary monument was to be a new library in Oxford, the iconic Radcliffe Camera (as it is now known). He stipulated that £40,000 should be spent on the purchase and demolition of the houses on Catte Street and the building of the library on the land thus acquired, between the University Church and the Bodleian Library. No doubt the Camera on its own would have been an extraordinary legacy, standing as the most distinctive and characteristic piece of Oxford architecture, but it was not the only visionary provision in the Doctor's will: the other was to allow his executors to apply the residuary income from his estate, after the new library was built, for such charitable purposes as they should think best at their absolute discretion. With this unusual, far-sighted and generous provision the Radcliffe Trust was created as one of the very first independent discretionary grant-making charities.

---

[88] Radcliffe refused to visit her deathbed claiming, probably with justice, that he should have been consulted sooner and that she was already beyond saving as a direct result of the treatments administered by medical colleagues who had been responsible for her care.

When the magnificent library was eventually completed in 1749, the Radcliffe trustees were at last able to turn their attention to their discretionary enterprises. The first of these was the Radcliffe Infirmary in the Woodstock Road, for which the foundation stone was laid in 1759, to be followed by the Radcliffe Observatory which was completed, after long delays, in 1799. Thus, at the start of the nineteenth-century the Radcliffe trustees had three very substantial undertakings in place and for the next century and a half the business of their meetings was almost entirely occupied with running them, especially the library and the observatory, both of which were institutions of national significance for which the Trustees had exclusive responsibility. The Infirmary, on the other hand, was from the outset a University building, governed by University officers and staffed by medical Fellows of the colleges until 1885.

The Trust's income derived entirely from the Buckinghamshire estate which Dr Radcliffe had acquired shortly before his death, and as time went on it became increasingly clear that the operation of a major library, let alone a leading astronomical establishment, would not be viable indefinitely within the Trust's limited resources. Gradually therefore, responsibility for the operation of the Library was transferred to the Bodleian Library, and soon afterwards ownership of the building itself was also transferred. As for the astronomical operations of the Observatory, these were re-located in the 1930s to the Transvaal in South Africa, greatly superior to Oxford for observing the stars, and eventually the Transvaal observatory was sold for a respectable sum to the South African government. Shortly thereafter most of the Trust's Buckinghamshire agricultural holdings were compulsorily purchased, to provide the site for the new town of Milton Keynes. Thus by the 1960s, the trustees had shed all of their historical recurrent commitments and had significantly more cash at their disposal, so they were, after 250 years, again in a position to re-define the 'charitable purposes at their absolute discretion' which Radcliffe's will allowed them to pursue. Sir Ralph Verney was already Chairman by this time and, since his interests included music and traditional craft skills, he seized the opportunity to steer the Trust's grant-making in these directions. These remain the two main interests of the Radcliffe Trust.

I had served on the Music Advisory panel for almost twenty years when I was invited to join the trustee board and I initially resisted this promotion on the reasonable grounds that I knew a good deal about music but little about equity investment or the management of agricultural holdings (which for historical reasons continue to make up a disproportionate percentage of the trust's portfolio), and not a great deal about the craft sector which accounted for something over half of the trust's grant-making programme[89]. But my resistance was, to be honest, half-hearted and I soon persuaded myself that so long as the trustees continued to have discretion in their grant-making, music should have an advocate on the board, willing to fight a 'musical corner' in the event of a future challenge to existing policies. I must admit, too, that there is pleasure in joining a board of this kind and being able to count amongst predecessors so many eminent men (for they were until recently all men), including former prime ministers (William Gladstone and Robert Peel), many peers including William Wilberforce, the Marquess of Salisbury and, in the twentieth-century, the Astronomer Royal Fred Hoyle, the aforementioned Anthony Quinton, and many others.

Sir Ralph Verney had retired by now and the Trust was chaired by Lord Cottesloe, a retired naval officer and lord lieutenant of Buckinghamshire (the county in which Dr Radcliffe had, late in life, become a landowner). Two years later, on Cottesloe's retirement, I became chairman of an organisation clearly in some need of change to make it fit for purpose in a new century. In particular the administration of the Trust was still in the hands of the Lincoln's Inn lawyers whose services were efficient enough but seemed excessively expensive in our more cost-conscious age. Thus, one of my first actions as chairman was to move the administrative functions out of London and into the hands of The Trust Partnership, an organisation set up to offer just the kind of governance services the Trust required. At a stroke this made more money available for grants, which was satisfying enough, but the most unexpected discovery in the course of the handover was that our lawyer-administrators had, with excessive caution, accumulated a quite unnecessarily substantial cash reserve of over £600,000 of unspent income which had been sitting in a separate account of which the trustees had been unaware.

I had already been thinking about how, if at all, we should mark the upcoming 300th anniversary of the Radcliffe Trust, a date which would fall in 2014, so it was a stroke of great good luck to benefit from such a windfall which,

---

[89] I feared that my promotion to the Board would be an example of the 'Peter Principle', the proposition that within any organisation its employees rise to their 'level of incompetence': if you are doing a job well you are very likely to be promoted until you reach a point when you are doing a job badly. Here you are likely to remain.

as unspent income, we arguably had a duty to distribute, and could do so on special 'tercentenary' projects without disturbing the regular ongoing grant-giving programmes. The Trustees thus had the enjoyable task of planning the celebration of this notable landmark without too many constraints.

The Trust has no staff, so is not equipped to promote or manage its own events. For this reason we needed partners for all of our special tercentenary projects, and an obvious starting point was Oxford University itself which had benefited so conspicuously from Dr Radcliffe's legacy. Also, as it happened, the University had recently embarked on its largest building project for a century, naming the whole venture the New Radcliffe Quarter, so it seemed possible that the university might 'adopt' the Radcliffe tercentenary, using it as an example for modern-day philanthropists of how major gifts can achieve if not immortality, at least something very close to it.

Unfortunately, the development of the decorative and artistic aspects of the New Radcliffe Quarter project had been out-sourced to a consultancy with whom there was no meeting of minds. They had a baleful 'vision' which seemed mainly to involve the provision of inter-active installations aimed at primary school children, or possibly adults with the mental capacity of children. When my co-trustee, Christopher Butcher, and I suggested such worthy projects as an exhibition about Radcliffe as an example for modern-day philanthropists, or the idea of commissioning a public statue of the doctor, we were greeted with patronising disdain. Clearly such ideas were unfit for the 21st Century. What, I wonder, has now become of these 'visionary' politically correct cardboard cut outs? I seem to have forgotten their names.

As soon as we had decided to go it alone, everything began to fall into place. We persisted with the exhibition idea and found a willing host in the Bodleian Library itself, 'Remembering Radcliffe' curated by the Bodleian Library, was appropriately enough the last exhibition to be mounted in the small exhibition space alongside the Divinity School. The Library was then in the midst of its major (and rather wonderful) refurbishment which, when completed, was to include a new exhibition space in the newly configured main building, but it seemed very appropriate that Radcliffe should bring to a close one Bodleian 'chapter' just as another, looking to the future, was about to open.

We persisted, too, with the commissioning of a statue of Dr Radcliffe from the eminent sculptor Martin Jennings, who lived not far from Oxford but had not previously had any Oxford commissions. As we now knew, such a work would not be welcomed as part of the Radcliffe Quarter but we were fortunate that one of our trustees, Timothy Wilson, re-established the historic connection with Green Templeton College, whose site includes the Radcliffe Observatory, and abuts the new Radcliffe Quarter on its northern side. The upshot was an agreement to place our statue on the small lawn outside the Observatory (conveniently a parcel of land not belonging to the University, so beyond the baleful influence of their so-called artistic consultants) so that our eight-foot bronze Radcliffe, when completed, would cast his own disdainful eye from this Grade 1-listed location across the modernist brutality which he had so narrowly avoided as his future home.

Martin Jennings proved an inspired choice as creator of our statue. The difficulties of creating a likeness of a man who died over three hundred years earlier are not to be underestimated, and with this project there were two in particular: the first was that Radcliffe was not often portrayed during his lifetime. There is one portrait, by his one-time next-door neighbour Sir Godfrey Kneller, and there is a small figure and a bust, both of modest aesthetic merit, one in University College and the other in the Camera itself. So the dearth of images was a significant challenge.

The second difficulty was of a different kind: Martin's extraordinary skill is to capture in his work something essential in the character of his subject, and we certainly wanted an honest, rather than an idealised, representation. The problem, in this regard, was that, during his lifetime, John Radcliffe evidently had very little interest in making himself likeable.

It is probably just a kind of laziness which leads us to assume, without much thought, that great philanthropists must by definition be nice people. Indeed the opposite may be more likely to be true: isn't there something rather vainglorious about the determination to memorialise yourself in a building? In Radcliffe's case he had a most terrific self-confidence and was famously contemptuous of his medical colleagues and downright rude to his patients, especially if he detected any tendency towards hypochondria. Yet in an age befogged by medical superstition, he spurned the commonly practiced but often fatal treatments, such as bleeding and the application of leeches (as had been applied to Queen Anne), and threw open the window on cures characterised by common sense. His feet were more firmly planted on the ground than those of his professional peers, and he certainly knew it.

Personally likeable or not, there is no disputing the enduring power of Dr Radcliffe's legacy in Oxford. In honour of the three hundredth anniversary of his death the Vice Chancellor of the university, Andrew Hamilton, proposed a reception, to be held in early December 2014, in the Radcliffe Camera followed by the grandest of dinners in that most beautiful of interiors, the Divinity School, the very building in which the Doctor had lain in state 300 years before. It was only the second time in three centuries that refreshments of any kind had been permitted within the hallowed walls of the Doctor's library, and a little research revealed that the previous occasion had not ended well. The event was also a centenary celebration, in this case the 100th anniversary of the Trust: in 1814 a sensational dinner was held in the Camera with tables radiating out in a kind of asterisk arrangement from a single central table. Although originally planned to celebrate the Radcliffe centenary, the event had been expanded to include a celebration of the fall of Paris and abdication of the Emperor Napoleon earlier that year and, in particular, the triumph of the Triple Alliance of England, Russia and Prussia which had achieved this great victory. So, although the dinner was formally hosted by the then chairman of the Radcliffe Trust, Lord Sidmouth (a former Prime Minister and current Home Secretary), the quite extraordinary guest list was headed by the Prince Regent (later to be George IV) and the Tsar of Russia, Emperor Alexander I. The Chancellor of the University, Lord Grenville (another former prime minister) sat at the centre of the central circular table, with the Tsar on his right, and on his left the King of Prussia, Frederick William. Also at the centre table, in addition to the Prince Regent and Lord Sidmouth, were the Prince of Orange, Prince Metternich and Marshall Blücher (soon to be of Waterloo fame). Some unwise member of the University had made the curious decision to open this unusual event to the public, as if dining were a kind of spectator sport, but the Camera's galleries are narrow and became so overcrowded and unruly that the army had to be summoned from their base in Headington to restore order. Our own tercentenary event at the Camera, although unable to compete with the social prestige of that earlier centenary dinner, could at least boast that military force was not called upon to maintain public order and decency.

I have now been involved with The Radcliffe Trust as adviser, trustee and chairman, for almost forty years, so will soon be passing on this venerable three-hundred-year-old baton to a new generation of trustees. I would not presume to advise them on how to continue the trust's work, because their challenges will be different from ours. What I can do, though, is reflect on how the grant-making environment has changed since I first encountered it back in the 1970s. We live now in an 'Age of Regulation', in which articulating policy, establishing procedures, accountability, accessibility, equality of opportunity and so on are all expected to be systematised and measured. This can be seen as a perfectly reasonable search for objectivity and procedural fairness, but the very same measured objectivity can all too easily become a lazy substitute for subjective judgements of merit or quality. This is the trap into which the arts bureaucrats tend to fall, and as independent grant-makers, we must avoid it by continuing to have confidence in our own judgements and the courage to take risks. I hope the Radcliffe Trust will continue to support high culture and exceptional skills and, if so, we must accept not only that the requisite cultural appreciation and technical expertise will be in the possession of a relatively small number of people, but also that this is not necessarily a bad thing. We must not fear accusations of elitism: any system of education must recognise that there exist skills and knowledge to which everyone should aspire, but (and this is perhaps harder to admit) not everyone will have the capacity to absorb or apply them. The danger is that our 'Age of Regulation' becomes a smokescreen to impose a kind of value neutral approach to education: this must be resisted, for it is surely a fundamental tenet of cultural education that there is a difference between good and bad, meaningful and meaningless, profound or shallow, exciting or banal, and we must be bold enough to keep pointing this out.

The Radcliffe Trust has the great advantage that it is not accountable to the public (except as represented by the Charity Commission). Unlike the Arts Council, it does not spend taxpayers' money, so it is vital to resist the temptation to become a mini-Arts Council. Its trustees are in a privileged position, able to back their judgements with financial support and they must remain confident and clear-eyed in defending the traditional skills and values they choose to favour against all threats, especially those from the dead hands of bureaucracy and fashion. If the Radcliffe Trust continues in the future to support unpopular causes and specialised interests and skills, I shall be happy.

Chapter 8
Coda

It feels somehow dangerous in a book of this frivolous kind to devote a chapter to the decidedly unfrivolous subject of politics, but I do so because my adult life thus far has been so neatly book-ended by the issue of the UK's troubled relationship with continental Europe, with referendums on membership of the European Economic Community in 1975 (when I was twenty-three) and of the re-named European Union in 2016 (when I was not). In 1975 I voted to remain but by 2016, after 40 years of membership, I voted to leave. And although my vote for Brexit meant that I had been on the winning side nationally in both votes I nevertheless feel that my despair of the EU, which caused such bafflement and anger amongst my London-based friends and colleagues requires some explanation.

It will be many years before the consequences of Brexit can be dispassionately assessed, so my intention here is not to make forecasts, but simply to record why I voted confidently for the leave side. For, if the received opinion of the liberal establishment proves to be correct and dire outcomes follow our EU departurewe 'leavers' will either look stupid and ignorant (as we were often told, immediately before and after the referendum, that we are), or at best deluded; all the more important then to remember how things appeared at the time. On the other hand if, as I expect, the forecast catastrophes and humiliations do not happen, I expect the prophecies of doom soon to be completely forgotten and history re-written, so this too is a worthwhile reason to record opinion as it was at the time. I should also record that I am writing this in January 2018, some considerable time before the 29 March 2019 departure date fixed by Article 50 (the legislative mechanism governing leaving) and in the midst of more or less desperate parliamentary attempts to stick to the timetable, or to postpone the date or to cancel Brexit altogether. Nothing is yet settled.

The Brexit referendum victory was forecast by almost no-one, with even one of the leading protagonists of the 'No' campaign[90] reportedly going to bed on the evening of the count in the belief that the 'Yes' side would win by ten percentage points. The result was such a shock because it was achieved against the combined forces of the political establishment, City money and the expectations of almost all media commentators including broadsheet newspapers and the BBC. However undesirable referendums may be as a policy-making mechanism, this victory for the Leave campaign, against such a weight of establishment opinion, should, you might have thought, have prompted some reflections amongst the defeated establishment opinion-formers who claim to speak for the nation, but the very opposite was the case. Attitudes hardened, and in the months following the vote, 'Remain' opinions seemed to survive unscathed despite the reality that over seventeen million people voted to leave, a larger number than had voted for the Labour Party at the previous two General Elections put together. We have since had academic papers, political speeches and TV documentaries offering all sorts of theories about why people voted as they did, everything from racism, or class, or anti-globalisation to a love of imperial weights and measures. Yet these self-appointed commentators have predominantly looked inwards to domestic politics in their search for explanations, and few have yet admitted that the shock result was perhaps because voters had finally rumbled the truth that the EU is rubbish. The institution was trenchantly described by Michael Gove, admittedly with a touch of campaigning hyperbole, as a, "Dysfunctional, anti-democratic, growth-strangling, job-destroying, market-rigging, hope-shredding empire of failed dreams."

The Remain campaign was aptly named 'Project Fear.' Voters were told that a new recession would follow a vote to leave, property prices would crash by 15%, a special austerity budget was planned for later that year, the City would lose its pre-eminence, unemployment and inflation would rise and so on and so forth. One particularly absurd forecast, by Chancellor George Osborne, was that all households would be £4,200 worse off by 2020. Given the Treasury's startlingly poor record of economic forecasting even six months ahead, the idea that they could predict to within a single pound the income of every household in the country in five years' time was beyond parody. We, the voters, did not understand, we were told, what would be in our own interests, and this from the same 'experts' who brought you the 2008 crash and recession, the

---

[90] Michael Gove, Minister for Agriculture, Fisheries and Food at the time of writing.

recommendation to adopt the euro and so on. To quote Michael Gove again, "...the reformed EU we were being invited to stay in was fundamentally unchanged and this latest promise that the Union would mend its ways was, like all the other pledges of reform from Maastricht onwards, as empty as Jean-Claude Juncker's burgundy bottle after lunch."

In the months following the vote, only one of the forecast 'dire' consequences in fact happened. There was a moderate devaluation of the pound, a fall which some believed was desirable in any case and which actually produced some significant benefits. The stock market was at or near an all-time high throughout 2017. Every negative event or bump in economic performance continued to be blamed on Brexit, while good economic news was either not reported at all or prefaced with the words 'despite Brexit'. The 'dire consequences' were, it seemed, simply deferred until the next year when catastrophic events remained inevitable; or perhaps the year after. And one truth of which the establishment elite seemed unaware, so certain were they of their own superior wisdom, was that, even if some of their forecasts were to come true, they were unlikely to gain much support from their opponents by calling them stupid. This was never likely to be a persuasive strategy.

And the post-referendum battle continues. In the pages of The Times a doleful Matthew Parris laments that the Brexit winners are now in charge but none has any idea what to do. This, he says, is a betrayal of the 17 million people who thought there was a plan and when they realise there isn't, "Their revenge will be terrible." This is a strange prediction—surely the much more likely victims of 'terrible revenge' by those who voted to leave would be politicians who defy the democratic will of the people, either by failing to deliver a sensible Brexit or, even more so, by seeking to reverse the referendum result. Meanwhile these pessimists talk as though the terms of the UK's departure from the EU are entirely in the gift of Brussels and that Brussels is in a mood to punish our effrontery. Worse still, there is a disagreeable tendency for the bureaucratic and political classes to continue to patronise: their jobs depend on persuading the rest of us that leaving the EU is fiendishly complicated, requiring skilled and experienced negotiators working diligently for at least ten years to negotiate trade deals of such complexity as we Leavers could never comprehend. In other words, we need men just like them to steer the ship of state into a position as close as possible to that which we are already in. As a mere layman, I can only comment that a trade deal between the EU and the UK <u>should</u> be one of the simplest, for we start from a position of having no existing trade barriers with the EU, and with no difference in standards and regulations. We have, after all, been members of the same club for forty-five years. When everyone's posturing is set aside it must surely be clear that an orderly exit is in everyone's interest, but the UK will not be in the single market because we do not want to accept the unconditional movement of people across borders, and we will not be in the customs union because this means accepting high trade tariffs against most of the world's largest economies. We should not need to spend years striking a complex deal for trade with our European allies because we are fortunate to have tariff-free trade already, so why not just keep it as it is. After all, they sell much more to us than we do to them, so why would this not be in their interest? If, in an attempt to prevent others from leaving their club, the EU rejects this generous offer, the UK will have regained the right to adjust its own financial model by keeping a substantial proportion of the £39 billion price of leaving, reducing tax and regulation, and increasing infrastructure spending so as to become, in due course, the destination of choice for investors, inventors and innovation.

~~~

The vote to leave the EU was a demand for politicians to speak plainly and honestly: to stop pretending that the EU was entirely a force for good, and to be honest about the limitations it imposed on politicians' scope for action on many of the most pressing domestic problems. The voters knew that immigration could not be cut to, "the tens of thousands", despite this appearing repeatedly in Conservative Party manifestos (and, extraordinarily, even in the Theresa May manifesto of 2017); they knew that the EU was a threat to our security given its insistence on free movement across borders; they knew that the Euro project was in deep trouble so long as the economies of southern Europe remain unable to devalue in order to stimulate growth and reduce their high levels of unemployment. They knew, too, that the optimistic claim that the EU had accepted any meaningful reform in David Cameron's laughably inadequate renegotiation was wishful thinking at best, but more probably an outright lie.

Despite these generalisations, individual voters on the Brexit side had divergent priorities: there were certainly some who wanted, above all, to curb immigration, others, such as me, who were mainly stirred to action by the dreadful democratic deficit in the EU, there may have been a few 'little

Englanders' who yearned for a return to the comparative (though imagined) simplicities of an earlier age, there were even alleged (by Remainers) to be some who wanted, above everything, to return to pounds and ounces, and pounds, shillings and pence. But the key point was that David Cameron and the Remain campaign failed, despite huge efforts, to persuade these people that the vote was primarily about economics. The BBC's coverage of European issues was always framed in economic terms—it was all about how impossible it would be for the British economy to prosper outside the EU, and there was little or nothing on the feeble and undemocratic nature of the EU political institutions, and the fact that its accounts were rejected by the auditors year after year was scarcely reported, let alone subjected to any analysis. EU parliamentary elections were of course given plenty of airtime but no one dared mention how pathetic this parliamentary fig leaf was when it came to EU policy-making and power-broking.

The essential dishonesty of this unbalanced approach, both during the referendum campaign and indeed in the years before it, was a vital contributor to the outcome. The truth was that many people did not greatly care about the economic costs of leaving; as Roger Scruton acutely pointed out, their vote was about identity and sovereignty. For such people the question was not, "What will make us better off?" but rather, "Who are we, and what holds us together in a shared political order? And to whom should we give authority to govern us?"

These are not altogether simple questions: after all, we already live in a political union consisting of four nationalities, the United Kingdom, and one of the little foreseen consequences of ceding political control to Brussels has been the rise of nationalism in the UK's celtic fringes as real power moves ever further towards a central European state. Nor is the rise of separatist movements confined to the UK: the Belgian coalition of nationalities has caused paralysis in their government (and in the ratification of the Canadian trade deal), the future of the Spanish state remains uncertain following the vote (in another referendum) for Catalan independence. Meanwhile the Italian political establishment is threatened by rising populism as is the stability of many of the old Eastern bloc countries who also face growing nationalist revivals. Above all, the EU has failed, try as it might, to persuade people to think of themselves as Europeans, rather than, say, as Poles or Portuguese.

In truth, the attempt to persuade people to think of themselves primarily as citizens of Europe has only been explicit in comparatively recent times. One key difference between the referendum campaigns of 1975 and 2016 is that back then there was very little mention of what we now know as the 'European Project'. There were a few who warned of a hidden integrationist agenda, but these voices were very much on the political fringes, and the public were specifically assured, on the rare occasions such questions arose, that we were in a limited 'economic' union, not a political movement towards a United States of Europe, and that each nation state had the right to veto unacceptable political proposals. It is hard to avoid the conclusion that the public have been repeatedly misled on the matter of the so-called 'hidden agenda' of political union, and yet it is surprising, with the benefit of hindsight, that the goal of a United States of Europe should ever have been thought of as 'hidden'.

The man often referred to as the 'founding father' of the European Union is Jean Monnet whose vision of a United States of Europe (he was at first quite explicit about it) was formulated shortly after the First World War (yes, I do mean the First). Almost a century ago, Monnet proposed a new form of 'supranational' government, beyond the control of national governments, politicians and electors. The elimination of the nation state was, he argued, a necessary step towards building a new world order. More than 20 years, and another World War, later, Monnet had become a leading civil servant in post-war France and was at last in a position to pursue his enormously ambitious project. He had by this time realised that it would be necessary to proceed by stealth: the project should develop one step at a time, with the key elements of his supranational government machine to be put in place one by one. Only when enough of the machine was irreversibly in place could the guiding political purpose be fully acknowledged. The first step turned out to be the creation of a largely forgotten institution called the European Coal and Steel Community (ECSC) which began a process of dismantling cross-border trade barriers with the limited aim (according to the narrative of the time) of creating a common market for those industries.

Incremental steps continued for decades: Jacques Delors' attempt (aided by the French and German leaders Mitterand and Helmut Kohl and at first by Margaret Thatcher too) to develop the EU along a United States model, was probably always doomed. But certainly so by the premature adoption of the single currency, the Euro. Structurally flawed, the Euro turned public disenchantment in most of the non-central EU countries into disillusion, consigned their economies to recession, and poured fuel on growing national hostilities which are only now beginning to surface in political form.

Then, at the beginning of our present century, the project moved towards the supposed endgame: the European Union now consisted of twenty-five nations, and delegates from all of them gathered in Brussels, at the grandiose headquarters of the European Parliament, for the opening of a convention for the drafting of a constitution for a 'United Europe'. The participating delegates were no doubt mindful of the parallels with the 1787 convention in Philadelphia which led to the drafting of a constitution for the United States of America, but there cannot have been more than a tiny number of people amongst the 500 million or so population of the European participating countries, in whose name all this was happening, who had any real grasp of what was being done in their names.

~~~

Back in the 1960s the UK had actually made two unsuccessful attempts to join the EEC, both of which were blocked by French veto. I am old enough to remember the shock of President de Gaulle's famous 'Non', a rejection of the MacMillan government's first attempt to take the UK into membership of the European club (a mere six countries at that time), and I was in my teens when Edward Heath did eventually take us into membership of the EEC (without a referendum), and cast my vote, as a novice, in the 1975 referendum, called by Harold Wilson following his re-negotiation of membership terms. I confess that I do not remember that referendum campaign in great detail, perhaps because, as with younger voters now, my choice was made not on specific policy issues but rather on the basis of what I thought was an inevitable historical tide flowing towards greater European co-operation. Also, because the UK had hitherto always been on the outside, it was easier to be persuaded that influence could only be exercised from within, as a member of the club. So, the positive approach was to join and seek change from within.

And even then it was obvious that change was needed, especially to the much-vilified Common Agricultural Policy which had originally been conceived in a post-war era when the destruction of much agricultural infrastructure meant that feeding a growing population was a legitimate political concern. Such immediate post-war concerns could no longer be justified in the mid-1970s, and the CAP appeared to have become a mechanism to protect mainly, but not exclusively, French farmers from the consequences of their own inefficiency.[91]

The reasons for the eventual French change of heart concerning UK membership were articulated most clearly by Christopher Booker and Richard North in their book 'The Great Deception'. In brief, the argument goes, the French economy had become dangerously reliant on agricultural subsidies which, by the mid-60s had become obviously unsustainable. Agriculture accounted for 20% of the French economy (the comparable figure in the UK was 4%), but a drive to rationalise the number of inefficient small-holdings was bound to lead to a migration from rural areas to cities which were already struggling to provide employment for their existing citizens, let alone a flood of new arrivals. Agricultural reform was in any case politically unacceptable. To solve this dilemma de Gaulle turned to the EEC, and the French administrators began to devise what came to be known as the Common Agricultural Policy (CAP). In 1960, at the time of the first serious UK attempt to join the EEC, it was belatedly realised in the French government that Britain would refuse to agree entry terms which would require them to provide massive subsidies for French farmers. It followed that UK membership could not be allowed until the CAP was so firmly embedded in EEC structures that it could be presented as non-negotiable in any future British attempt at membership. It would have to be 'swallowed whole' or not at all. A decade later, when Edward Heath's government again applied to join, the CAP was in place, with its pillars being tariffs on imported non-EEC produce and the continuation of agricultural subsidies which favoured, or at least did not penalise, small farms. What was now needed were new sources of income to finance the subsidies in the future, so UK membership of the EEC could now be seen as a solution, not a problem. Willi Brandt, the German Chancellor, was left in no doubt that the French price for lifting the veto on expansion of the EEC was German agreement to the CAP arrangements. And the costs were indeed huge: according to *The Guardian*[92]

---

[91] The inefficiency of French farming has been a constant refrain throughout the history of the EU and I have often wondered how much this was caused by their system of Napoleonic law, under which the guiding principal of inheritance is not primogeniture, as in the Common Law system, but to divide estates between all the immediate male inheritors. In an agricultural context this must surely lead to the creation of ever smaller agricultural holdings, and consequent inefficiency.

[92] *The Guardian*, 14 December 1970

newspaper the annual cost of the CAP alone was the equivalent of what the Americans were spending on landing on the moon.

Edward Heath had been MacMillan's chief negotiator in the abortive 1960 application. By 1970, he was Prime Minister and determined to take the UK into membership, more or less at any price. Public attention was focussed during the negotiations on trade matters, especially on the fate of imports from Britain's historic Commonwealth trading partners, especially New Zealand, Australia and Canada, but also to a lesser extent the Caribbean (including bananas, the measurement of whose parabolic curvature later became a powerful symbol of Brussels' bureaucratic overreach). More significant in the long run was the agreement on Britain's future budget contributions. A transitional 8% of the total budget was agreed, to rise to nearly 20% in due course, and with no guarantee that the proportion would not increase further. The UK became then, as it has been ever since, the second highest budget contributor after Germany.

Within a few years Heath had been replaced by Harold Wilson (as a result of the 'Who governs Britain,' election triggered by the first of Arthur Scargill's miners' strikes). The Labour Party was split on the European question (just as was the Conservative Party in 2016): Labour had opposed the legislation which took the UK in but there had been a sufficient number of pro-Europe members (led by Roy Jenkins) to help the Conservative government carry the day with a majority above 100. Labour's opposition was based primarily on the terms of membership but also, to an extent, on the claim that the UK electorate had not been properly consulted. There was some truth in this because all three main political parties had, since 1964, favoured entry, and the European issue had scarcely been mentioned during the 1970 election campaign which had brought the Heath government to power. Thus it was that in the 1974 General Election Harold Wilson promised to re-negotiate the terms of entry and to put the new deal to the people in a referendum. The people would decide.

In 1975, just as in 2016, the overwhelming majority of 'establishment' opinion was ranged on the 'Remain' side with support from every living Prime Minister and every ex-Foreign Secretary, the CBI, 415 out of 419 chairmen of leading companies surveyed by *The Times*, plus the vast majority of press and TV commentators. In the anti-Europe ranks, on the other hand, the right-wing Conservatives who had so fiercely resisted their own leader when the UK first joined were surprisingly absent from the 'Leave' campaign. Perhaps this was because they could not bring themselves to share a platform, literally and metaphorically, with the Labour left-wingers who led that campaign, notably Tony Benn, Michael Foot, Barbara Castle and Edward Short. But in their absence the 'Remain' side was able to portray their opponents as dangerous socialist mavericks, and they also succeeded in focusing the debate on conventional (in electioneering terms) economic issues. Their left-wing political opponents would in any case have been well outside their comfort zone had they raised questions of sovereignty, democratic accountability and 'taking back control' (to borrow an effective 2016 slogan). In 1975, then, these larger issues of principle were not at the centre of debate, such as it was, and of plans for a common currency there was almost no mention at all. Above all, voters were persuaded (at least I was, and for a rare change found myself in the majority) a) that any fear of further political European integration could always be stopped by using the veto which each member state could exercise and b) that the UK could only exert real influence by having a seat at the European table. Looking back, we might think that had the voters been told the truth about the EEC in 1970 they would never have accepted joining, but, as mentioned earlier, they were not asked their opinion. It was, as Tony Benn said at the time, a *coup d'état* by a political class who did not believe in popular sovereignty, the clearest possible example of victory for undemocratic liberalism over illiberal democracy.

The 2016 referendum was a one-off event in which voters were offered a binary, yes or no, choice, so a victory for Tony Benn's so-called 'illiberalism' was an obvious risk, however improbable it was thought to be at the time. But does the result represent a wider, more existential threat to liberalism, as many commentators have suggested? Liberalism is, broadly speaking, an approach to politics which attempts, through rational debate, to navigate changes in such a way as to protect individual liberties while meeting social needs. This approach is a kind of mediation between left-of-centre and right-of-centre political attitudes, between right-wing libertarianism and left-wing social collectivism, and its operators are found in the centre ground of political parties of both left and right. The achievements of the liberal consensus have been real—think of civil rights, universal suffrage, religious tolerance to name but three—and it seemed as relatively recently as 1989, with the fall of the Berlin Wall, and the apparent death of the Communist threat, that it was approaching a total victory. There was talk, admittedly never very convincing, of the End of History, and British politics in the subsequent years seemed to have settled firmly in the middle ground. Tony Blair adopted much of what Margaret Thatcher had achieved, and David Cameron was widely described as the heir to Blair. The Labour Party's left wingers were marginalised and the threat, such as it was, to Conservative administrations came from the Liberal Democrats, not from UKIP nationalists. With hindsight, the first signs of real trouble for this cosy liberal consensus may be traced to the rise of UKIP during the post-2010 Cameron coalition administration. The very decision to hold the European Union membership referendum was, after all, an attempt to win back to the Conservative fold the anti-EU UKIP supporters. That it failed so spectacularly to achieve its aim is an indication that the purveyors of broadly 'consensus politics' had become so alarmingly detached from their own people as to be unceremoniously sandbagged. They just did not see it coming; but it is surely now much too late for our liberal Remainer MPs, in both Conservative and Labour parties, to refuse to be bound by the referendum result. They dug this hole for themselves: there was never any suggestion that the outcome would not be binding. Parliament voted by a large majority to go ahead with the bill enabling the referendum vote and both major parties fought the 2017 General Election promising to honour the outcome. MPs handed the decision to the people, so it is particularly disingenuous now to attempt to justify overturning the result on the grounds that they, as MPs, are representatives and not delegates. They delegated their authority on this issue.

How did the MPs and commentators within the so-called 'Westminster bubble' miss the signs of this 'peoples' revolt'? During the 1980s and 90s the centre-ground consensus was that we would inevitably, as a society, embrace a kind of hyper-capitalism, which later became known as globalisation. This may even have been beneficial (in short-term economic terms) for a while but can now be seen to have led to major trauma amongst traditional industrial communities; domestic manufacturing (both in the UK and the US) was sacrificed on the altar of this new globalisation. A second act of faith, which with hindsight seems equally misguided, was to enter a toxic debt-fuelled alliance with the banking industry driven by lending policies which relied on heroic assumptions about the invulnerability of the property market. Thirdly, the liberal consensus (and here to be fair there was significant opposition too) was that there were righteous wars to be fought all round the world, in Iraq, Afghanistan, Libya, Syria and elsewhere. The long-term consequences are as yet unclear but the rise of radical Islamism was certainly not foreseen and has brought a huge step backwards in terms of all those liberal advances, such as women's rights, religious toleration and so on, which the liberal elite rightly took pride in. And of course, the most recent and disturbing consequence has been the creation of another irreversible tide, but this one is a tide of refugees.

All these developments, and the uncertainty and bitter sense of exclusion which they prompted, led to widespread attitudinal changes which were expressed in the 'peoples' vote'. Some would perhaps have happened anyway, so to that extent they would have been inevitable, but some of them will surely come to be seen simply as bad political decisions, and these kinds of bad decisions did not arise in a vacuum: a cheerleader for all the attitudes characteristic of the liberal consensus from which they emerged was the BBC, the dominant force, by virtue of its sheer size and reach, in a media consensus. The BBC has a duty, in which it takes great pride, of impartiality and it is probably the most trusted source of news and comment in the world. However, there are issues, such as immigration and Brexit to take two current and related examples, which cause the organisation great difficulty: there is no doubt which side of the Brexit debate the great majority of university-educated, metropolitan-living BBC employees are on; their instinctive collective leaning towards left-of-centre politics and social liberalism meant that the narrative running through all BBC political coverage of Brexit has been that 'Remain' was the 'grown-up' position and 'Leave' an historic aberration based on an out-dated and discredited nationalism. The BBC has always regarded itself as having a global responsibility, as opposed to being merely a 'voice of the nation' (captured in the very title The World Service) and, as such, feels bound to give equality of respect, largely unqualified, to overseas stories, attitudes and politicians as against domestic stories. Thus the pronouncements of officials on EU negotiating positions in Brussels are reported with unqualified deference, while comparable UK positions are always to be closely interrogated. In a wider social context, the BBC is an uncritical promoter of a kind of multiculturalism which goes far beyond Brexit and which is even more insidious: all minorities are to be presented as oppressed and given an easy ride in interviews, while opposing opinion is to be closely questioned or simply ignored. This approach to social and political questions leads to some curious bedfellows: Islam, for instance, is treated with the same deference to victimhood as feminism, for fear of being vilified as homophobic or Islamophobic, without it ever being articulated that Islam and feminism are themselves utterly irreconcilable.

Immigration, even more so than Islam or feminism, is an issue on which the BBC (and other news media) finds its 'world view' to be at odds with the views of many ordinary people, and its consequent lack of honesty in the reporting and analysis of events has actually exacerbated the problem: it would be far easier to make a strong moral case for accepting large numbers of refugees if there had been any credible effort to distinguish between actual refugees and the much less needy economic migrants. But politicians and the media have been complicit in denying that such a distinction can be made[93]. The worst culprit, simply in terms of numbers of 'refugees', may have been Germany's Angela Merkel, but the impact of this mistake on politics in the UK compounded the Blair government's earlier decision to open the borders to immigration from Eastern Europe ahead of the EU-agreed timetable. The result in this country was a widely held perception (rightly or wrongly) of immigration as a bad thing, depressing wages, reducing job opportunities for the indigenous communities and putting enormous pressure on public services. Worse, the failure of the 'liberal elite' to even acknowledge a problem came to be perceived as a conspiracy to change the country by stealth.

A bleakly compelling view of the EU's current travails can be found in Douglas Murray's book 'The Strange Death of Europe'. His argument, in brief, is that Europe is committing suicide by embracing the mass immigration of millions from the Islamic world while not encouraging them to embrace our enlightened values. There is a crisis of confidence in European culture, according to Murray, attributable to the erosion of our own religion. Mass immigration, imposed on people without their consent, gave rise to the doctrine of multiculturalism in which all faiths and cultures are treated as equal. But here is the catch: in order to achieve equality, the only 'culture' which cannot be promoted is the one which allowed all the others to be celebrated in the first place, western civilisation. And this brings us back to the threat of Islamism: a Europe devoid of self-belief is dangerously exposed to the existential threat posed by a religious Islamic culture driven by an aggressive certainty and a mission to overwhelm rival religions. The European Parliament was recently told that Muslims will soon outnumber Christians in Europe, yet even to raise this as

---

[93] Is it coincidence that so many of those seeking refuge from 'persecution' in their home countries seem to be able-bodied young men between the ages of 18 and 30? If all those wanting to come to Europe were refugees in the usual sense of the word they would surely include a much greater proportion of women, children and the elderly.

a legitimate concern is to invite accusations of nationalistic racism. Similar concerns about London's population have been dismissed as scaremongering (and some less polite epithets) despite the fact that in 23 of its 32 boroughs white Christians are now in a minority. In Murray's bleak analysis, the EU itself was born out of this cultural demoralisation: in the wake of world wars it seemed that 'the problem of Germany' (that Germany is too large, hence too dominant, in relation to other European countries) had been aggravated by nationalism; hence the need for transnational institutions, specifically the EU, to introduce an age of borderless neighbourly harmony and the abolition of prejudice. However, this noble aim is being overwhelmed by the religious intolerance of immigrant peoples who are, in effect, taking Europe back to its earlier history: long before the European wars between nation states the great European wars were religious, mainly power struggles between the Catholic and Protestant faiths. If Murray's view is accepted, the UK's decision to leave the EU gives the UK a last chance to reclaim its own culture through laws made as an independent nation. This is more clearly perceived in Britain than in much of continental Europe, with its more recent history of invasions, shifting borders and tyrannical regimes. So Murray concludes, "An entire political class have failed to appreciate that many of us who live in Europe love the Europe that was ours. We do not want our politicians, through weakness, self-hatred, malice, tiredness or abandonment to change our home into an utterly different place." It says much for the strength of Britain's democratic traditions that the British people have so far been the only citizens of the EU to be asked their opinion. Why was it such a surprise that the voters expressed their disenchantment with all this at the first opportunity they were given?

A vote for Brexit was, on this view, a rational response to a multiplicity of inter-related policy failures which came to be epitomised by the European Commission which exists in a state of unelected complacency, presiding over an institution which itself stands on the brink of actual failure. The electorate were offered a chance to seize the initiative through the referendum, and, inspired by a Brexit campaign armed with a much more persuasive narrative than that of their opponents, they took it. The democratic risk, and consequent severe stress on the democratic system, does not stem from the peoples' vote but from their elected representatives who do not share their view.

As for the EU itself, it is (or at any rate was) a great liberal project which now seems not to be working, and it may be beyond rescue in its current form.

Europe is governed not by its people nor by its ideals but by a 'board' of unelected functionaries. This was the inevitable consequence of the anti-democratic empire-building of the founders who knew that if they put their pan-European vision to the democratic test it would be rejected. The relationships between the central Brussels authority and the member states were, from the beginning, conflicting, in principle unresolved and in practice deliberately obscure. The prevailing notion, implicit in Jean Monnet's original governance methodology, that Europe's fate was best determined by a cadre of 'Platonic Guardians' was always deeply flawed because it lacked any serious democratic component.

The difficulties now facing the EU are indeed numerous and serious and the feeble attempts of the Brussels 'government' to manage them are met with failure on all fronts. Overambitious policy aims in finance, energy and IT have all failed as Europe's power shrinks relative to China, the US and India. At the same time the influx of millions of unwanted economic migrants is setting member states against each other, and before long there will be families to join the (mostly) young men who have somehow made it to Europe. As a consequence we are seeing the rise of grassroots nationalist (and populist) politics in response to the failure of the centre and the real weakness of the so-called Schengen Agreement on free movement which can scarcely survive unreformed. 'President' Jean-Claude Juncker himself has warned that, "If the Schengen agreement fails, the single currency will no longer make sense. And the single currency is one of the main pillars in the construction of Europe." And even if Schengen survives the migration crisis, another major terrorist attack could shatter it overnight. For the time being, though, the European 'project' staggers on from one crisis to the next.

~~~

If the 'big picture' tells the story of a resurgence of nationalism as a result of the failure of Europe to find solutions to transnational problems, there is also a small picture based on individual experiences of dealing with the impenetrable and inflexible bureaucracies of the European government machine. Looking, as it were, from the bottom up there are deep cultural differences in so many spheres of social and cultural life. Such cultural differences run deep and cannot be changed at the stroke of a bureaucratic pen.

A trivial example, but one which caused me amusement at the time, of cultural incompatibility was provided by the neighbouring house to an Umbrian villa in which my family spent some weeks a few summers ago: this substantial building proudly sported a sign which identified it as the headquarters of, 'The National Society for the Shooting of Rare Birds'. As an inhabitant of the country of origin of the Royal Society for the Protection of Birds, as well as of many other animal protection charities, this sign seemed to symbolise how the European nations were doomed always to diverge.[94]

Our bird-free Italian holiday coincided with my first and last attempt to access EU funding for The English Concert of which I was then in charge. I spent many days of my life working on an application to one of the Brussels-inspired collaborative programmes whose Kafka-esque opacity slowly but inexorably drained the will to live. Simply reading the guidance notes for applicants was a dispiriting experience, partly because these programmes were clearly more about achieving political goals than about artistic value: for example, to qualify for a grant, a project required at least three collaborating organisations from different European 'regions'. You needed to read the rules carefully because you might be forgiven for assuming that this means three different countries. Not so. The map of Europe had been redrawn: the newly defined regions straddled traditional borders so that, for example, the 'region' called northern France included the county of Kent. Having toiled through this kind of contrived, if rather sinister, nonsense, you eventually reach the application form itself which, in this case, comprised a 360-page email. Almost a page for every day of the year. And when this marathon application was submitted there was no way to discover who would be assessing it, and no feedback given in the event of rejection. All that was available was a list of successful projects from previous years, of which I can remember a few, not because of any inherent merit but simply because I was so annoyed at my lack of success that they left a scar. The EU cultural programme, I learned, was awarding substantial grants to something called, "E(U)quality", a project designed to answer the question, "How useful is the EU for women?" and to explore, "What expectations and needs women have towards the EU?" The questions were to be answered by establishing eleven E(U)quality discussion cafés in various Austrian, Slovak and German regions (those 'regions'

---

[94] It was notable, too, that although our villa was surrounded by extensive mature woodland there was almost no evidence of bird life. It seemed that the society devoted to their assassination had been so successful as to render all birds rare.

again) in order to provide women, "An opportunity to approach the EU which they often experience in an abstract way." How could my project, an Anglo-Austrian-German collaborative production of a Haydn opera for puppets, possibly compete with a Slovakian discussion café for abstracted women?

Another famous so-called 'cultural' project saw Greek potato farmers receive funding from the Common Agricultural Policy budget to promote their potatoes in Sweden. You might wonder why this was necessary in Sweden of all places, where their own farmers easily meet the admittedly high demand for potatoes from their own resources. Brochures extolling the wonders of Greek potatoes were sent to every Swedish household, apparently translated using the Google translator, which of course resulted in language which was hilariously odd. Of course it is easy to mock such ludicrous misjudgements, but the serious point is the unaccountability of the process; if the Arts Council or the Turner Prize or other award-making committees make absurd decisions, at least we can know who sits on these panels, even if we can't directly fire them. As a last resort, we can point a public finger at the guilty men or women.

The EU cultural budgets were of course miniscule when compared with the CAP, which, as we have seen, was comparable to the cost of landing on the Moon. The absurdities of the CAP could be (and surely have been) the subject of a separate study, so I will confine myself to a single example, a letter to *The Times* from one Nigel Johnson-Hill addressed to the then Secretary of State at the Department for the Environment, Food and Rural Affairs (DEFRA), which captures the spirit:

'Dear Secretary of State,

'A friend, who is in farming at the moment, has recently received a cheque for £3,000 from the Rural Payments Agency for not rearing pigs and I would like to join the 'not rearing pigs' business.

'In your opinion, what is the best kind of farm not to rear pigs on, and which is the best breed of pigs not to rear? I want to be sure I approach this endeavour in keeping with all government policies, as dictated by the EU under the Common Agricultural Policy. I would prefer not to rear bacon pigs, but if this is not the type you want not rearing, I will gladly not rear porkers. Are there any advantages in not rearing rare breeds such as Saddlebacks or Gloucester Old Spots, or are there too many farmers not rearing these already?

'As I see it, the hardest part of this programme will be keeping an accurate record of just how many pigs I haven't reared. Are there any Government or Local Authority courses on this?

'My friend is very satisfied with this business. He has been rearing pigs for forty years or so, and the best annual return he ever made on them was £1,422 in 1978; that is, until this year, when he received your cheque for £3,000 for not rearing any.

'If I were to get £3,000 for not rearing fifty pigs, will I be entitled to £6,000 for not rearing one hundred? I plan to operate on a small scale at first, holding myself down to about 4,000 pigs not raised, which will mean about £240,000 for the first year. However, as I become more expert in not rearing pigs, I plan to be more ambitious, perhaps increasing to, say, forty thousand pigs not reared in my second year, for which I should expect about £2.4 million from your department. Incidentally, I wonder if I would be eligible to receive tradable carbon credits for all these pigs not producing harmful and polluting methane gases?

'Another point: these pigs that I plan not to rear will not eat 2,000 tonnes of cereals. I understand you also pay farmers not to grow crops, so will I qualify for payments for not growing cereals in order not to feed the pigs I don't rear?

'In order to diversify, I am also considering the 'not milking cows' business, so please send any information leaflets you have on that too, please. Would you also include the current DEFRA advice on set-aside fields? Can this be done on an e-commerce basis of 'virtual' fields of which I seem to have several thousand hectares.

'In view of the above, you will realise that I shall be totally unemployed and will, therefore, qualify for unemployment benefits over and above the monies that I shall receive from DEFRA's Rural Payments Agency.

'I shall of course be voting for your party at the next General Election.

'Yours faithfully.

'Etc.'

This letter inspired a number of replies in the same vein, pointing out the potential downsides of the new, not rearing pigs business. These included the absence of barriers to entry, meaning that others would soon be on the bandwagon, driving down the price of not reared pigs. Animal rights activists were also a potential threat: unless the latest humane methods of not rearing pigs are used, the animal rights people may invade your not land and interfere with your not rearing activities. Then there is the danger of not Swine Flu, with the obvious risk that all not reared pigs could be quarantined, lengthening the not rearing process, thereby reducing income generation potential. The last threat (rather prescient this) was that sooner or later those clever people in the banks will take the not reared pigs, collateralise them, bundle them into a new type of derivative and sell the not reared pigs on to people with no proper understanding of the business. There would be a bubble followed by the inevitable crash, at which point not reared pigs could not even be given away, resulting in government bail-out of the banks, and driving the economy to the brink of bankruptcy.

~~~

We stand now on the brink of a new independence for the UK (admittedly subject to the economic/financial pressures and constraints of a 'globalised' world) and I hope our politicians will begin to articulate a vision for the future.

This vision should include a return to our homegrown Common Law system and a divergence from the Civil Law of continental Europe. This may seem like another large abstract concept but it affects many aspects of our public and private lives and institutions. Far be it from me to attempt an account of the relationships between these two systems, but the influence of Magna Carta on the development of the English system illustrates some fundamental differences: Magna Carta, although written within a completely feudal framework, gives the clearest articulation to the concept of the Rule of Law, and at the same time declares that there are certain fundamental rights which every freeman enjoys without any specific conferment from the King. Roman Law, by contrast, is seen, at least by its Common Law rivals, as authoritarian and absolutist. Its description of the relationship between ruler and subject, in which legal authority flows from a single central source, is perceived as fundamentally undemocratic. This was the basis for the philosopher Leszek Kolakowski's summary of the differences between European legal cultures, "In Britain, everything is permitted unless it is forbidden; in Germany everything is forbidden unless it is permitted; in France everything is permitted, even if it is forbidden; and in Russia everything is forbidden even if it is permitted."

Returning to the political world, it is a curious paradox that the rejection of the long-dominant liberal consensus, both in the UK and with the Trump presidency in the States, has left us with right-wing governments in both countries. After all, the section of the electorate which has delivered these huge shocks to the political landscape comprises, in the main, those people who feel left behind in the jobs market, or whose employment, if it continues at all, has been undermined by stagnant wages. Some also feel overwhelmed by immigration, which can lower wage levels and put pressure on public services such as hospital care and school places. All of these are people who should provide fertile territory for the politics of the left, yet we have right wing governments in the UK and the USA, as well as growing right-wing parties in continental Europe (even if these have not yet acquired the momentum to win elections). Why is this?

Part of the reason seems to be in the language of left-wing politics, based as it is on the historic revolutionary slogans of *liberté, fraternité* and *egalité*. When it comes to liberty and fraternity there is little to choose between the main political parties (even if the Labour Party, within its own organisation, shows scant fraternal tolerance for those unwilling to toe the Momentum line), but when it comes to equality there could be important differences. The left traditionally stresses equality and the fairness of equal shares, but there are signs that social attitudes have moved against the simplistic notion of 'equal shares for all' towards a more nuanced approach. Rather than insisting on actual equality for everyone, which is seen as unachievable, the desire instead is for a sense of fairness, which includes a notion of reciprocity: we co-operate with each other not for any dogmatic or idealistic reasons, but because it works for us; if I do you a favour you will do me one in return. In other words, there is a relationship between what you put in and what you get out. Equality says nothing about the contribution a person makes, and seems in this respect clearly unfair. One of the more toxic of political issues is the perception that society is becoming full of people who are taking something for nothing or for no added contribution, be they unemployed immigrants, MPs fiddling their expenses, bankers awarding themselves huge bonuses, or simply men being paid more than women for the same work. The left can score some easy points against bankers, of course, but the public resentment against bankers pay seems to arise more from the idea of reciprocity than from equality: for years we did not much mind bankers being very highly paid because their businesses appeared to be making a lot of money and they, personally and corporately, contributed large tax revenues. But when the banks crashed and the bonus culture continued, this offended against the idea of reciprocity; as a consequence of bail-outs, the tax payer was now a contributor to, and in some cases even a part-owner of, the banking system, so the bankers themselves, who were seen to have brought many of their troubles upon themselves, were no longer contributing enough to justify their continuing rewards.

If we look at welfare through a lens of equality, our primary concern should be that recipients of welfare receive enough to live on. But in reality the political debate is increasingly focused (rightly or often wrongly) on welfare fraud; are recipients of benefits putting in enough to justify what they take out? Crime is an even starker example, because it is literally a case of criminals taking what others have worked hard to earn. But immigration also powerfully illustrates the difficulty for 'pure' egalitarians: there is a perception (again I do not comment on the truth of it) that immigrants are unfairly benefiting from public services funded by others, and the argument that they also contribute through working does not seem to very much change this perception. The politicians of the Left are much too quick to categorise the resentments which such conceptions give rise to as racism, and the Labour Party will not win back its own traditional voters unless it can itself find a more nuanced response to the Brexit vote and its motivations.

It is not yet clear where the UK's newfound independence will lead, nor what the eventual effect will be on the EU when it eventually loses one of its largest net contributors. My guess, for what it's worth, is that Brexit will in the long run be a catalyst for change for the better, possibly with a central core of some of the original EU members (perhaps minus Italy) and a looser combination of other countries, including the UK, around the edges. A re-ordering of the EU seems inevitable in the wake of Brexit, the only question being whether it is an orderly or disorderly process.